The Risālah of Ibn Abī Zayd al-Qayrawānī

The Risālah

Ibn Abī Zayd al-Qayrawānī

Arabic-English edition

Translated by Aisha Bewley

Risalah Ibn Abi Zayd al-Qayrawani, Arabic-English edition

Published by: Diwan Press Ltd.
311 Allerton Road
Bradford
BD15 7HA
UK
Website: www.diwanpress.com
E-mail: info@diwanpress.com

Author: Ibn Abi Zayd al-Qayrawani
Translation: Aisha Bewley
Editor: Abdalhaqq Bewley
A catalogue record of this book is available from the British Library.

ISBN-13: 978-1-908892-93-5 (casebound)
978-1-908892-94-2 (paperback)
978-1-908892-95-9 (ePub & Kindle)

Contents

4.1 Istinjā' (Cleansing with water in the lavatory); 4.2 Istijmār (Cleansing with stones); 4.3 Washing one's hands before wuḍū'; 4.4 Sunnahs and obligations of wuḍū'; 4.5 Obligatory elements of wuḍū'; 4.6 How to perform wuḍū'; 4.7 The reward for wuḍū'; 4.8 The purpose of wuḍū'

Table of Transliteration

ء	ʾ	ض	ḍ
ا	a	ط	ṭ
ب	b	ظ	ẓ
ت	t	ع	ʿ
ث	th	غ	gh
ج	j	ف	f
ح	ḥ	ق	q
خ	kh	ك	k
د	d	ل	l
ذ	dh	م	m
ر	r	ن	n
ز	z	ه	h
س	s	و	w
ش	sh	ي	y
ص	ṣ		

Long vowel		Short vowel	
ا	ā	َ	a [fatḥah]
و	ū	ُ	u [ḍammah]
ي	ī	ِ	i [kasrah]
أَوْ	aw		
أَيْ	ay		

In the name of Allah, All-Merciful, Most Merciful.
May Allah bless our Master Muḥammad and his family and Companions and give him peace.

Ibn Abī Zayd's Prologue

Abū Muḥammad 'Abdullāh ibn Abī Zayd al-Qayrawānī, may Allah be pleased with him and make him pleased, says:

Praise be to Allah Who begins the creation of man as a blessing from Him and fashions him in the womb by His wisdom and brings him out into His tender care and to the provision to which He eases him, and teaches him what he did not know – Allah's favour to him is indeed immense.

Allah makes him aware of Himself through the effects of what He has made and has left no excuse for him by virtue of what has come on the tongues of His Messengers, the best of His creation. He guides, by His favour, those to whom He has granted success and He leads astray, by His justice, those whom He has debased. He eases the believers to ease and opens their hearts to the Reminder. So they believe in Allah, articulating that belief with their tongues, being sincere about it in their hearts and acting according to what has come down to them through His Messengers and His Books. They learn what He teaches them and stop at the limits He has prescribed for them. They are satisfied with what He has made *ḥalāl* for them and avoid what He has made *ḥarām* for them.

May Allah assist both us and you in taking care of what He has entrusted us with and in holding to His *sharī'ah.*

بسم الله الرحمن الرحيم
وصلى الله على سيدنا محمد وآله وصحبه
وسلم تسليما

مقدمة:

قال أبو محمد عبد الله بن أبي زيد، القيرواني رضي الله عنه وأرضاه:

الحمد لله الذي ابتدأ الإنسان بنعمته، وصوره في الأرحام بحكمته، وأبرزه إلى رفقه وما يسر له من رزقه، وعلمه ما لم يكن يعلم، وكان فضل الله عليه عظيما.

ونبهه بآثار صنعته، وأعذر إليه على ألسنة المرسلين الخيرة من خلقه، فهدى من وفقه بفضله، وأضل من خذله بعدله، ويسر المؤمنين لليسرى، وشرح صدورهم للذكرى، فآمنوا بالله بألسنتهم ناطقين، وبقلوبهم مخلصين، وبما أتتهم به رسله وكتبه عاملين، وتعلموا ما علمهم، ووقفوا عند ما حد لهم، واستغنوا بما أحل لهم عما حرم عليهم.

(أما بعد) أعاننا الله وإياك على رعاية ودائعه، وحفظ ما أودعنا من شرائعه.

You have asked me to write a short treatise for you about what is obligatory in the *dīn*, those things which should be pronounced by the tongue, believed by the heart and acted upon by the limbs; about those *sunnahs* which are associated with these obligatory actions – the confirmed (*mu'akkadah*), the supererogatory (*nāfilah*) and the desirable (*raghībah*); something about the courtesies (*adab*) associated with them; along with certain of the key principles and derived rulings in jurisprudence (*fiqh*) according to the *madhhab* and way of Imam Malik ibn Anas ﷺ; and in addition to mention what the great men of knowledge and *fiqh* have said about unclear matters in the *madhhab* in order to make them easier to understand.

You have made this request because of your desire to teach these things to children in the same way that you teach them how to read the Qur'an, so that they may first of all gain an understanding of the *dīn* of Allah and His *sharī'ah* in their hearts, which will hopefully bring them blessing and a praiseworthy end. I have responded to this out of the same hope of gaining for both myself and you something of the reward of those who teach the *dīn* of Allah or call to it.

Know that the best of hearts is the one which contains the most good, and those hearts which are most likely to gain good are the ones that no evil has been able to enter. That which the people of sincere advice are most concerned about and which those who desire its reward most want, is to put good into the hearts of the children of the believers so that it becomes firmly established in them; and to make them aware of the fundamentals of the *dīn* and the limits of the *sharī'ah* so that they may be satisfied with that, and to make their hearts believe those things in the *dīn* that they have to accept and that their limbs are required to do. It is related that teaching the Book of Allah to young children extinguishes the anger of Allah and also that teaching something to someone in their childhood is like engraving

فإنك سألتني أن أكتب لك جملة مختصرة من واجب أمور الديانة مما تنطق به الألسنة، وتعتقده القلوب، وتعمله الجوارح، وما يتصل بالواجب من ذلك من السنن من مؤكدها ونوافلها ورغائبها وشيء من الآداب منها وجمل من أصول الفقه وفنونه، على مذهب الإمام مالك بن أنس رحمه الله تعالى وطريقته، مع ما سهل سبيل ما أشكل من ذلك من تفسير الراسخين، وبيان المتفقهين،

لما رغبت فيه من تعلم ذلك للولدان كما تعلمهم حروف القرآن، ليسبق إلى قلوبهم من فهم دين الله وشرائعه ما ترجى لهم بركته، وتحمد لهم عاقبته، فأجبتك إلى ذلك رجوته لنفسي ولك من ثواب من علم دين الله أو دعا إليه.

واعلم أن خير القلوب أوعاها للخير، وأرجى القلوب للخير ما لم يسبق الشر إليه، وأولى ما عني به الناصحون، ورغب في أجره الراغبون، إيصال الخير إلى قلوب أولاد المؤمنين ليرسخ فيها، وتنبيههم على معالم الديانة وحدود الشريعة ليراضوا عليها وما عليهم أن تعتقده من الدين قلوبهم، وتعمل به جوارحهم، فانه روي أن تعليم الصغار لكتاب الله يطفىء غضب الله، وأن تعليم الشيء في الصغر كالنقش في الحجر، وقد مثلت لك من ذلك ما ينتفعون- إن شاء الله - بحفظه ويشرفون بعلمه، ويسعدون باعتقاده والعمل به.

it on stone. I have made these things clear, and if Allah wills, they will get benefit from learning them, nobility from knowing them and happiness from believing them and acting according to them.

It has come down to us that children should be ordered to do the prayer at seven years old, be chastised for not doing it at ten years old and also at that time be separated in their beds. Similarly, they should be taught before they reach puberty those words and actions which Allah has made obligatory for people so that when they reach puberty these things are fixed in their hearts and they are at ease with them and their limbs are used to doing them. Allah has made certain beliefs obligatory for the heart and certain acts of obedience obligatory for the limbs.

I will arrange what I have undertaken to talk about in chapters so that it will be easier, if Allah wills, for those who are studying it to understand. It is Him we ask for guidance and Him we ask for help. And there is no power nor strength except by Allah, the High, the Mighty. May Allah bless our Master Muḥammad, His Prophet, and his family and Companions and grant them much peace.

وقد جاء أن يؤمروا بالصلاة لسبع سنين، ويضربوا عليها لعشر، يفرق بينهم في المضاجع. فكذلك ينبغي أن يعلموا ما فرض الله على العباد من قول وعمل قبل بلوغهم، ليأتي عليهم البلوغ وقد تمكن ذلك من قلوبهم، وسكنت إليه أنفسهم، وأنست بما يعملون به من ذلك جوارحهم.

وقد فرض الله سبحانه على القلب عملا من الاعتقادات، وعلى الجوارح الظاهرة عملا من الطاعات. وسأفصل لك ما شرطت لك ذكره بابا بابا ليقرب من فهم متعلميه إن شاء الله تعالى، وإياه نستخير، وبه نستعين، ولا حول ولا قوة إلا بالله العلي العظيم. وصلى الله على سيدنا محمد نبيه وآله وصحبه وسلم وتسليما كثيرا.

1. Creeds

The obligatory matters of the *dīn* that the tongue should give expression to and the heart should believe

These obligatory tenets include believing in the heart and expressing with the tongue that Allah is One God and there is no god other than Him, nor is there any like Him nor any equal to Him. He has had no child. He had no father. He has no wife. He has no partner. There is no beginning to His firstness nor any end to His lastness.

Those who try to describe Him can never adequately do so nor can thinkers encompass Him in their thought. Thinkers may derive lessons from His signs but should not try to think about the nature of His Essence.

"But they cannot grasp any of His knowledge save what He wills. His Footstool encompasses the heavens and the earth, and their preservation does not tire Him. He is the Most High, the Magnificent." (2:255)

He is the All-Knowing and the All-Aware, the Arranger and the All-Powerful, the All-Hearing and the All-Seeing, the High and the Great. He is above His Throne, Glorious in His Essence.

He is everywhere through His knowledge. He created man and He knows what his self whispers to him and He is nearer to him than his jugular vein. (50:16)

"No leaf falls without Him knowing of it nor is there any seed in the darkness of the earth, nor any fresh thing nor any dry thing, that is not in a Clear Book." (6:59)

He is settled on His throne and has absolute control over His kingdom.

١ - باب ما تنطق به الألسنة وتعتقده الأفئدة من واجب أمور الديانة

ومن ذلك الإيمان بالقلب، والنطق باللسان، أن الله اله واحد لا إله غيره، ولا شبيه له ولا نظير له، ولا ولد له ولا والد له، ولا صاحبة له ولا شريك له، ليس لأوليته ابتداء، ولا لآخريته انقضاء

لا يبلغ كنه صفته الواصفون، ولا يحيط بأمره المتفكرون، يعتبر المتفكرون بآياته، ولا يتفكرون في ماهية ذاته.

وَلَا يُحِيطُونَ بِشَيْءٍ مِّنْ عِلْمِهِۦٓ إِلَّا بِمَا شَآءَ ۚ وَسِعَ كُرْسِيُّهُ ٱلسَّمَٰوَٰتِ وَٱلْأَرْضَ ۖ وَلَا يَـُٔودُهُۥ حِفْظُهُمَا ۚ وَهُوَ ٱلْعَلِىُّ ٱلْعَظِيمُ ﴿٢٥٥﴾

العالم الخبير، المدبر القدير، السميع البصير، العلي الكبير، وانه فوق عرشه المجيد بذاته.

وهو في كل مكان بعلمه. خلق الإنسان ويعلم ما توسوس به نفسه وهو أقرب إليه من حبل الوريد.

وَمَا تَسْقُطُ مِن وَرَقَةٍ إِلَّا يَعْلَمُهَا وَلَا حَبَّةٍ فِى ظُلُمَٰتِ ٱلْأَرْضِ وَلَا رَطْبٍ وَلَا يَابِسٍ إِلَّا فِى كِتَٰبٍ مُّبِينٍ ﴿٥٩﴾

على العرش استوى، وعلى الملك احتوى.

He has the most Beautiful Names and the most sublime Attributes and He has always had all these Names and Attributes. He is exalted above any of His Attributes ever having been created or any of His Names having been brought into temporal existence.

He spoke to Musa with His speech which is an attribute of His Essence and not something created. He manifested Himself to the mountain and it disintegrated through exposure to His majesty.

The Qur'an is the speech of Allah, not something created which must therefore die out, nor the attribute of something created which must therefore come to an end.

Also included is belief in the Decree, both the good of it and the evil of it, the sweet of it and the bitter of it. All of this has been decreed by Allah, our Lord. The way things are decided is entirely in His control; and the way they happen is according to His decree. He knows all things before they come into existence and they take place in the way He has already decided.

There is nothing that His servants say or do which He has not decreed and does not have knowledge of.

"Does He Who created not then know?
He is the All-Pervading, the All-Aware?" (67:14)

He leads astray whomever He wills and in His justice debases them, and He guides whomever He wills and in His generosity grants them success. In that way everyone is eased by Him to what He already has knowledge of and has previously decreed as to whether they are to be one of the fortunate or the wretched.

He is exalted above there being anything He does not desire in His kingdom, or that there should be anything not dependent on Him, or that there should be any creator of anything other than Him. He is the Lord of all people, the Lord of their actions, the One who decrees their movements and decrees the time of their death.

وله الأسماء الحسنى، والصفات العلى، لم يزل بجميع صفاته وأسمائه، تعالى أن تكون صفاته مخلوقة، وأسماؤه محدثة.

كلم موسى بكلامه الذي هو صفة ذاته لا خلق من خلقه، وتجلى للجبل فصار دكا من جلاله.

وأن القرآن كلام الله ليس بمخلوق فيبيد، ولا صفة لمخلوق فينفد.

والإيمان بالقدر خيره وشره حلوه ومره، وكل ذلك قد قدره الله ربنا، ومقادير الأمور بيده، ومصدرها عن قضائه. علم كل شيء قبل كونه فجرى على قدره.

لا يكون من عباده قول ولا عمل إلا وقد قضاه وسبق علمه به.

أَلَا يَعْلَمُ مَنْ خَلَقَ وَهُوَ ٱللَّطِيفُ ٱلْخَبِيرُ ﴿١٤﴾

يضل من يشاء فيخذله بعدله، ويهدي من يشاء فيوفقه بفضله، فكل ميسر بتيسيره إلى ما سبق من علمه وقدره من شقي أو سعيد.

تعالى أن يكون في ملكه ما يريد أو يكون لأحد عنه غنى، أو يكون خالق لشيء إلا هو رب العباد ورب أعمالهم، والمقدر لحركاتهم وآجالهم.

He has sent Messengers to people so that they would have no argument against Him. He sealed this Messengership, warning, and Prophethood with his Prophet Muḥammad ﷺ whom He made the last of the Messengers, a bringer of good news and a warner,

"and a caller to Allah by His permission and a light-giving lamp." (33:45-46)

He sent down His Wise Book on him and by means of him He explained His upright *dīn* and guided people to the Straight Path.

Also part of what must be believed is that the Final Hour is coming – there is no doubt about it.

It must be believed that Allah will resurrect all who have died: As He brought them into existence the first time so they will be brought back again. (21:104)

It must be believed that Allah, glory be to Him, multiplies the reward of the good actions of His believing servants. He pardons them for their major wrong actions by virtue of their repentance (*tawbah*) and He forgives them for their minor wrong actions by virtue of their avoidance of the major wrong actions.

Those who do not repent of their major wrong actions become subject to His will.

"Allah does not forgive anything being associated with Him, but He forgives whomever He wills for anything other than that." (4:48)

If He punishes someone with His Fire, He will remove him from it on account of any belief he has and by this He will cause him to enter His Garden.

"Whoever does an atom's weight of good will see it." (99:7)

Any of the community of the Prophet ﷺ who have committed major wrong actions and for whom he intercedes, will be brought out of the Fire through his intercession.

الباعث الرسل إليهم لإقامة الحجة عليهم. ختم الرسالة والنذارة والنبوة بمحمد نبيه صلى الله عليه وسلم فجعله آخر المرسلين بشيرا ونذيرا،

وَدَاعِيًا إِلَى ٱللَّهِ بِإِذْنِهِۦ وَسِرَاجًا مُّنِيرًا ﴿٤٦﴾

وأنزل عليه كتابه الحكيم، وشرح به دينه القويم، وهدى به الصراط المستقيم،

وأن الساعة آتية لا ريب فيها

وأن الله يبعث من يموت، كما بدأهم يعودون،

وأن الله سبحانه ضاعف لعباده المؤمنين الحسنات، وصفح لهم بالتوبة عن كبائر السيئات، وغبر لهم الصغائر باجتناب الكبائر،

وجعل من لم يتب من الكبائر صائرا إلى مشيئته

إِنَّ ٱللَّهَ لَا يَغْفِرُ أَن يُشْرَكَ بِهِۦ وَيَغْفِرُ مَا دُونَ ذَٰلِكَ لِمَن يَشَآءُ

ومن عاقبه بناره أخرجه منها بإيمانه فأدخله به جنته.

فَمَن يَعْمَلْ مِثْقَالَ ذَرَّةٍ خَيْرًا يَرَهُۥ ﴿٧﴾

ويخرج منها بشفاعة النبي صلى الله عليه وسلم من شفع له من أهل الكبائر من أمته.

Allah has created the Garden and has prepared it as an everlasting abode for His friends (*awliyā'*). He will honour them in it with the vision of His Noble Face. This is the same Garden from which He sent down Adam, His Prophet and Caliph, to the earth, which was as it had already been decreed in His foreknowledge.

He has created the Fire and has prepared it as an everlasting abode for those who disbelieve in him and deny His Signs and Books and Messengers, and He keeps them veiled from seeing Him.

Allah ﷻ will come on the Day of Rising, together with the angels rank upon rank. All the different peoples will be confronted with their accounts and their punishment or reward.

The balances will be set up to weigh people's actions –

> "*Those whose scales are heavy, they are the successful.*" (23:102)

People will be given pages on which their actions are recorded. Whoever is given his Book in his right hand, will be given an easy reckoning. But whoever is given his book behind his back, will be roasted in a Searing Blaze. (84:7-13)

The Bridge (*ṣirāṭ*) is true and people will cross it according to their actions. Those who cross it and achieve safety from the Fire do so at different speeds, while the actions of others cast them to their destruction in the Fire.

Also included is belief in the Basin (*ḥawḍ*) of the Messenger of Allah ﷺ which his community will come to drink from after which they will never feel thirst again. But those who made any changes or alterations in the *dīn* will be driven away from it.

Belief consists in what you say with the tongue, what you believe sincerely in the heart, and what you do with the limbs. Belief increases when your actions increase, and decreases when they decrease. So it is through actions or the lack of them that increase and decrease in faith occurs.

وأن الله سبحانه قد خلق الجنة فأعدها دار خلود لأوليائه، وأكرمهم فيها بالنظر إلى وجهه الكريم، وهي التي أهبط منها آدم نبيه وخليفته إلى أرضه بما سبق في سابق علمه.

وخلق النار فأعدها دار خلود لمن كفر به، والحد في آياته وكتبه ورسله، وجعلهم محجوبين عن رؤيته.

وأن الله تبارك وتعالى يجيء يوم القيامة والملك صفا صفا لعرض الأمم وحسابها وعقوبتها وثوابها.

وتوضع الموازين لوزن أعمال العبادة

فَمَن ثَقُلَتْ مَوَٰزِينُهُۥ فَأُو۟لَٰٓئِكَ هُمُ ٱلْمُفْلِحُونَ ﴿١٠٢﴾

ويؤتون صحائفهم بأعمالهم، فمن أوتي كتابه بيمينه فسوف يحاسب حسابا يسيرا، ومن أوتي كتابه وراء ظهره فأولئك يصلون سعيرا،

وأن الصراط حق يجوزه العباد بقدر أعمالهم، فناجون متفاوتون في سرعة النجاة عليه من نار جهنم وقوم أو بقتهم فيها أعمالهم.

والإيمان بحوض رسول الله صلى الله عليه وسلم ترده أمته لا يظمأ من شرب منه، ويذاد عنه من بدل وغير،

وأن الإيمان قول باللسان وإخلاص بالقلب وعمل بالجوارح، يزيد بزيادة الأعمال، وينقص بنقصها، فيكون فيها النقص وبها الزيادة.

The statement of belief is not complete without action. Neither are the statement nor action complete without intention. And neither the statement nor the intention are complete unless they are in accordance with the *sunnah*.

No Muslim becomes an unbeliever through wrong actions.

Martyrs (*shuhadā'*) are alive, receiving their provision in the presence of their Lord.

The spirits of the fortunate remain in bliss until the day they are raised again. The spirits of the wretched are tormented until the Day of Judgment.

The believers are tried and questioned in their graves.

"Allah makes those who believe firm with the Firm Word in the life of this world and the Next World." (14:27)

People have recording angels over them who write down their actions. Nothing people do escapes the knowledge of their Lord.

The Angel of Death seizes people's spirits by the permission of his Lord.

The best generation are those who saw the Messenger of Allah ﷺ and believed in him, then those who followed them and then those who followed them.

The best of the Companions (*Ṣaḥābah*) are the Rightly-Guided Caliphs, firstly, Abū Bakr, then 'Umar, then 'Uthman, then 'Alī رضي الله عنهم.

None of the Companions of the Messenger should be mentioned except in the best way, and silence should be maintained concerning any disagreements that broke out between them. They are the people who are most worthy of being considered in the best light possible and the people whose opinions should be most respected.

ولا يكمل قول الإيمان إلا بالعمل، ولا قول وعمل إلا بالنية، ولا قول وعمل ونية إلا بموافقة السنة.

وأنه لا يكفر أحد بذنب من أهل القبلة.

وأن الشهداء أحياء عند ربهم يرزقون.

وأرواح أهل السعادة باقية ناعمة إلى يوم يبعثون، وأرواح أهل الشقاوة معذبة إلى يوم الدين.

وأن المؤمنين يفتنون في قبورهم ويسألون.

يُثَبِّتُ ٱللَّهُ ٱلَّذِينَ ءَامَنُوا۟ بِٱلْقَوْلِ ٱلثَّابِتِ فِى ٱلْحَيَوٰةِ ٱلدُّنْيَا وَفِى ٱلْءَاخِرَةِ

وأن على العباد حفظة يكتبون أعمالهم، ولا يسقط شيء من ذلك عن علم ربهم.

وأن ملك الموت يقبض الأرواح بإذن ربه.

وأن خير القرون القرن الذين رأوا رسول الله صلى الله عليه وسلم وآمنوا به، ثم الذين يلونهم، ثم الذين يلونهم.

وأفضل الصحابة الخلفاء الراشدون المهديون: أبو بكر ثم عمر ثم عثمان ثم علي رضي الله عنهم أجمعين.

ويجب أن لا يذكر أحد من صحابة الرسول إلا بأحسن ذكر، والإمساك عما شجر بينهم، وأنهم أحق الناس أن يلتمس لهم أحسن المخارج، ويظن بهم أحسن المذاهب.

Obedience to the leaders of the Muslims, both their rulers and their men of knowledge, is obligatory.

It is also obligatory to follow the righteous Salaf, tread in their footsteps and ask Allah to grant them forgiveness.

It is also obligatory to avoid wrangling and argumentation regarding the *dīn* and to avoid every new thing which people have introduced into it.

May Allah bless and give much peace to our Master Muḥammad, His Prophet, and his family and his wives and his descendants.

والطاعة لأئمة المسلمين من ولاة أمورهم وعلمائهم،

وإتباع السلف الصالح واقتفاء آثارهم والاستغفار لهم،

وترك المراء والجدال في الدين وترك كل ما أحدثه المحدثون.

وصلى الله على سيدنا محمد نبيه وعلى آله وأزواجه وذريته، وسلم تسليما كثيرا.

2. What necessitates *wuḍū'* and *ghusl*

You must do *wuḍū'* after urinating or defecating or passing wind and when the liquid known as *madhy* emerges from the penis, in which case it is also necessary to wash the entire penis. *Madhy* is a thin, white liquid which comes out at times of sexual excitement when the penis is erect, either during sexual foreplay or when thinking about it. *Wady* is a thick white liquid which comes out, usually after urinating, and it carries the same ruling as urine. Sperm – *maniy* – is the white liquid ejaculated at orgasm during sexual intercourse which smells similar to the pollen of the date-palm. The liquid which comes from a woman is a thin yellow fluid and necessitates purification, purification of the whole body, as is the case after menstruation.

In the case of bleeding which continues beyond the normal period of menstruation (*istiḥāḍah*), only *wuḍū'* is required, although in such circumstances it is recommended for a woman to repeat *wuḍū'* for every prayer. This is also the case for someone suffering from incontinence (*salas*) of urine.

You must do *wuḍū'* after loss of consciousness caused by either deep sleep, or fainting, or intoxication or a bout of madness. *Wuḍū'* is also necessary when you touch someone to gain sexual pleasure or have bodily contact with them for the same reason or kiss them for sexual pleasure.

A man must do *wuḍū'* if he touches his penis. But there is difference of opinion about whether a woman has to do *wuḍū'* if she touches her vagina.

You must do *ghusl* when, as has already been mentioned, sperm (*maniy*) is ejaculated accompanied by sexual pleasure either during sleep or when

٢ - باب ما يجب منه الوضوء والغسل

الوضوء يجب لما يخرج من أحد المخرجين من بول أو غائط أو ريح، أو لما يخرج من مذى مع غسل الذكر كله منه، وهو ماء أبيض رقيق يخرج عند اللذة بالإنعاظ عند الملاعبة أو التذكار. وأما الودي فهو ماء أبيض خاثر يخرج بإثر البول يجب منه ما يجب من البول. وأما المني فهو الدافق الذي يخرج عند اللذة الكبرى بالجماع، رائحته كرائحة الطلع. وماء المرأة ماء رقيق أصفر يجب منه الطهر، فيجب من هذا طهر جميع الجسد كما يجب من طهر الحيضة.

وأما دم الاستحاضة فيجب منه الوضوء، ويستحب لها ولسلس البول أن يتوضأ لكل صلاة.

ويجب الوضوء من زوال العقل بنوم مستثقل أو إغماء أو سكر أو تخبط جنون. ويجب الوضوء من الملامسة للذة والمباشرة بالجسد للذة والقبلة للذة

ومن مس الذكر، واختلف في مس المرأة فرجها في إيجاب الوضوء بذلك.

ويجب الطهر مما ذكرنا من خروج الماء الدافق للذة في نوم أو يقظة من

awake, whether from a man or woman. It is also necessary at the end of the blood of menstruation and when abnormal bleeding (*istiḥāḍah*) stops and at the end of the period of bleeding which follows childbirth (*nifās*).

Ghusl must also be done if the head of the penis penetrates the vagina even if no ejaculation takes place. Just as the penetration of the vagina by the head of the penis necessitates *ghusl*, it also necessitates the *ḥadd* punishment (for *zinā*), the payment of the dowry, gives married couples the status of being *muḥṣan*, makes a woman who has gone through a triple divorce lawful for her original husband and invalidates *ḥajj* and fasting.

A woman should do *ghusl* immediately she sees the white liquid (*qaṣṣah*) which comes at the end of menstruation, or when she notices dryness, even if she notices this after a day or two days or only an hour. If bleeding starts again or if she sees any yellowish discharge, she must stop doing the prayer and then, when the bleeding stops again, she should do *ghusl* and start praying once more. When this situation occurs, it is considered a single menstrual period when reckoning the period of *'iddah* (after divorce or being widowed) or the period of *istibrā'* (in the case of a slavegirl).

If there is a considerable interval between the two periods of bleeding, such as eight or ten days, then the second one is considered to be a new menstrual period. If menstrual bleeding continues longer than fifteen days, then it is considered to be *istiḥāḍah* (false menstruation) and the woman should do a *ghusl*, fast, pray, and her husband can have sexual intercourse with her.

If the bleeding after childbirth (*nifās*) stops soon after the birth, a woman should do *ghusl* straightaway and start doing the prayer. However, if bleeding continues longer than sixty nights, then she performs a *ghusl* anyway, the bleeding is considered to be *istiḥāḍah*, and she does the prayer and fasts and her husband can have sexual intercourse with her.

رجل أو امرأة، أو انقطاع دم الحيضة أو الاستحاضة أو النفاس،

أو بمغيب الحشفة في الفرج وإن لم ينزل. ومغيب الحشفة في الفرج يوجب الغسل، ويوجب الحد، ويوجب الصداق، ويحصن الزوجين، ويحل المطلقة ثلاثا للذي طلقها، ويفسد الحج، ويفسد الصوم.

وإذا رأت المرأة القصة البيضاء تطهرت، وكذلك إذا رأت الجفوف تطهرت مكانها، رأته بعد يوم أو يومين أو ساعة، ثم إن عاودها دم أو رأت صفرة أو كدرة تركت الصلاة، ثم إذا انقطع عنها اغتسلت وصلت، ولكن ذلك كله كدم واحد في العدة والاستبراء

حتى يبعد ما بين الدمين مثل ثمانية أيام أو عشرة، فيكون حيضا مؤتنفا. ومن تمادى بها الدم بلغت خمسة عشر يوما، ثم هي مستحاضة تتطهر وتصوم وتصلى ويأتيها زوجها،

وإذا انقطع دم النفساء فإن كان قرب الولادة اغتسلت وصلت، وإن تمادى بها الدم جلست ستين ليلة ثم اغتسلت وكانت مستحاضة تصلي وتصوم وتوطأ.

3. Purity of Water, Clothing and the Place of Prayer

and What Can Be Worn When Performing the Prayer

When you do the prayer you are talking to your Lord. You must therefore prepare yourself for this by performing *wuḍū'*, or *ghusl* if a *ghusl* is necessary. This must be done using pure water which is uncontaminated by any impurity.

You cannot use water whose colour has been changed by something mixed in with it, whether that thing is pure or impure, unless the change of colour has been caused by something intrinsic to the ground where the water is, such as salt deposits or mud or similar things. Any water coming from the sky or from springs or wells or the sea is good, pure and purifies impurities.

If the colour of the water has been changed by something pure which has got into it, it remains pure but cannot be used for purification either in *wuḍū'* or *ghusl* or for removing impurities. Water that has been changed by something impure getting into it is not pure and cannot be used for purification purposes. A small amount of impurity makes a small amount of water impure even if there is no change in the water.

It is *sunnah* to use a small amount of water when doing *wuḍū'* provided you perform it thoroughly. Using an excessive amount is extremism and innovation. The Messenger of Allah ﷺ did *wuḍū'* with one *mudd* of water, which is equivalent to 1 1/3 *riṭl*s (about 1 litre), and he did *ghusl* with one *ṣā'*, which is four *mudd*s measuring by his *mudd* ﷺ.

It is obligatory for the place where you are going to do the prayer to be pure. Your clothing must also be pure. It is said by some that

٣ - ما طهارة الماء والثوب والبقعة وما يجزي من اللباس في الصلاة

والمصلى يناجي ربه، فعليه أن يتأهب لذلك بالوضوء أو بالطهر إن وجب عليه الطهر. و يكون ذلك بماء طاهر غير مشوب بنجاسة ولا ماء قد تغير لونه لشيء خالطه من شيء نجس أو طاهر، إلا ما غيرت لونه الأرض التي هو بها من سبخة أو حمأة أو نحوهما.

وماء السماء وماء العيون وماء الآبار وماء البحر طيب طاهر مطهر للنجاسات،

وما غير لونه بشيء طاهر حل فيه فذلك الماء طاهر غير مطهر في وضوء أو طهر أو زوال نجاسة، وما غيرته النجاسة فليس بطاهر ولا مطهر. وقليل الماء ينجسه قليل النجاسة وإن لم تغيره،

وقلة الماء مع إحكام الغسل سنة، والسرف منه غلو وبدعة. وقد توضأ رسول الله صلى الله عليه وسلم بمد، وهو وزن رطل وثلث، وتطهر بصاع، وهو أربعة أمداد بمده عليه الصلاة والسلام.

وطهارة البقعة للصلاة واجبة، وكذلك طهارة الثوب، فقيل: إن ذلك فيهما واجب وجوب الفرائض، وقيل وجوب السنن المؤكدة.

the nature of the obligation referred to here is that of an absolute obligation (*farḍ*) and by others that it has the obligatory status of a confirmed *sunnah* (*mu'akkadah*).

You should not do the prayer in places where camels congregrate, or in the middle of a road, or on top of the Ka'bah, or in a public bath – if you are not certain whether it is pure or not – or on a rubbish heap or in a slaughter house, or in the graveyards of non-Muslims and places of worship of non-Muslims.

The least clothing in which a man can do the prayer is something which covers his *'awrah* (everything between his navel and his knees) such as a long shirt or a piece of cloth he can wrap round him. However, it is disliked to do the prayer wearing something that does not cover the shoulders, but if this does happen the prayer need not be repeated.

The least clothing in which a woman can do the prayer is a thick full-length garment covering her whole body including the top of the feet and something covering her head. A woman should touch the ground with the palms of her hands in prostration just as a man does.

وينهى عن الصلاة في معاطن الإبل، ومحجة الطريق، وظهر بيت الله الحرام، والحمام حيث لا يوقن منه بطهارة، والمزبلة والمجزرة ومقبرة المشركين وكنائسهم.

وأقل ما يصلي فيه الرجل من اللباس ثوب ساتر من درع أو رداء، والدرع القميص. ويكره أن يصلي بثوب ليس على أكتافه منه شيء، فإن فعل لم يعد.

وأقل ما يجزىء المرأة من اللباس في الصلاة الدرع الحصيف السابغ الذي يستر ظهور قدميها، وخمار تتقنع به، وتباشر بكفيها الأرض في السجود مثل الرجل.

4. On how to perform *wuḍū'*

and what is *farḍ* and *sunnah* in it – how to clean yourself after going to the lavatory with water (*istinjā'*) or with stones and other things (*istijmār*)

Cleaning yourself with water after going to the lavatory should not be considered a part of *wuḍū'*, being neither one of its *sunnah* nor its *farḍ* aspects. However, you have to do it in order to ensure that all impurities are removed before performing the prayer. You do not have to make a special intention before doing it. The same thing applies when washing impurities off clothes.

The way you wash yourself after going to the lavatory (*istinjā'*) is first of all to wash your hand and then the end of the penis where the urine comes out. You then wipe any impurity from your anus using hard earth or other things or your left hand, which you should then wipe on the ground and wash. After this you wash your anus by pouring water over it, which you continue to do while at the same time relaxing it a little, rubbing the area thoroughly with the left hand until it is clean. You do not have to wash the inside of either of the two openings. You should not do *istinjā'* on account of having broken wind.

When doing *istijmār* it is sufficient to use only three stones provided that the last one comes out clean, but using water is more purifying, pleasanter and is preferred by scholars.

If someone has neither urinated nor defecated but is performing *wuḍū'* because he has broken it in some other way or has been asleep or done something else which makes it necessary for him to perform *wuḍū'*, he should wash his hands before he puts them into whatever water container he is using.

٤ - صفة الوضوء ومسنونه ومفروضه وذكر الاستنجاء والاستجمار

وليس الاستنجاء مما يجب أن يوصل به الوضوء لا في سنن الوضوء ولا في فرائضه، وهو من باب إيجاب زوال النجاسة به أو بالاستجمار، لئلا يصلي بها في جسده، ويجزىء فعله بغير نية، وكذلك غسل الثوب النجس.

وصفة الاستنجاء أن يبدأ بعد غسل يده فيغسل مخرج البول ثم يمسح ما في المخرج من الأذى بمدر أو غيره أو بيده ثم يحكها بالأرض ويغسلها، ثم يستنجي بالماء ويواصل صبه ويسترخي قليلا ويجيد عرك ذلك بيده حتى يتنظف، وليس عليه غسل ما بطن من المخرجين. ولا يستنجى من ريح،

ومن استجمر بثلاثة أحجار يخرج آخرهن نقيا أجزأه، والماء أطهر وأطيب وأحب إلى العلماء.

ومن لم يخرج منه بول ولا غائط وتوضأ لحدث أو نوم أو لغير ذلك مما يوجب الوضوء فلا بد من غسل يديه قبل دخولهما في الإناء.

The *sunnahs* of *wuḍū'* include: washing the hands before putting them into the water container, rinsing the mouth, sniffing up water into the nose and blowing it out again, and wiping the ears. These are all *sunnah* actions, the rest being obligatory (*farḍ*).

Some of the men of knowledge state that when you go to perform *wuḍū'* because you have been asleep or for any other reason you should begin by saying "بِسْمِ اللهِ *bismillah*" ("In the Name of Allah"), whereas others say that this is not part of doing *wuḍū'* correctly.

It is easier to get at the water if the container is on your right hand side. You begin by washing your hands three times before putting them into the water container, except if you have just urinated or defecated in which case you wash off any traces of impurity before starting to perform *wuḍū'*. You then put your right hand into the container, take some water, and rinse your mouth out three times, using either one handful or three as you wish. It is also good to rub your teeth with your finger.

You then sniff up water into your nose and blow it out again three times, holding your nose as you do when you blow it. It is all right if you do this rinsing and sniffing less than three times. It is also all right to do all of this with only one handful of water, but three handfuls is preferable.

Then you take water, either with both hands together, or with the right hand bringing the hands together afterwards, and using both hands pour the water onto your face. Then using both hands you wash the face from the top of the forehead – which is marked by the hairline – to the end of the chin, covering the whole area of the face from the jawbones to where the ears start, making sure you include the eye sockets, any wrinkles on the forehead and the bottom of the nose. You wash your face in this way three times taking water to it.

ومن سنن الوضوء غسل اليدين قبل دخولهما في الإناء، والمضمضة، والاستنشاق، والاستنثار، ومسح الأذنين سنة، وباقيه فريضة. فمن قام إلى وضوء من نوم أو غيره فقد

قال بعض العلماء: يبدأ فيسمي الله، ولم يره بعضهم من الأمر بالمعروف،

وكون الإناء على يمينه أمكن له في تناوله، ويبدأ فيغسل يديه قبل أن يدخلهما في الإناء ثلاثا، فإن كان قد بال أو تغوط غسل ذلك منه ثم توضأ، ثم يدخل يده في الإناء، فيأخذ الماء فيمضمض فاه ثلاثا من غرفة واحدة إن شاء أو ثلاث غرفات، وإن استاك بأصبعه فحسن،

ثم يستنشق بأنفه الماء ويستنثره ثلاثا، يجعل يده على أنفه كامتخاطه، ويجزئه أقل من ثلاث في المضمضة والاستنشاق، وله جمع ذلك في غرفة واحدة، والنهاية أحسن،

ثم يأخذ الماء إن شاء بيديه جميعا، وإن شاء بيده اليمنى فيجعله في يديه جميعا ثم ينقله إلى وجهه فيفرغه عليه غاسلا له من أعلى جبهته، وحده منابت شعر رأسه إلى طرف ذقنه ودور وجهه كله من حد عظمي لحييه إلى صدغيه، ويمر يديه على ما غار من ظاهر أجفانه وأسارير جبهته وما تحت مارنه من ظاهر أنفه، يغسل وجهه هكذا ثلاثا، ينقل الماء إليه

When washing your face you rub the beard with both palms to make sure that water gets into it, since hair has a natural tendency to repel water. According to Mālik you do not have to put your fingers through your beard when doing *wuḍū'*. You merely rub your hands over your beard down to the end.

You then wash your right hand and forearm three times, or twice, pouring water over it and rubbing it with the left hand, making the fingers of one hand go between the fingers of the other. Then you wash the left hand and forearm in the same way with the right hand. When washing the arms you wash them right up to the elbows, including them in the washing. It has also been said that you only wash up to the elbows and that it is not necessary to include them, but it is better to include them in order to remain on the safe side.

Then you take water with your right hand, pour it onto the left hand and, using both hands, you wipe over your head, beginning at the hairline at the front of the head. You place your fingertips together, with the thumbs at the temples, then wipe over your head with both hands as far as the hairline at the back of the neck. Then you bring them back to the place you started, bringing your thumbs up behind your ears back to the temples. Whatever way you wipe your head is acceptable as long as the whole head is covered, but the way mentioned is better. If you were to put both hands into the container, then lift them out wet, and wipe over your head with them this is also acceptable.

Then you pour water over your index fingers and thumbs, or if you like dip them into the water, and with them you wipe the outside and inside of both ears. Women wipe their heads and ears in the same way, but they have to wipe over any hair that is hanging loose and cannot wipe over any head covering. They should put their hands under their plaits when bringing their hands back to the front.

ويحرك لحيته في غسل وجهه بكفيه ليداخلها الماء لدفع الشعر لما يلاقيه من الماء، وليس عليه تخليلها في الوضوء في قول مالك، ويجري عليها يديه إلى آخرها،

ثم يغسل يده اليمنى ثلاثا أو اثنتين. يفيض عليها الماء ويعركها بيده اليسرى ويخلل أصابع يديه بعضها ببعض، ثم يغسل اليسرى كذلك، ويبلغ فيهما بالغسل إلى المرفقين يدخلهما في غسله. وقد قيل: إليهما حد الغسل فليس بواجب إدخالهما فيه، وإدخالهما فيه أحوط، لزوال تكلف التحديد،

ثم يأخذ الماء بيده اليمنى فيفرغه على باطن يده اليسرى، ثم يمسح بها رأسه يبدأ من مقدمه من أول منابت شعر رأسه، وقد قرن أطراف أصابع يديه بعضها ببعض على رأسه، وجعل إبهاميه على صدغيه، ثم يذهب بيديه ماسحا إلى طرف شعر رأسه مما يلي قفاه، ثم يردهما إلى حيث بدأ، ويأخذ بإبهاميه خلف أذنيه إلى صدغيه، وكيفما مسح أجزأه إذا أوعب رأسه، والأول أحسن، ولو أدخل يديه في الإناء ثم رفعهما مبلولتين ومسح بهما رأسه أجزأه،

ثم يفرغ الماء على سبابتيه وإبهاميه، وإن شاء غمس ذلك في الماء، ثم يمسح أذنيه ظاهرهما وباطنهما. وتمسح المرأة كما ذكرنا، وتمسح على دلاليها ولا تمسح على الوقاية، وتدخل يديها من تحت عقاص شعرها في رجوع يديها في المسح،

You then wash both feet, pouring water onto your right foot with your right hand and rubbing it with your left hand little by little. You do this thoroughly three times. If you want, you can put your fingers between your toes. If you do not do this it does not matter, but doing so is more satisfactory. You then rub your heels and ankles and any part which water does not get to easily due to hardening or cracking of the skin. You should make sure you do this well, pouring water on the area with your hand, because there is a hadith which says, "Woe to the heels from the Fire." The "heel" of a thing is its extremity or end. You then do the same thing with the left foot.

Washing each of the limbs three times is not an actual command. You can do it less but three is the most you should do. If you can do it thoroughly with less than that it is acceptable as long as you do not leave anything out. Not everyone is the same regarding the amount of water they require to do *wuḍū'* thoroughly. The Messenger of Allah ﷺ said, "Anyone who does *wuḍū'* and does it well and then raises his eyes to the sky and says:

Ashhadu an lā ilāha illa-llāhu waḥdahu lā sharīka lahu, wa ashhadu anna Muḥammadan 'abduhu wa rasūluh

"'I bear witness that there is no god but Allah alone, without any partner and I bear witness that Muḥammad is His slave and Messenger,' will have the eight gates of the Garden opened for him and he can enter by any of them he chooses."

Some scholars commend saying when you finish *wuḍū'*:

Allāhumma-j'alni mina-t-tawwabin wa-j'alni mina-l-mutaṭahhirin

"O Allah, make me one of those who turn back to You and make me one of those who purify themselves."

You must do *wuḍū'* with full awareness that you are doing it for Allah as He has ordered you to, hoping that it will be accepted and that you will get the reward for it and that it will purify you of your

ثم يغسل رجليه يصب الماء بيده اليمنى على رجله اليمنى، ويعركها بيده اليسرى قليلا قليلا، يوعبها بذلك ثلاثا، وإن شاء خلل أصابعه في ذلك، وإن ترك فلا حرج، والتخليل أطيب للنفس، ويعرك عقبيه وعرقوبيه، وما لا يكاد يداخله الماء بسرعة من جساوة أو شقوق، فليبالغ بالعرك مع صب الماء بيديه. فإنه جاء الأثر (ويل للأعقاب من النار)، وعقب الشيء: طرفه وآخره. ثم يفعل باليسرى مثل ذلك، وليس تحديد غسل أعضائه ثلاثا بأمر لا يجزىء دونه ولكنه أكثر ما يفعل، ومن كان يوعب بأقل من ذلك أجزأه إذا أحكم ذلك، وليس كل الناس في إحكام ذلك سواء. وقد قال رسول الله صلى الله عليه وسلم من توضأ فأحسن الوضوء، ثم رفع طرفه إلى السماء فقال:

أَشْهَدُ أَنْ لَآ إِلَهَ إِلاَّ اللهُ وَحْدَهُ لَا شَرِيكَ لَهُ، وَأَشْهَدُ أَنَّ مُحَمَّدًا عَبْدُهُ وَرَسُولُهُ، فتحت له أبواب الجنة الثمانية يدخل من أيها شاء.

وقد استحب بعض العلماء أن يقول بإثر الوضوء:

اَللَّهُمَّ اجْعَلْنِي مِنَ التَّوَّابِينَ وَاجْعَلْنِي مِنَ الْمُتَطَهِّرِينَ

ويجب عليه أن يعمل عمل الوضوء احتسابا لله تعالى لما أمره به يرجو تقبله وثوابه وتطهيره من الذنوب به، ويشعر نفسه أن ذلك تأهب

wrong actions. You should feel in yourself that it is a preparation and a cleansing for speaking to your Lord and standing in front of Him to carry out the acts He has made obligatory on you with humility in your bowing and prostration. You should perform *wuḍū'* with a certainty of this, taking good care to do it properly, for no action is complete without the right intention behind it.

وتنظف لمناجاة ربه والوقوف بين يديه لأداء فرائضه والخضوع له بالركوع والسجود، فيعمل على يقين بذلك وتحفظ فيه، فإن تمام كل عمل بحسن النية فيه.

5. *Ghusl*

You must do a *ghusl* on account of *janābah* or at the end of menstruation and the bleeding after childbirth. If someone starts their *ghusl* without doing *wuḍū'* it is acceptable but it is better to begin by doing *wuḍū'*, having first washed off any impurity from the private parts or the rest of the body. After that you do *wuḍū'* as you would for the prayer. If you want to, you can include your feet, or if you want, you can leave them to the end.

Then you should immerse your hands completely in the water container, take them out without holding any water in them and rub the roots of your hair with your fingertips. You then take out three handfuls of water washing your head thoroughly with each one. Women do the same as this. They should gather up their hair but do not have to undo their plaits.

You then pour water over your right side, then over the left, rubbing the body with both hands immediately the water has been poured so that the whole body is covered. If you have any doubt about water reaching any part of your body you pour water over it again, rubbing with your hand until you are certain every part of your body has been covered. You must make sure that you include the inside of the navel, under your chin, that you run your fingers right through your beard, that you rub under your armpits, between your buttocks and thighs, behind your knees, not forgetting the heels and the soles of your feet. You also make sure you rub between each finger. If you have delayed washing your feet, then you wash them last, thereby completing both your *ghusl* and your *wuḍū'*.

You should be careful not to touch your penis with the inside of

٥ - باب في الغسل

أما الطهر فهو من الجنابة ومن الحيضة والنفاس سواء، فإن اقتصر المتطهر على الغسل دون الوضوء أجزأه، وأفضل له أن يتوضأ بعد أن يبدأ بغسل ما بفرجه أو جسده من الأذى، ثم يتوضأ وضوء الصلاة، فإن شاء غسل رجليه وإن شاء أخرهما إلى آخر غسله،

ثم يغمس يديه في الإناء ويرفعهما غير قابض بهما شيئا، فيخلل بهما أصول شعر رأسه، ثم يغرف بهما على رأسه ثلاث غرفات غاسلا له بهن، وتفعل ذلك المرأة وتضغث شعر رأسها، وليس عليها حل عقاصها،

ثم يفيض الماء على شقه الأيمن، ثم على شقه الأيسر، ويتدلك بيديه بإثر صب الماء حتى يعم جسده. وما شك أن يكون الماء أخذه من جسده عاوده بالماء ودلكه بيده حتى يوعب جميع جسده، ويتابع عمق سرته وتحت حلقه، ويخلل شعر لحيته وتحت جناحيه وبين أليتيه ورفغيه وتحت ركبتيه وأسافل رجليه، ويخلل أصابع يديه، ويغسل رجليه آخره ذلك يجمع ذلك فيهما لتمام غسله ولتمام وضوئه إن كان أخر غسلهما،

ويحذر أن يمس ذكره في تدلكه بباطن كفه، فإن فعل ذلك وقد

your hand when rubbing your body but if you do, having already completed your *ghusl*, you have to do *wuḍū'* again. If you touch it at the beginning of your *ghusl*, after having washed the areas included in *wuḍū'*, you should then go over them again with water in the proper sequence and with the intention of doing *wuḍū'*.

أوعب طهره أعاد الوضوء، وإن مسه في ابتداء غسله وبعد أن غسل مواضع الوضوء منه فليمر بعد ذلك بيديه على مواضع الوضوء بالماء على ما ينبغي من ذلك وينويه.

6. *TAYAMMUM* AND ITS DESCRIPTION

If you are on a journey and you cannot find water, you must do *tayammum* if you do not expect to find any water before the time for the prayer has finished. You must also do *tayammum*, even when there is water available, whether on a journey or staying in one place, if you are unable to use water on account of illness or are disabled by illness to such an extent that, although you could use it, you are unable to get to it and cannot find anyone else to bring it to you. The same applies to someone travelling who is near water but prevented from reaching it because of fear of thieves or wild animals.

If a traveller reckons that he will get to water within the time of the prayer, he avoids doing *tayammum* until the end of the time. If he reckons he will not get to water he should perform *tayammum* at the beginning of the time. If he does not know whether he will get to water or not, he should perform *tayammum* in the middle of the time. This also applies to someone who is afraid that he will not be able to get to water but nevertheless hopes that he will.

If, under any of these circumstances, you do *tayammum* and do the prayer and then come across water within the time of the prayer the following rulings apply:

- A sick person who could not find anybody to bring water to him should perform the prayer again.
- This also applies to someone who was afraid of wild animals or other dangers of that sort.
- It also applies to a traveller who was afraid he would not reach water but still hoped that he would.

٦ - باب فيمن لم يجد الماء وصفة التيمم

التيمم يجب لعدم الماء في السفر إذا يئس أن يجده في الوقت، وقد يجب مع وجوده إذا لم يقدر على مسه في سفر أو حضر لمرض مانع، أو مريض يقدر على مسه ولا يجد من يناوله إياه، وكذلك مسافر يقرب منه الماء ويمنعه منه خوف لصوص أو سباع.

وإذا أيقن المسافر بوجود الماء في الوقت أخر إلى آخره، وإن يئس منه تيمم في أوله، وإن لم يكن عنده منه علم تيمم في وسطه، وكذلك إن خاف أن لا يدرك الماء في الوقت ورجا أن يدركه فيه.

ومن تيمم من هؤلاء ثم أصاب الماء في الوقت بعد أن صلى،

فأما المريض الذي لم يجد من يناوله إياه فليعد،

وكذلك الخائف من سباع ونحوها، و

كذلك المسافر الذي يخاف أن لا يدرك الماء في الوقت ويرجو أن يدركه فيه،

- If you have done *tayammum* for any other reason than these three, you should not repeat the prayer.

You should not pray two *farḍ* prayers with one *tayammum* unless you are ill and cannot touch water because of some harm to your body that would last at least until the time of the next prayer. Although there are some who say that even in this situation you should perform *tayammum* again for each prayer. It has been related from Mālik that someone who remembers not having done a number of prayers can do them with one *tayammum*.

Tayammum is done using the pure surface of the earth, that is any substance on the earth's surface such as soil, sand, stones, or salt deposits. To do *tayammum* you pat the ground with the palms of both hands, shaking off lightly anything that clings to them. Then, using both hands, you wipe over your whole face. Then you pat the ground with both hands again and wipe over your right hand and arm with your left hand. To do this you put the fingers of your left hand on the tips of the fingers of your right and slide your fingers down the back of your right hand and arm, as far as the elbow, folding your fingers round it as you do so, wiping it thoroughly. Then you put your palm on the inside of your arm and, gripping your arm, slide your hand from your elbow back as far as your wrist and then run the inside of the left thumb over the outside of your right thumb.

You then wipe over the left hand and arm in the same way and finally, after reaching the wrist, you wipe your right palm with the left down to the tips of the fingers. If you wipe the right with the left or the left with the right in some other way that you find easy, that is acceptable as long as it is done thoroughly.

If someone is in a state of *janābah*, or a woman has been menstruating, and they cannot find any water to do *ghusl* with, they should do

ولا يعيد غير هؤلاء

ولا يصلي صلاتين بتيمم واحد من هؤلاء إلا مريض لا يقدر على مس الماء لضرر بجسمه مقيم، وقد قيل: يتيمم لكل صلاة. وقد روي عن مالك فيمن ذكر صلوات أن يصليها بتيمم واحد.

والتيمم بالصعيد الطاهر، وهو ما ظهر على وجه الأرض منها من تراب أو رمل أو حجارة أو سبخة. والتيمم بالصعيد الطاهر، وهو ما ظهر على وجه الأرض منها من تراب أو رمل أو حجارة أو سبخة. يضرب بيديه الأرض، فإن تعلق بهما شيء نفضهما نفضا خفيفا، ثم يمسح بهما وجهه كله مسحا، ثم يضرب بيديه الأرض، فيمسح يمناه بيسراه، يجعل أصابع يده اليسرى على أطراف أصابع يده اليمنى ثم يمر أصابعه على ظاهر يده وذراعه، وقد حنى عليه أصابعه حتى يبلغ المرفقين، ثم يجعل كفه على باطن ذراعه من طي مرفقه قابضا عليه حتى يبلغ الكوع من يده اليمنى، ثم يجري باطن بهمه على ظاهر بهم يده اليمنى، ثم يمسح اليسرى باليمنى هكذا، فإذا بلغ الكوع مسح كفه اليمنى بكفه اليسرى إلى آخر أطرافه، ولما مسح اليمنى باليسرى واليسرى باليمنى كيف شاء وتيسر عليه وأوعب المسح لأجزأه.

وإذا لم يجد الجنب أو الحائض الماء للطهر تيمما وصليا، فإذا وجد الماء تطهرا ولم يعيدا ما صليا.

tayammum for the prayer and then, when they find water, they should do *ghusl*. They do not have to repeat any prayers they have done.

A man may not have sexual intercourse with his wife if she has just finished menstruating or bleeding after childbirth and she has only purified herself through *tayammum* until there is enough water for her to do *ghusl* first and both of them to do *ghusl* afterwards.

Other matters relating to *tayammum* will be mentioned in the general chapter on the prayer.

ولا يطأ الرجل امرأته التي انقطع عنها دم الحيض أو نفاس بالطهر بالتيمم حتى يجد من الماء ما تتطهر به المرأة ثم ما يتطهران به جميعا.

وفي باب جامع الصلاة شيء من مسائل التيمم.

7. Wiping Over Leather Socks

You may wipe over leather socks, either when travelling or otherwise, provided you have not taken them off. This is as long as you put them on after you had washed your feet as part of *wuḍū'* for doing the prayer. It is in this situation that, if you then break *wuḍū'*, you are entitled to wipe over your leather socks when doing *wuḍū'*. In any other case it is not permitted.

The way you do the wiping is to put your right hand on the top of your right foot beginning at the toes and your left hand underneath. Then you pass your hands over your foot as far as the ankle. You do the same thing with the left foot except that you put the left hand on top and the right hand underneath. If there is any mud or dung on your leather socks, you cannot wipe over them until you have wiped or washed it off.

Some people say you should start at the ankles and wipe to the tip of the toes so that any dust on the socks that might get wet does not end up at the ankle end of your socks. But if there is any actual mud on the bottom of your socks you should not wipe over it until it has been removed in any case.

٧ - باب في المسح على الخفين

وله أن يمسح على الخفين في الحضر والسفر ما لم ينزعهما، وذلك إذا أدخل فيهما رجليه بعد أن غسلهما في وضوء تحل به الصلاة، فهذا الذي إذا أحدث وتوضأ مسح عليهما وإلا فلا.

وصفة المسح أن يجعل يده اليمنى من فوق الخف من طرف الأصابع، ويده اليسرى من تحت ذلك، ثم يذهب بيديه إلى حد الكعبين، وكذلك يفعل باليسرى، ويجعل يده اليسرى من فوقها واليمنى من أسفلها. ولا يمسح على طين في أسفل خفه أو روث دابة حتى يزيله بمسح أو غسل.

وقيل: يبدأ في مسح أسفله من الكعبين إلى أطراف الأصابع لئلا يصل إلى عقب خفه شيء من رطوبة ما مسح من خفيه من القشب، وإن كان في أسفله طين فلا يمسح عليه حتى يزيله.

8. The Times of the Prayers and Their Names

According to the people of Madīnah "*the middle prayer*" (2:238) is the early morning prayer, namely the dawn prayer. The beginning of the time for this prayer is when dawn breaks and the light spreads out in the extreme east, going from the *qiblah* to behind the *qiblah*,[1] until it rises up and fills the whole horizon. The end of its time is when the light has got very bright so that someone ending the prayer says the *salām* just as the edge of the sun appears over the horizon. Any time between these two points is acceptable but the beginning of the time is the best.

The time of *Ẓuhr* is from when the sun has passed the zenith, and that is when the shadows start to get longer. It is recommended to delay the prayer in summer until the shadow of an object reaches a quarter of the length of that object added to the length of its shadow at noon. It is also said that this practice is only recommended for mosques so that more people can catch the prayer, and that it is better for a man praying by himself to do the prayer at the beginning of the time. It is also said that, when the heat is fierce, it is better to delay the prayer until it is a little cooler even if you are praying by yourself, since the Prophet ﷺ said, "Delay the prayer until it gets a little cooler because the fierceness of the heat is from the flames of Hell." The end of the time of *Ẓuhr* is when the shadow of an object is the same length as that object in addition to the length of its shadow at noon.

The beginning of the time of *'Aṣr* is the end of the time of *Ẓuhr* and its end is when the shadow of an object is twice the length of that object in addition to the length of its shadow at noon. It is also

٨ - باب في أوقات الصلاة وأسمائها

أما صلاة الصبح فهي الصلاة الوسطى عند أهل المدينة، وهي صلاة الفجر، فأول وقتها انصداع الفجر المعترض بالضياء في أقصى المشرق ذاهبا من القبلة إلى دبر القبلة حتى يرتفع فيعم الأفق، وآخر الوقت الإسفار البين الذي إذا سلم منها بدا حاجب الشمس. وما بين هذين وقت واسع وأفضل ذلك أوله.

ووقت الظهر إذا زالت الشمس عن كبد السماء وأخذ الظل في الزيادة، ويستحب أن تؤخر في الصيف إلى أن يزيد ظل كل شيء ربعه بعد الظل الذي زالت عليه الشمس، وقيل: إنما يستحب ذلك في المساجد ليدرك الناس الصلاة، وأما الرجل في خاصة نفسه فأول الوقت أفضل له، وقيل: أما في شدة الحر فالأفضل له أن يبرد بها وإن كان وحده، لقول النبي صلى الله عليه وسلم: "أبردوا بالصلاة فإن شدة الحر من فيح جهنم". وآخر الوقت أن يصير ظل كل شيء مثله بعد ظل نصف النهار.

وأول وقت العصر آخر وقت الظهر، وآخره أن يصير ظل كل شيء مثليه بعد ظل نصف النهار، وقيل: إذا استقبلت الشمس بوجهك

said that if, standing upright facing the sun with your eyes looking straight ahead, you can see the sun, then the time of *'Aṣr* has arrived. If you cannot see the sun the time has not yet begun. If the sun has descended right into your field of vision, then you are well into the time. According to Mālik ﷺ the time for *'Aṣr* lasts until the sun begins to turn yellow.

The time of *Maghrib* – also known as the prayer of the resident, in that a traveller does not shorten it but prays it in the same way as someone who is resident – is at sunset. When the sun has completely disappeared below the horizon, the prayer is due and it should not be delayed. This moment is the time for this prayer and it should not be delayed beyond it.

The time of the prayer of darkness (*al-'atamah*) or *'Ishā'*, the latter being the better name for it, is when the redness remaining in the sky from the remaining rays of the sun after sunset has disappeared. When all yellowness and redness are gone, the time of the *'Ishā'* prayer has arrived. No attention need be paid to any whiteness that may remain on the western horizon. The time for *'Ishā'* extends from this time until a third of the night has passed for those who want to delay doing it because of working or some other good reason. It is better to do it as early as possible although there is no harm in delaying it a little in mosques to allow time for people to gather. Sleeping before praying *'Ishā'* is disliked, as is talking after it, unless there is a good reason for doing so.

وأنت قائم غير منكس رأسك ولا مطأطىء له، فإن نظرت إلى الشمس ببصرك فقد دخل الوقت، وإن لم ترها ببصرك فلم يدخل الوقت، وإن نزلت عن بصرك فقد تمكن دخول الوقت. والذي وصف مالك رحمه الله أن الوقت فيها ما لم تصفر الشمس.

ووقت المغرب وهي صلاة الشاهد، يعني الحاضر، يعني أن المسافر لا يقصرها ويصليها كصلاة الحاضر، فوقتها غروب الشمس، فإذا توارت بالحجاب وجبت الصلاة لا تؤخر، وليس لها إلا وقت واحد لا تؤخر عنه.

ووقت صلاة العتمة، وهي صلاة العشاء، وهذا الاسم أولى بها غيبوبة الشفق، والشفق: الحمرة الباقية في المغرب من بقايا شعاع الشمس، فإذا لم يبق في المغرب صفرة ولا حمرة فقد وجب الوقت، ولا ينظر إلى البياض في المغرب، فذلك لها وقت إلى ثلث الليل ممن يريد تأخيرها لشغل أو عذر، والمبادرة بها أولى، ولا بأس أن يؤخرها أهل المساجد قليلا لاجتماع الناس، ويكره النوم قبلها، والحديث لغير شغل بعدها.

9. The *Adhān* and the *Iqāmah*

It is obligatory to call the *adhān* in mosques and wherever people meet regularly to do the prayer. If you are alone it is good to give the *adhān*. A man must do the *iqāmah* but for a woman it is only recommended and, if she does not do it, it does not matter. The *adhān* for a prayer should not be given before the time of that prayer except in the case of *Ṣubḥ* when there is no harm in calling the *adhān* in the last sixth of the night.

The *adhān* consists of the words:

Allāhu akbar. Allāhu akbar. Ash-hadu an lā ilāha illa-llāh. Ash-hadu an lā ilāha illa-llāh. Ash-hadu anna Muḥammadan rasūlu-llāh. Ash-hadu anna Muḥammadan rasūlu-llāh.

"Allah is greater. Allah is greater. I testify that there is no god but Allah. I testify that there is no god but Allah. I testify that Muḥammad is the Messenger of Allah. I testify that Muḥammad is the Messenger of Allah."

Then you repeat the testimony in a louder voice than the first time, saying again:

Ash-hadu an lā ilāha illa-llāh. Ash-hadu an lā ilāha illa-llāh. Ash-hadu anna Muḥammadan rasūlu-llāh. Ash-hadu anna Muḥammadan rasūlu-llāh.

Then you say:

Ḥayya 'ala-ṣ-ṣalāh. Ḥayya 'ala-ṣ-ṣalāh. Ḥayya 'ala-l-falāḥ. Ḥayya 'ala-l-falāḥ.

"Come to the prayer. Come to the prayer. Come to success. Come to success."

Then if you are calling the *adhān* for *Ṣubḥ* you add here:

Aṣ-ṣalātu khayrun mina-n-nawm. Aṣ-ṣalātu khayrun mina-n-nawm.

٩ - باب في الأذان والإقامة

والأذان واجب في المساجد والجماعات الراتبة، فأما الرجل في خاصة نفسه، فإن أذن فحسن، ولا بد له من الإقامة، وأما المرأة فإن أقامت فحسن، وإلا فلا حرج. ولا يؤذن لصلاة قبل وقتها إلا الصبح، فلا بأس أن يؤذن لها في السدس الأخير من الليل.

والأذان:

اَللهُ أَكْبَرُ. اَللهُ أَكْبَرُ. أَشْهَدُ أَن لاَّ إِلَهَ إِلاَّ اللهُ. أَشْهَدُ أَن لاَّ إِلَهَ إِلاَّ اللهُ. أَشْهَدُ أَنَّ مُحَمَّدًا رَسُولُ اللهِ. أَشْهَدُ أَنَّ مُحَمَّدًا رَسُولُ اللهِ.

ثم ترجع بأرفع من صوتك أول مرة: فتكرر التشهد فتقول:

أَشْهَدُ أَن لاَّ إِلَهَ إِلاَّ اللهُ. أَشْهَدُ أَن لاَّ إِلَهَ إِلاَّ اللهُ. أَشْهَدُ أَنَّ مُحَمَّدًا رَسُولُ اللهِ. أَشْهَدُ أَنَّ مُحَمَّدًا رَسُولُ اللهِ.

حَيَّ عَلَى الصَّلاَةِ. حَيَّ عَلَى الصَّلاَةِ. حَيَّ عَلَى الْفَلاَحِ. حَيَّ عَلَى الْفَلاَحِ.

فإن كنت في نداء الصبح زدت هاهنا:

"Prayer is better than sleep. Prayer is better than sleep."

This is not said in the *adhān* for any other prayer. Finally you say:

Allāhu akbar. Allāhu akbar. Lā ilāha illa-llāh.

"Allah is greater. Allah is greater. There is no god but Allah."

The last phrase is only said once.

The phrases in the *iqāmah* [apart from *Allāhu akbar*] are said only once. It consists of:

Allāhu akbaru, Allāhu akbaru, ash-hadu an lā ilāha illa-llāhu, ash-hadu anna Muḥammadan rasūlu-llāhi, ḥayya 'ala-ṣ-ṣalāti, ḥayya 'ala-l-falāḥi, qad qāmati-ṣ-ṣalātu, Allāhu akbaru, Allāhu akbaru, lā ilāha illa-llāh.

"Allah is greater, Allah is greater, I testify that there is no god but Allah, I testify that Muḥammad is the Messenger of Allah, come to the prayer, come to success, the time for prayer has come, Allah is greater, Allah is greater, there is no god but Allah."

الصَّلاَةُ خَيْرٌ مِنَ النَّوْمِ. الصَّلاَةُ خَيْرٌ مِنَ النَّوْمِ.

لا تقل ذلك في غير نداء الصبح،

اَللّٰهُ أَكْبَرُ. اَللّٰهُ أَكْبَرُ. لاَ إِلَهَ إِلاَّ اللّٰهُ،

مرة واحدة.

والإقامة وتر:

اَللّٰهُ أَكْبَرُ، اَللّٰهُ أَكْبَرُ، أَشْهَدُ أَن لاَّ إِلَهَ إِلاَّ اللّٰهُ، أَشْهَدُ أَنَّ مُحَمَّدًا رَسُولُ اللّٰهِ، حَيَّ عَلَى الصَّلاَةِ، حَيَّ عَلَى الْفَلاَحِ، قَدْ قَامَتِ الصَّلاَةُ، اَللّٰهُ أَكْبَرُ، اَللّٰهُ أَكْبَرُ، لاَ إِلَهَ إِلاَّ اللّٰهُ.

10. How to perform the prayers

THE *FARḌ* AND THE *SUNNAH* AND *NĀFILAH* PRAYERS CONNECTED TO THEM

Going into the state of *iḥrām* for the prayer is achieved by saying "*Allāhu akbar*". No other expression is acceptable. At the same time you raise your hands level with your shoulders, or lower, and then begin the recitation.

If you are praying *Ṣubḥ* you recite the *Fātiḥah* out loud. You do not say *bismi-llāhi-r-raḥmāni-r-raḥīm* for the *Fātiḥah* nor for the *sūrah* which comes after it. If you are by yourself or behind an imam you say *āmīn* after the words, *wa la-ḍ-ḍāllīn*, but you do not say it out loud. An Imam does not say *āmīn* if he is reciting aloud but he does if the recitation is silent. There is, however, a difference of opinion about whether the imam should say *āmīn* when the recitation is out loud. After that you recite one of the longer *sūrah*s from the *Mufaṣṣal*.[2] If the *sūrah* you recite is longer than that, that is fine so long as it is not getting too light. The *sūrah* is also recited out loud.

When you have finished the *sūrah* you say "*Allāhu akbar*" as you go down into *rukūʿ* – the bowing position of the prayer. You put your hands on your knees, straightening your back so it is parallel to the ground. You do not lift your head nor do you let it drop. You make sure that the insides of your arms are held away from your sides. In both *rukūʿ* and *sujūd* you should be aware of your state of complete submission. You do not make *duʿā'* while you are in *rukūʿ* but if you like, you can say:

2 The *Mufaṣṣal* is the last part of the Qur'an containing the shorter *sūrahs*, beginning with *Sūrat al-Ḥujurāt* (49), although there are other opinions about where it starts.

١٠ - باب في صفة العمل في الصلوات المفروضة وما يتصل بها من النوافل والسنن

والإحرام في الصلاة أن تقول : ٱللَّهُ أَكْبَرُ، لا يجزئ غير هذه الكلمة، وترفع يديك حذو منكبيك أو دون ذلك، ثم تقرأ،

فإن كنت في الصبح قرأت جهراً بأم القرآن، لا تستفتح ببسم الله الرحمن الرحيم في أم القرآن ولا في السورة التي بعدها، فإذا قلت ولا الضالين، فقل:آمين، إن كنت وحدك أو خلف إمام، وتخفيها، ولا يقولها الإمام فيما جهر فيه، ويقولها فيما أسر فيه، وفي قوله إياها في الجهر اختلاف، ثم يقرأ سورة من طوال المفصل، وإن كانت أطول من ذلك فحسن بقدر التغليس، وتجهر بقراءتها.

فإذا تمت السورة كبرت في انحطاطك للركوع، فتمكن يديك من ركبتيك، وتسوي ظهرك مستويا، ولا ترفع رأسك ولا تطأطئه، وتجافي بضبعيك عن جنبيك وتعتقد الخضوع بذلك بركوعك وسجودك، ولا تدعو في ركوعك، وقل إن شئت:

Subḥāna rabbiya-l-'aẓīmi wa biḥamdihi

"Glory be to My Lord the Great and with His praise."

It does not matter how many times you say this or how long you take in saying it.

Then you come up again, at the same time saying:

Sami'a-llāhu liman ḥamidah

"Allah hears the one who praises Him."

And then, if you are by yourself, you say:

Allāhumma rabbanā wa laka-l-hamd

"O Allah, our Lord, all praise belongs to You."

The imam does not say this. Someone praying behind an imam does not say "*sami'a-llāhu liman ḥamidah,*" but he does say, "*Allāhumma rabbanā wa laka-l-hamd.*"

You then stand up straight, still, until the limbs have settled and then go down into *sujūd* without going into a sitting position on the way. As you go down into *sujūd* you say, "*Allāhu akbar.*" You put your forehead and nose on the ground, with your palms flat on the ground, fingers facing *qiblah*, on a level with your ears or further back – there being no fixed position for the hands – although you must make sure your forearms are not touching the ground. Your arms should not be close against your sides but should be held out a little. During *sujūd* your feet should be upright with your toes on the ground facing forwards.

When you are in *sujūd*, you can say if you like:

Subhānaka rabbī, ẓalamtu nafsī wa 'amiltu sū'an fa-ghfir lī

"Glory be to You my Lord. I have wronged myself and acted badly, so forgive me."

Or if you like, you can say something else. You can also make *du'ā'* in your *sujūd* if you want. There is no particular limit to the length of time you may stay in *sujūd* but the shortest is the time it takes for the whole body to become still.

سُبْحَانَ رَبِّيَ الْعَظِيمِ وَبِحَمْدِهِ

وليس في ذلك توقيت قول، ولا حد في اللبث،

ثم ترفع رأسك وأنت قائل:

سَمِعَ اللهُ لِمَنْ حَمِدَهُ

ثم تقول:

اَللَّهُمَّ رَبَّنَا وَلَكَ الْحَمْدُ

إن كنت وحدك، ولا يقولها الإمام، ولا يقول المأموم: سمع الله لمن حمده، ويقول : اللهم ربنا ولك الحمد.

وتستوي قائما مطمئنا مترسلا، ثم تهوي ساجدا لا تجلس، ثم تسجد وتكبر في انحطاطك للسجود، فتمكن جبهتك وأنفك من الأرض، وتباشر بكفيك الأرض باسطا يديك مستويتين إلى القبلة، تجعلهما حذو أذنيك، أو دون ذلك، وكل ذلك واسع، غير أنك لا تفترش ذراعيك في الأرض، ولا تضم عضديك إلى جنبيك، ولكن تجنح بهما تجنيحا وسطا، وتكون رجلاك في سجودك قائمتين وبطون إبهاميهما إلى الأرض، وتقول إن شئت في سجودك:

سُبْحَانَكَ رَبِّي، ظَلَمْتُ نَفْسِي وَعَمِلْتُ سُوءً فَاغْفِرْ لِي

أو غير ذلك إن شئت، وتدعو في السجود إن شئت، وليس لطول ذلك وقت، وأقله أن تطمئن مفاصلك متمكنا،

Then, saying, "*Allāhu akbar*", you come up and sit back. In the sitting position between the two *sajdah*s your left foot is folded underneath and your right foot remains upright and you lift your hands from the ground and place them on your knees. You then go into *sujūd* again repeating what you did the first time.

Then you stand up again directly from *sujūd* pushing yourself up with your hands. You do not go back to the sitting position and stand up from there but rather you do as I have described. As you stand up you say, "*Allāhu akbar.*" You then recite as much as you did in the first *rak'at* or a little less and do the same again except that (in *Ṣubḥ*) you also recite the *qunūt* after doing *rukū'*. You can, however, if you want, recite it before *rukū'* after finishing your recitation of Qur'an.

The *qunūt* consists of the words:

Allāhumma innā nasta'īnuka wa nastaghfiruka wa nu'minu bika wa natawakkalu 'alayka wa nakhna'u laka wa nakhla'u wa natruku man yakfuruk. Allāhumma iyyāka na'budu wa laka nuṣallī wa nasjud. Wa ilayka nas'ā wa naḥfid. Narjū raḥmataka wa nakhāfu 'adhābaka-l-jidd. Inna 'adhābaka bi-l-kāfirīna mulḥiq.

"O Allah, we seek help from You and ask forgiveness of You and believe in You and rely on You. We humble ourselves before you and renounce all other *dīn*s and we abandon all who reject You. O Allah it is You we worship and to You that we pray and prostrate and for You that we strive and struggle. We hope for Your mercy and fear Your certain punishment. Your punishment will surely come to those who disbelieve."

Then you do the same regarding your *sujūd* and sitting as has already been described. When you sit back again after your two *sajdah*s you keep your right foot upright with the toes pointing forward and fold your left foot underneath with your left buttock resting on the ground, not on your left foot. If you want, your right foot can be

ثم ترفع رأسك بالتكبير، فتجلس فتثني رجلك اليسرى في جلوسك بين السجدتين، وتنصب اليمنى، وبطون أصابعها إلى الأرض، وترفع يديك عن الأرض على ركبتيك، ثم تسجد الثانية كما فعلت أولا، ثم تقوم من الأرض كما أنت معتمدا على يديك لا ترجع جالسا لتقوم من جلوس، ولكن كما ذكرت لك، وتكبر في حال قيامك، ثم تقرأ كما قرأت في الأولى أو دون ذلك، وتفعل مثل ذلك سواء، غير أنك تقنت بعد الركوع، وإن شئت قنت قبل الركوع بعد تمام القراءة.

والقنوت:
اللَّهُمَّ إنَّا نَسْتَعِينُكَ وَنَسْتَغْفِرُكَ وَنُومِنُ بِكَ وَنَتَوَكَّلُ عَلَيْكَ. نَشْكُرُكَ وَلاَ نَكْفُرُكَ وَنَخْنَعُ لَكَ وَنَخْلَعُ وَنَتْرُكُ مَنْ يَكْفُرُكَ. اَللَّهُمَّ إيَّاكَ نَعْبُدُ وَلَكَ نُصَلِّي وَنَسْجُدُ، وَإلَيْكَ نَسْعَى وَنَحْفِدُ. نَرْجُو رَحْمَتَكَ وَنَخَافُ عَذَابَكَ الْجِدَّ. إنَّ عَذَابَكَ بِالْكَافِرِينَ مُلْحِقٌ.

ثم تفعل في السجود والجلوس كما تقدم من الوصف. فإذا جلست بعد السجدتين نصبت رجلك اليمنى، وبطون أصابعها إلى الأرض، وثنيت اليسرى، وأفضيت بأليتك إلى الأرض، ولا تقعد على رجلك اليسرى. وإن شئت حنيت اليمنى في انتصابها فجعلت جنب بهمها

at an angle, with the side of the big toe resting on the ground. Both of these positions are acceptable.

You then say the *tashahhud*, which consists of the words:

At-taḥiyyātu lillāh. Az-zākiyātu lillāh. Aṭ-ṭayyibātu-ṣ-ṣalawātu lillāh. As-salāmu 'alayka ayyuha-n-nabiyyu wa raḥmatu-llāhi wa barakātuh. As-salāmu 'alaynā wa 'alā 'ibādi-llāhi-ṣ-ṣāliḥīn. Ash-hadu an lā ilāha illa-llāhu. Wa ash-hadu anna Muḥammadan 'abduhu wa rasūluh.

"Greetings are for Allah, good actions are for Allah, good words and prayers are for Allah. Peace be upon you, O Prophet, and the mercy of Allah and His blessings. Peace be upon us and upon the righteous slaves of Allah. I bear witness that there is no god except Allah and I bear witness that Muḥammad is His slave and His Messenger."

If you then say the *salām* at this point, your prayer is valid.

You can also add to this, one possibility being:

Wa ash-hadu anna-lladhī jā'a bihi Muḥammadun ḥaqq, wa anna-l-jannata ḥaqq, wa anna-n-nāra ḥaqq, wa anna-s-sā'ata ātiyatun lā rayba fīhā, wa anna-llāha yab'athu man fi-l-qubūr. Allāhumma ṣalli 'alā Muḥammadin wa 'alā āli Muḥammadin wa-rḥam Muḥammadan wa āla Muḥammadin wa bārik 'alā Muḥammadin wa 'alā āli Muḥammadin kamā ṣallayta wa raḥimta wa bārakta 'alā Ibrāhīma wa 'alā āli Ibrāhīma fi-l-'ālamīna, innaka ḥamīdun majīd. Allāhumma ṣalli 'alā malā'ikatika-l-muqarrabīna wa 'alā anbiyā'ika wa-l-mursalīna wa 'alā ahli ṭā'atika ajma'īn. Allāhumma-ghfir lī wa liwālidayya wa li a'immatinā wa liman sabaqanā bi-l-īmani maghfiratan 'azmā. Allāhumma innī as'aluka min kulli khayrin sa'alaka minhu Muḥammadun nabiyyuka, wa a'ūdhu bika min kulli sharrin ista'ādhaka minhu Muḥammadun nabiyyuk. Allāhumma-ghfir lanā mā qaddamnā wa mā akhkharnā wa mā asrarnā wa mā a'lannā wa mā anta a'lamu bihi minnā. Rabbanā ātina fi-d-dunyā ḥasanatan wa fi-l-ākhirati ḥasanatan wa qinā 'adhāba-n-nār, wa a'ūdhu bika min fitnati-l-maḥyā

إلى الأرض فواسع. ثم تتشهد.

والتشهد:

اَلتَّحِيَّاتُ لِلّٰهِ. اَلزَّاكِيَّاتُ لِلّٰهِ. اَلطَّيِّبَاتُ الصَّلَوَاتُ لِلّٰهِ. اَلسَّلاَمُ عَلَيْكَ أَيُّهَا النَّبِيُّ وَرَحْمَةُ اللّٰهِ وَبَرَكَاتُهُ. اَلسَّلاَمُ عَلَيْنَا وَعَلَى عِبَادِ اللّٰهِ الصَّالِحِينَ. أَشْهَدُ أَن لآ إِلَهَ إِلاَّ اللّٰهُ وَأَشْهَدُ أَنَّ مُحَمَّدًا عَبْدُهُ وَرَسُولُهُ

فإن سلمت بعد هذا أجزأك.

ومما تزيده إن شئت:

وَأَشْهَدُ أَنَّ الَّذِي جَاءَ بِهِ مُحَمَّدٌ حَقٌّ، وَأَنَّ الْجَنَّةَ حَقٌّ، وَأَنَّ النَّارَ حَقٌّ، وَأَنَّ السَّاعَةَ آتِيَةٌ لَا رَيْبَ فِيهَا، وَأَنَّ اللّٰهَ يَبْعَثُ مَنْ فِي الْقُبُورِ. اَللَّهُمَّ صَلِّ عَلَى مُحَمَّدٍ وَعَلَى آلِ مُحَمَّدٍ، وَارْحَمْ مُحَمَّدًا وَآلَ مُحَمَّدٍ، وَبَارِكْ عَلَى مُحَمَّدٍ وَعَلَى آلِ مُحَمَّدٍ، كَمَا صَلَّيْتَ وَرَحِمْتَ وَبَارَكْتَ عَلَى إِبْرَاهِيمَ وَعَلَى آلِ إِبْرَاهِيمَ فِي الْعَالَمِينَ، إِنَّكَ حَمِيدٌ مَجِيدٌ. اَللَّهُمَّ صَلِّ عَلَى مَلَائِكَتِكَ الْمُقَرَّبِينَ، وَعَلَى أَنْبِيَائِكَ وَالْمُرْسَلِينَ، وَعَلَى أَهْلِ طَاعَتِكَ أَجْمَعِينَ. اَللَّهُمَّ اغْفِرْ لِي وَلِوَالِدَيَّ وَلِأَئِمَّتِنَا وَلِمَنْ سَبَقَنَا بِالْإِيمَانِ مَغْفِرَةً عَزْمًا. اَللَّهُمَّ إِنِّي أَسْأَلُكَ مِنْ كُلِّ خَيْرٍ سَأَلَكَ مِنْهُ مُحَمَّدٌ نَبِيُّكَ، وَأَعُوذُ بِكَ مِنْ كُلِّ شَرٍّ اِسْتَعَاذَكَ مِنْهُ مُحَمَّدٌ نَبِيُّكَ. اَللَّهُمَّ اغْفِرْ لَنَا مَا قَدَّمْنَا وَمَا أَخَّرْنَا وَمَا أَسْرَرْنَا وَمَا أَعْلَنَّا وَمَا أَنْتَ أَعْلَمُ

wa-l-mamāti wa min fitnati-l-qabri wa min fitnati-l-masīḥi-d-dajjāli wa min 'adhābi-n-nāri wa sū'i-l-maṣīr. As-salāmu 'alayka ayyuha-n-nabiyyu wa raḥmatu-llāhi wa barakātuh. As-salāmu 'alaynā wa 'alā 'ibādi-llāhi-ṣ-ṣāliḥīn.

"And I bear witness that what Muḥammad brought is true. And that the Garden is true. And that the Fire is true. And that the Hour is coming and there is no doubt about it. And that Allah will raise up those in the graves. O Allah bless Muḥammad and the family of Muḥammad and have mercy on Muḥammad and the family of Muḥammad as you blessed and had mercy on and sent *bārakah* on Ibrāhīm and the family of Ibrāhīm. In all the worlds, You are praiseworthy, glorious. O Allah, bless Your angels and those brought near and Your Prophets and Messengers and all the people who obey You. O Allah, forgive me and my parents and our imams and those who have gone before us with faith with complete forgiveness. O Allah, I ask You for every good thing that Muḥammad, Your Prophet, asked You for and I seek refuge in You from every evil that Muḥammad, Your Prophet, sought refuge in You from. O Allah, forgive us for what we have done and for what we have put off doing, for what we have kept hidden and what we have done openly and for what You have more knowledge about than us. Our Lord give us good in this world and good in the next world and protect us from the torment of the Fire. I seek refuge in You from the trials of life and death and from the trials of the grave and from the trials of the Dajjal and from the torment of the Fire and from an evil end. Peace be upon you, O Prophet and the mercy of Allah and His blessings. Peace be upon us and upon the right-acting slaves of Allah."

Then you say, "*As-salāmu 'alaykum*" once, starting facing the front and turning to the right a little as you say it. This is what is done by

بِهِ مِنَّا، رَبَّنَا آتِنَا فِي الدُّنْيَا حَسَنَةً وَفِي الْآخِرَةِ حَسَنَةً وَقِنَا عَذَابَ النَّارِ، وَأَعُوذُ بِكَ مِنْ فِتْنَةِ الْمَحْيَى وَالْمَمَاتِ، وَمِنْ فِتْنَةِ الْقَبْرِ، وَمِنْ فِتْنَةِ الْمَسِيحِ الدَّجَّالِ، وَمِنْ عَذَابِ النَّارِ وَسُوءِ الْمَصِيرِ. السَّلَامُ عَلَيْكَ أَيُّهَا النَّبِيُّ وَرَحْمَةُ اللهِ وَبَرَكَاتُهُ، السَّلَامُ عَلَيْنَا وَعَلَى عِبَادِ اللهِ الصَّالِحِينَ

ثم تقول: السلام عليكم. تسليمة واحدة عن يمينك، تقصد بها قبالة وجهك وتتيامن برأسك قليلا، هكذا يفعل الإمام والرجل وحده.

the imam or anyone doing the prayer on their own. If you are doing the prayer behind an imam you say the *salām* once, turning a little to the right, then you return the *salām* of the imam towards the front and then, if there is anyone on your left who has said the *salām*, you greet them in return. You do not say the *salām* to the left if no one has said it to you.

While you are saying the *tashahhud* you place your hands on your thighs, clenching all the fingers of the right hand except your forefinger which you extend with its side uppermost. There is some difference of opinion as regards the movement of this finger. There are those who say that by holding it straight you are indicating that Allah is one God, while those who move it say that doing so repels *shayṭān*. I think they mean by this that you will be reminded in your prayer by moving your finger which will prevent you, if Allah wills, from becoming forgetful and distracted. Your left hand is laid flat on your left thigh and you neither move it nor point with it.

It is recommended to do *dhikr* immediately after the prayer. You say 'سُبحان اللهِ *Subḥāna-llāh*' (Glory be to Allah) thirty-three times, 'اَلْحَمْدُ لِلّٰهِ *Al-ḥamdulillāh*' (Praise be to Allah) thirty-three times, and 'اَللّٰهُ أَكْبَرُ *Allāhu akbar*' (Allah is greater) thirty-three times. Then you seal the hundred by saying:

Lā ilāha illa-llāhu waḥdahu lā sharīka lah. Lahu-l-mulku wa lahu-l-ḥamd. Wa huwa 'alā kulli shay'in qadīr.

"There is no god but Allah alone without partner. His is the kingdom and praise is His and He has power over all things."

It is also recommended, after *Ṣubḥ*, to continue to do *dhikr* and ask forgiveness and glorify Allah and make *du'ā'* up until sunrise or near to sunrise, but this is not obligatory. There are also the two *rak'at*s of *Fajr* which you do before *Ṣubḥ* after the break of dawn. In each *rak'at* you recite just the *Fātiḥah* silently.

وأما المأموم فيسلم واحدة يتيامن بها قليلا، ويرد أخرى على الإمام قبالته، يشير بها إليه، ويرد على من كان سلم عليه على يساره. فإن لم يكن سلم عليه أحد لم يرد على يساره شيئا،

ويجعل يديه في تشهده على فخذيه، ويقبض أصابع يده اليمنى، ويبسط السبابة يشير بها وقد نصب حرفها إلى وجهه. واختلف في تحريكها، فقيل: يعتقد بالإشارة بها أن الله إله واحد، ويتأول من يحركها أنها مقمعة للشيطان، وأحسب تأويل ذلك أن يذكر بذلك من أمر الصلاة ما يمنعه إن شاء الله عن السهو فيها والشغل عنها. ويبسط يده اليسرى على فخذه الأيسر ولا يحركها، ولا يشير بها.

ويستحب الذكر بإثر الصلوات، يسبح الله ثلاثا وثلاثين، ويختم المائة بـ:

لاَ إِلَهَ إلاَّ اللهُ وَحْدَهُ لاَ شَرِيكَ لَهُ، لَهُ الْمُلْكُ وَلَهُ الْحَمْدُ، وَهُوَ عَلَى كُلِّ شَيْءٍ قَدِيرٌ

ويستحب بإثر صلاة الصبح التمادي في الذكر والاستغفار والتسبيح والدعاء إلى طلوع الشمس أو قرب طلوعها، وليس بواجب، ويركع ركعتي الفجر قبل صلاة الصبح بعد الفجر يقرأ في كل ركعة بأم القرآن يسرها.

Your recitation for *Ẓuhr* should be from *sūrah*s like the ones you recite at *Ṣubḥ* or a little shorter, but in *Ẓuhr* none of the recitation is done out loud. In both the first and the second *rak'at*s you recite the *Fātiḥah* and another *sūrah* silently and in the last two *rak'at*s you recite just the *Fātiḥah* silently. You do the *tashahhud* in the first sitting as far as the phrase, '*wa ash-hadu anna Muḥammadan 'abduhu wa rasūluh.*'

After that you stand up but do not say '*Allāhu akbar*' until you are fully upright. This is what is done by someone leading the prayer or someone doing the prayer by himself. If you are doing the prayer behind an imam you stand up after the imam has said, '*Allāhu akbar*', and, when you are fully upright, you say, '*Allāhu akbar*'. Apart from that, the rest of the prayer, in terms of the *rukū'*, *sujūd* and sitting, is the same as has been mentioned for *Ṣubḥ*. It is recommended to pray four *nāfilah rak'at*s after *Ẓuhr*, saying the *salām* after each two *rak'ats*. It is also recommended to do the same before *'Aṣr*

For *'Aṣr* you do exactly the same as we have detailed for *Ẓuhr* except that in the first two *rak'at*s, after reciting the *Fātiḥah*, you recite one of the short *sūrah*s such as "*Wa-ḍ-ḍuḥā*" (93) or "*Innā anzalnāhu*" (97).

For *Maghrib* you do the recitation out loud in the first two *rak'at*s, in each *rak'at* reciting the *Fātiḥah* and one of the short *sūrah*s. In the third *rak'at* you recite the *Fātiḥah* on its own and do the *tashahhud* and say the *salām*. It is recommended to pray two *nāfilah rak'at*s after *Maghrib* and if you do more than this, that is good. Six *rak'at*s are specifically recommended. Doing *rak'at*s in the time between *Maghrib* and *'Ishā'* is also strongly recommended. As for the other aspects of *Maghrib*, they are the same as has already been mentioned regarding the other prayers.

والقراءة في الظهر بنحو القراءة في الصبح من الطوال أو دون ذلك قليلا، ولا يجهر فيها بشيء من القراءة، ويقرأ في الأولى والثانية في كل ركعة بأم القرآن وسورة سرا، وفي الأخيرتين بأم القرآن وحدها سرا. ويتشهد في الجلسة الأولى إلى قوله. وأشهد أن محمدا عبده ورسوله.

ثم يقول فلا يكبر حتى يستوي قائما، هكذا يفعل الإمام والرجل وحده. وأما المأموم فبعد أن يكبر الإمام يقوم المأموم أيضا، فإذا استوى قائما كبر، ويفعل في بقية الصلاة من صفة الركوع والسجود والجلوس نحو ما تقدم ذكره في الصبح، ويتنفل بعدها. ويستحب له أن يتنفل بأربع ركعات يسلم من كل ركعتين. ويستحب مثل ذلك قبل صلاة العصر.

ويفعل في العصر كما وصفنا في الظهر سواء، إلا أنه يقرأ في الركعتين الأوليين مع أم القرآن بالقصار من السور مثل ﴿والضحى﴾ و﴿إنا أنزلناه﴾ ونحوهما.

وأما المغرب فيجهر بالقراءة في الركعتين الأوليين منها، ويقرأ في كل ركعة منهما بأم القرآن وسورة من السور القصار، وفي الثالثة بأم القرآن فقط. ويتشهد ويسلم. ويستحب أن يتنفل بعدها بركعتين، وما زاد فهو خير، وإن تنفل بست ركعات فحسن، والتنفل بين المغرب والعشاء مرغب فيه. وأما غير ذلك من شأنها فكما تقدم ذكره في غيرها.

For the last prayer, *'Ishā'* – which is also known as *al-'Atamah* although the name *'Ishā'* is more appropriate – you pray the first two *rak'at*s out loud, reciting in both of them the *Fātiḥah* and another *sūrah.* The *sūrah*s chosen should be a little longer than those chosen for *'Aṣr.* In each of the last two *rak'at*s you recite the *Fātiḥah* to yourself. The other parts of the prayer are done as has already been described. Sleeping before *'Ishā'* is disliked, as is talking after it unless there is a special need to do so.

The expression 'reciting to yourself' as far as the prayers are concerned means moving the tongue as you articulate the words of the Qur'an. The expression 'reciting out loud' means, if you are doing the prayer alone, that you recite loud enough for yourself and anyone standing close to you to hear. Women's recitation should be quieter than that of men. Otherwise they do the prayer in the same way as men except that they should keep their legs together and their arms close to their sides and keep themselves as gathered as possible when sitting and in *sujūd* and in the whole of the prayer in general.

Then you pray the *shaf'* (even) and *witr* (odd) out loud. In the same way it is recommended to do *nāfilah* prayers at night out loud whereas *nāfilah* prayers during the day should be done to yourself, although if you say them out loud during the day it is still acceptable. The least number of *rak'at*s you can do for *shaf'* is two. It is recommended that you recite the *Fātiḥah* and *Sūrat al-A'lā* (87) in the first *rak'at* and the *Fātiḥah* and *Sūrat al-Kāfirūn* (109) in the second followed by the *tashahhud* and the *salām.* You then pray the single *rak'at* of *witr,* reciting in it the *Fātiḥah, Sūrat al-Ikhlāṣ* (112) and the two *sūrah*s of protection.[3] If you do more than one pair of *rak'at*s for the *shaf'* you do the *witr* at the end.

The Messenger of Allah ﷺ used to pray twelve *rak'at*s at night

3 *Sūrat al-Falaq* and *Sūrat an-Nas.*

وأما العشاء الأخيرة وهي العتمة، واسم العشاء أخص بها وأولى، فيجهر في الأوليين بأم القرآن وسورة في كل ركعة، وقراءتها أطول قليلا من قراءة العصر، وفي الأخيرتين بأم القرآن في كل ركعة سرا، ثم يفعل في سائرها كما تقدم من الوصف، ويكره النوم قبلها والحديث بعدها لغير ضرورة.

والقراءة التي يسر بها في الصلاة كلها هي بتحريك اللسان بالتكلم بالقرآن، وأما الجهر فأن يسمع نفسه ومن يليه عن كان وحده، والمرأة دون الرجل في الجهر، وهي في هيأة الصلاة مثله، غير أنها تنضم ولا تفرج فخذيها ولا عضديها، وتكون منضمة منزوية في جلوسها وسجودها وأمرها كله.

ثم يصلى الشفع والوتر جهرا. وكذلك يستحب في نوافل الليل الإجهار، وفي نوافل النهار الإسرار. وإن جهر في النهار في تنفله فذلك واسع. وأقل الشفع ركعتان، ويستحب أن يقرأ في الأولى بأم القرآن و﴿سبح اسم ربك الأعلى﴾ وفي الثانية بأم القرآن و﴿قل يا أيها الكافرون﴾ ويتشهد ويسلم، ثم يصلي الوتر ركعة يقرأ فيها بأم القرآن و﴿قل هو الله أحد﴾ والمعوذتين وإن زاد من الإشفاع جعل آخر ذلك الوتر.

وكان رسول الله صلى الله عليه وسلم يصلى من الليل اثنتي عشرة ركعة، ثم يوتر بواحدة، وقيل: عشر ركعات، ثم يوتر بواحدة.

making the number odd by praying one *rak'at* at the end. It is also said that he did twenty *rak'at*s making the number odd by adding one *rak'at* at the end. The best time for doing night prayers is the last part of the night. For this reason it is better to delay your *nāfilah* night prayers and your *witr* until the last part of the night. If, however, you are someone who does not usually wake up in time you should do your *witr*, along with any *nāfilah* prayers you want to do, at the beginning of the night and then if you do wake up in the last part of the night you can do whatever *nāfilah* prayers you want to in pairs, but you do not repeat the *witr*.

If you normally pray at the end of the night but oversleep, you can still do your night prayers overlapping the time of *Fajr* up to when it begins to get light. Then you pray your *witr* and pray *Ṣubḥ*. If you remember that you have not prayed the *witr* after you have prayed *Ṣubḥ* you do not make it up.

If you are in *wuḍū'* when you go into a mosque you should not sit down until you have prayed two *rak'at*s, provided it is at a time when you are allowed to pray. If you go into the mosque before you have done the two *rak'at*s of *Fajr* then they take the place of those two *rak'at*s. If you have already prayed the two *rak'at*s of *Fajr* before you go to the mosque, there is a difference of opinion about what you should do. Some people say you pray two *rak'at*s and some people say you do not. Between the break of dawn and sunrise there are no *nāfilah* prayers except the two *rak'at*s of *Fajr*.

وأفضل الليل آخره في القيام، فمن أخر تنفله ووتره إلى آخره فذلك أفضل إلا من الغالب عليه أن لا يتنبه فليقدم وتره مع ما يريد من النوافل أول الليل، ثم إن شاء إذا استيقظ في آخره تنفل ما شاء منها مثنى مثنى، ولا يعيد الوتر

ومن غلبته عيناه عن حزبه فله أن يصليه ما بينه وبين طلوع الفجر وأول الإسفار، ثم يوتر ويصلى الصبح. ولا يقضى الوتر من ذكره بعد أن صلى الصبح.

ومن دخل المسجد على وضوء فلا يجلس حتى يصلى ركعتين إن كان وقت يجوز فيه الركوع، ومن دخل المسجد ولم يركع الفجر أجزأه لذلك ركعتا الفجر، وأن ركع الفجر في بيته ثم أتى المسجد، فاختلف فيه، فقيل: يركع، وقيل: لا يركع، ولا صلاة نافلة بعد الفجر إلا ركعتا الفجر إلى طلوع الشمس.

11. On leading the prayer and rulings concerning the imam and those who pray behind an imam

The man who should lead a group of people in prayer is the best and most knowledgeable one among them. Women may not lead the prayer. This is the case whether the prayer is *farḍ* or *nāfilah* and whether the group in question consists of men or women. People praying behind an imam should recite to themselves when he recites to himself but should not recite with him when he recites out loud.

If you catch one or more *rak'at*s of a group prayer it is as if you have caught the whole prayer. You then make up the *rak'at*s you have missed after the imam has said the *salām*, making your recitation in them out loud or silent in the same way that the imam did. The other aspects of the prayer, such as your standing and sitting, are done as if you were continuing a prayer you had started by yourself.

If you have already done the prayer by yourself you can do it again with a group in order to obtain the excellence there is in doing that, except in the case of *Maghrib*. If you have caught one *rak'at* or more of a group prayer then you should not perform that prayer again with another group. But if you have only caught the *sujūd* or the *tashahhud* then you can, if you want, perform that prayer again with another group.

If there is just one man with the imam he stands on the imam's right. Two or more men stand behind the imam. If there is a woman there as well she stands behind the men. If there is just one man and a woman praying with the imam, the man stands on the imam's right and the woman stands behind them. If a man prays with his wife, she

١١ - باب في الإمامة وحكم الإمام والمأموم

ويؤم الناس أفضلهم وأفقههم، ولا تؤم المرأة في فريضة ولا نافلة، لا رجالا ولا نساء. ويقرأ المأموم مع الإمام فيما يسر فيه، ولا يقرأ معه فيما يجهر فيه.

ومن أدرك ركعة فأكثر فقد أدرك الجماعة، فليقض بعد سلام الإمام ما فاته على نحو ما فعل الإمام في القراءة. وأما في القيام والجلوس ففعله كفعل البانى المصلى وحده.

ومن صلى وحده فله أن يعيد في الجماعة، للفضل في ذلك، إلا المغرب وحدها. ومن أدرك ركعة فأكثر من صلاة الجماعة فلا يعيدها في جماعة. ومن لم يدرك إلا التشهد أو السجود فله أن يعيد في جماعة.

والرجل الواحد مع الإمام يقوم عن يمينه، ويقوم الرجلان فأكثر خلفه، فإن كانت امرأة معهما قامت خلفهما. وإن كان معها رجل صلى عن يمين الإمام والمرأة خلفهما. ومن صلى بزوجته قامت

stands behind him. If a young boy is praying with a man they stand side by side behind the imam as long as the boy is sensible enough not to run off and leave the man he is standing with on his own.

The prayer of the regular imam when he is alone is considered as a group prayer. It is disliked for there to be two group prayers for any one prayer in any mosque that has a regular imam. Someone who has already prayed a particular prayer cannot then be the imam for that same prayer for anyone else.

If the imam leaves out something in his prayer and does the *sujūd* of forgetfulness, those behind him follow him even though they themselves have not left anything out. No one should raise their head before the imam nor do any of the actions of the prayer until he has done them. You must begin the prayer after the imam has begun it, stand up after two *rak'at*s after he has stood up and say the *salām* after he has said the *salām*. With respect to any other of the actions of the prayer apart from these three, it is acceptable to do them at the same time as the imam but it is better to do them after him.

If anything is left out (*sahw*) by someone praying behind an imam, the responsibility for it is borne by the imam, except if it is something like not going into *rukū'* or *sujūd* or leaving out the "*Allāhu akbar*" that begins the prayer (*takbīrat al-iḥrām*) or the *salām* at the end or neglecting to make the intention for that specific prayer.

The imam should not stay in the same place after he has said the *salām* but should move away, except if he is in his own place in which case he can do either.

خلفه، والصبي إن صلى مع رجل واحد خلف الإمام قاما خلفه إن كان الصبي يعقل لا يذهب ويدع من يقف معه.

والإمام الراتب إن صلى وحده قام مقام الجماعة. ويكره في كل مسجد له إمام راتب أن تجمع فيه الصلاة مرتين. ومن صلى صلاة فلا يؤم فيها أحدا،

وإذا سها الإمام وسجد لسهوه فليتبعه من لم يسه معه ممن خلفه. ولا يرفع أحد رأسه قبل الإمام، ولا يفعل إلا بعد فعله، ويفتتح بعده، ويقوم من اثنتين بعد قيامه، ويسلم بعد سلامه، وما سوى ذلك فواسع أن يفعله معه، وبعده أحسن.

وكل سهو سهاه المأموم فالإمام يحمله عنه إلا ركعة أو سجدة أو تكبيرة الإحرام أو السلام أو اعتقاد نية الفريضة،

وإذا سلم الإمام فلا يثبت بعد سلامه، ولينصرف، إلا أن يكون في محله فذلك واسع.

12. On various aspects of the prayer

The least amount of clothing that is acceptable for a woman to do the prayer in is a robe which cannot be seen through that is long enough to cover the tops of her feet and a head covering through which the hair cannot be seen. The least which is acceptable for a man is a single garment. You should not cover your nose or your face in the prayer nor should you gather up your clothes or tie back your hair especially for it.

Any time you inadvertently add something to the prayer you should do two *sajdah*s after saying the *salām* and then do the *tashahhud* and say the *salām* again. If you miss something out of the prayer you should do two *sajdah*s before saying the *salām* after having finished the *tashahhud*. You then do the *tashahhud* again and say the *salām*. Some people say that it is not necessary to repeat the *tashahhud*. If you both leave something out and add something, then you do the two *sajdah*s before the *salām*. If you forget to do the two *sajdah*s which should be done after the *salām* you do them whenever you remember them even if a long time has elapsed. If you forget to do the two *sajdah*s which should be done before the *salām* then you do them straight away so long as the prayer is not long over. If quite some time has elapsed, however, you have to do the prayer again unless what you left out was not particularly critical such as only the *sūrah* which should follow the *Fātiḥah*, or two *takbīr*s, or saying the *tashahhud*s, or similar things in which case you need not do anything.

The two *sajdah*s of forgetfulness are not sufficient to make up for missing out a *rukū'* or *sujūd* or failing to recite the *Fātiḥah* in two *rak'at*s of any prayer (or, in case of *Ṣubḥ*, one *rak'at*). There is a difference of

١٢ - باب جامع في الصلاة

وأقل ما يجزئ المرأة من اللباس في الصلاة الدرع الخصيف السابغ الذي يستر ظهور قدميها، وهو القميص والخمار الخصيف. ويجزئ الرجل في الصلاة ثوب واحد، ولا يغطي أنفه ووجهه في الصلاة، أو يضم ثيابه، أو يكفت شعره.

وكل سهو في الصلاة بزيادة فليسجد له سجدتين بعد السلام، يتشهد لهما ويسلم منهما، وكل سهو بنقص فليسجد له قبل السلام إذا تم تشهده، ثم يتشهد ويسلم، وقيل: لا يعيد التشهد، ومن نقص وزاد سجد قبل السلام. ومن نسي أن يسجد بعد السلام فليسجد متى ذكره وإن طال ذلك، وإن كان قبل السلام سجد إن كان قريبا، وإن بعد ابتدأ صلاته إلا أن يكون ذلك من نقص شيء خفيف كالسورة مع أم القرآن، أو تكبيرتين، أو التشهدين وشبه ذلك فلا شيء عليه.

ولا يجزيء سجود السهو لنقص ركعة ولا سجدة ولا لترك القراءة في الصلاة كلها أو في ركعتين منها، وكذلك في ترك القراءة في ركعة

opinion about what you should do if you miss out the *Fātiḥah* in one *rak'at* of any prayer apart from *Ṣubḥ*. Some people say that you only have to do the two *sajdah*s before the *salām*; others say that the whole *rak'at* is invalidated and that you must do another *rak'at* to make up for it; yet others say that you do the two *sajdah*s before the *salām* without doing another *rak'at* but then repeat the whole prayer to make sure of being correct. This last ruling is the best if Allah wills.

If you forget to say one *takbīr* or to say '*sami'a-llāhu liman ḥamidah*' once or to do the *qunut* you do not have to do the *sajdah*s of forgetfulness. If you finish the prayer and then remember that you left out part of it, you should go back to it straightaway by saying a new *takbīr al-iḥrām* – provided that only a very little time has passed since you finished it – and then do whatever it was that you missed out. If, however, a long time has elapsed or you have left the mosque, you must begin the whole prayer again. That is also the case if someone forgets the *salām*.

If you do not know whether you have prayed three or four *rak'at*s you build on what you are certain of, repeating anything you are unsure about, in this case praying another *rak'at* to make sure of having prayed four. You then perform the *sajdah*s of forgetfulness after the *salām*. If you speak during the prayer inadvertently, you also perform the *sajdah*s of forgetfulness after the *salām*. If you are not sure whether you said the *salām* or not, you say it and do not do any *sajdah*s of forgetfulness.

Someone who finds themselves thinking all the time that they have made a mistake in the prayer should pay no attention to their doubts. They do not have to do anything in reparation but they should perform the two *sajdah*s after the *salām*. This refers to people who find this happening a lot and who are continually in doubt about whether they have added something to the prayer or left something out and never feel certain that they have prayed correctly. They should only

من الصبح، واختلف في السهو عن القراءة في ركعة من غيرها، فقيل: يجزيء فيه سجود السهو قبل السلام، وقيل يلغيها ويأتي بركعة وقيل: يسجد قبل السلام ولا يأتي بركعة ويعيد الصلاة احتياطا، وهذا أحسن ذلك إن شاء الله تعالى.

ومن سها عن تكبيرة أو عن قول سمع الله لمن حمده مرة أو القنوت فلا سجود عليه. ومن انصرف من الصلاة ثم ذكر أنه بقي عليه شيء منها فليرجع إن كان بقرب ذلك فيكبر تكبيرة يحرم بها. ثم يصلي ما بقي عليه، وإن تباعد ذلك أو خرج من المسجد ابتدأ صلاته، وكذلك من نسي السلام. ومن لم يدر ما صلى أثلاث ركعات أم أربعا بنى على اليقين وصلى ما شك فيه وأتى برابعة وسجد بعد سلامه. ومن تكلم ساهيا سجد بعد السلام. ومن لم يدر أسلم أم لم يسلم سلم ولا سجود عليه.

ومن استنكحه الشك في السهو فليله عنه ولا إصلاح عليه، ولكن عليه أن يسجد بعد السلام، وهو الذي يكثر ذلك منه، يشك كثيرا أن يكون سها زاد أو نقص ولا يوقن فليسجد بعد السلام فقط. وإذا أيقن بالسهو سجد بعد إصلاح صلاته، فإن كثر ذلك منه فهو يعتريه كثيرا أصلح صلاته ولم يسجد لسهوه.

perform the two *sajdah*s after the *salām*. On the other hand if they are certain that they have made a mistake, they should make the appropriate reparation and do the *sajdah*s of forgetfulness. If someone is always making a particular mistake in the prayer and this happens a lot, he should make the appropriate reparation but not do the *sajdah*s of forgetfulness.

If you begin to stand up directly from *sujūd* at the end of two *rak'at*s you should sit back down again as long as your hands and knees have not left the ground. If they have you should continue on up and not go back down and then do the *sajdah*s of forgetfulness before the *salām*.

If you have missed a prayer you should do it as soon as you remember in the same way that you would have done it if you had done it at its proper time. If you have already done the prayer of the time you are in you should do it again after making up the prayer you missed. If you have a lot of prayers to make up you can do them at any time of the day or night, including sunrise and sunset, according to what is convenient in your particular situation. If the number of prayers you have to make up is less than five you should do them before doing the prayer of the time you are in even if that means going beyond the time of that prayer. If the number of prayers you have to make up is greater than this and you are afraid that if you do them you will not be able to do the prayer of the time you are in in its time, you should pray that prayer first. If, while you are doing a prayer, you remember having missed a previous prayer, the prayer you are doing becomes invalid.

If you laugh while doing a prayer you have to repeat the prayer but you do not have to do *wuḍū'* again. If this happens when you are praying behind an imam you complete the prayer with him but then do it again afterwards. If you merely smile no reparation is necessary. Blowing in the prayer incurs the same ruling as talking – if it is intentional it invalidates your prayer.

ومن قام من اثنتين رجع ما لم يفارق الأرض بيديه وركبتيه، فإذا فارقها تمادى ولم يرجع وسجد قبل السلام.

ومن ذكر صلاة، صلاها متى ما ذكرها على نحو ما فاتته ثم أعاد ما كان في وقته مما صلى بعدها، ومن عليه صلوات كثيرة صلاها في كل وقت من ليل أو نهار، وعند طلوع الشمس وعند غروبها وكيفما تيسر له، وإن كانت يسيرة أقل من صلاة يوم وليلة بدأ بهن وإن فات وقت ما هو في وقته، وإن كثرت بدأ بما يخاف فوات وقته. ومن ذكر صلاة في صلاة فسدت هذه عليه،

ومن ضحك في الصلاة أعادها ولم يعد الوضوء، وإن كان مع إمام تمادى وأعاد. ولاشيء عليه في التبسم. والنفخ في الصلاة كالكلام، والعامد لذلك مفسد لصلاته.

If you make a mistake regarding the direction of *qiblah* you should do the prayer again if there is still time. The same applies if you do the prayer in clothes with some impurity on them or pray in an impure place. And the same also applies if you have done *wuḍū'* with water whose colour, taste, or smell has definitely changed: you must do the prayer again however much time has elapsed and, of course, repeat your *wuḍū'*.

It is permitted to join *Maghrib* and *'Ishā'* when there is heavy rain and also if it is muddy and the night is very dark. When this is the case the *adhān* for *Maghrib* is called at the beginning of the time outside the mosque. Then, according to Mālik, you should wait a little, then call the *iqāmah* inside the mosque and do the prayer. Then you call the *adhān* for *'Ishā'* inside the mosque and do the *iqāmah* and then do the prayer. Then everyone should leave while there is still some light left in the sky.

It is an obligatory *sunnah* to join together *Ẓuhr* and *'Aṣr* at Arafat at midday with an *adhān* and an *iqāmah* for each prayer. The same applies to joining *Maghrib* and *'Ishā'* on your arrival at Muzdalifah. If you are travelling hard you are permitted to join two prayers together – that is to pray *Ẓuhr* at the end of its time together with *'Aṣr* at the beginning of its time – and the same applies to *Maghrib* and *'Ishā'*. If you are starting your journey at the beginning of the time of the first prayer you may also join the two prayers together then.

Sick people are permitted to join the prayers, at the time of *Ẓuhr* or *Maghrib*, if they are afraid that their sickness will cause them to lose consciousness before the time of the next prayer. If joining the prayers makes things easier for someone suffering from dysentery or a similar illness, he can do the two prayers together either in the middle of the time of *Ẓuhr* or when the redness in the sky fades after *Maghrib*.

If you faint you do not have to make up any prayers whose time

ومن أخطأ القبلة أعاد في الوقت، وكذلك من صلى بثوب نجس أو على مكان نجس، وكذلك من توضأ بماء نجس مختلف في نجاسته، وأما من توضأ بماء قد تغير لونه أو طعمه أو ريحه أعاد صلاته أبدا ووضوءه.

ورخص في الجمع بين المغرب والعشاء ليلة المطر، وكذلك في طين وظلمة، يؤذن للمغرب أول الوقت خارج المسجد، ثم يؤخر قليلا في قول مالك، ثم يقيم في داخل المسجد ويصليها، ثم يؤذن للعشاء في داخل المسجد ويقيم ثم يصليها، ثم ينصرفون وعليهم إسفار قبل مغيب الشفق.

والجمع بعرفة بين الظهر والعصر عند الزوال سنة واجبة بأذان وإقامة لكل صلاة، وكذلك في جمع المغرب والعشاء بالمزدلفة إذا وصل إليها. وإذا جد السير بالمسافر فله أن يجمع بين الصلاتين في آخر وقت الظهر وأول وقت العصر، وكذلك المغرب والعشاء. وإذ ارتحل في أول وقت الصلاة الأولى جمع حينئذ.

وللمريض أن يجمع إذا خاف أن يغلب على عقله عند الزوال وعند الغروب، وإن كان الجمع أرفق به لبطن به ونحوه جمع وسط وقت الظهر وعند غيبوبة الشفق.

والمغمى عليه لا يقضي ما خرج وقته في إغمائه، ويقضي ما أفاق

finishes while you are still unconscious. If you regain consciousness, however, while there is still time to do at least one *rak'at* you must make up that prayer. The same applies to a menstruating woman when she becomes pure. If, after having a *ghusl* straight away, there is still enough of the daytime left to do five *rak'at*s, she should pray both *Ẓuhr* and *'Aṣr*. And if there is enough of the night left to do four *rak'at*s she should pray both *Maghrib* and *'Ishā'*. If there is less left of the day or night than that she should only pray the second of the two prayers.

If a woman's period starts with these same amounts of time left in the day or the night without her having done the prayers in question she does not have to make them up. However, if it starts in the daytime when there is only time for four *rak'at*s or less, even one *rak'at*, or at night when there is only time for three *rak'at*s or less, even one *rak'at*, she should only make up the first of the two prayers. There is a difference of opinion about the ruling if a woman's period starts when there is enough of the night left to pray four *rak'at*s. Some people say that the same applies and others say that since her period began in the time of both prayers she does not have to make either of them up.

If you are sure that you have done *wuḍū'* but not sure whether you have broken it or not since, then you should do *wuḍū'* again. If you remember missing out any *farḍ* aspect of *wuḍū'* soon after finishing it, you do the thing you missed out and whatever comes after it. If some time has elapsed you just do the thing you missed out, except if you missed it out deliberately, in which case you must do the whole *wuḍū'* again. If, in any of the above situations, you have already done the prayer you must do it over again no matter how much time has gone by, having put right *wuḍū'* as necessary. If you remember missing out something like rinsing out the mouth or snuffing up water or wiping the ears and only a short time has elapsed, you should do the thing you missed on its own. If a long time has passed, you must do the

في وقته مما يدرك منه ركعة فأكثر من الصلوات. وكذلك الحائض تطهر، فإذا بقي من النهار بعد طهرها بغير توان خمس ركعات صلت الظهر والعصر، وإن كان الباقي من الليل أربع ركعات صلت المغرب والعشاء، وإن كان من النهار أو من الليل أقل من ذلك صلت الصلاة الأخيرة،

وإن حاضت لهذا التقدير لم تقض ما حاضت في وقته، وإن حاضت لأربع ركعات من النهار فأقل إلى ركعة أو لثلاث ركعات من الليل إلى ركعة قضت الصلاة الأولى فقط، واختلف في حيضها لأربع ركعات من الليل، فقيل مثل ذلك وقيل: إنها حاضت في وقتهما فلا تقضيهما.

ومن أيقن بالوضوء وشك في الحدث ابتدأ الوضوء، ومن ذكر من وضوئه شيئا مما هو فريضة منه، فإن كان بالقرب أعاد ذلك وما يليه، وإن تطاول ذلك أعاده فقط، وإن تعمد ذلك ابتدأ الوضوء إن طال ذلك، وإن كان قد صلى في جميع ذلك أعاد صلاته أبدا ووضوءه، وإن ذكر مثل المضمضة والاستنشاق ومسح الأذنين، فإن كان قريبا فعل ذلك ولم يعد ما بعده، وإن تطاول فعل ذلك لما يستقبل، ولم يعد ما صلى قبل أن يفعل ذلك.

thing you missed before performing any other prayers. You do not have to repeat any prayer you have already done.

If a mat has some impurity on it but you do the prayer on a part which is pure, your prayer is valid. There is no harm in a sick man putting down a thick cloth which is pure over his bedding which has impurity on it and then doing the prayer on that. If a sick man cannot pray standing up he should pray sitting down, cross-legged if possible; if not then to the best of his ability. If he is not able to go into *sujūd* he should make a gesture of going into *rukū'* and *sujūd*, making what he does for *sujūd* lower than what he does for *rukū'*. If he cannot sit he should pray lying on his right side making gestures to indicate the various positions. If he is unable to do anything but lie on his back he should pray in that position. As long as he is in his right mind he should not delay the prayer and should do it as best as he is able.

If a sick person cannot use water because doing so would be harmful to him or because he cannot get anyone to bring him any, he should do *tayammum*. If he cannot find anyone to bring him earth, he should do *tayammum* using the wall at his side provided that it is made of clay or covered with clay. If, however, the wall is covered with plaster or whitewash, it cannot be used for *tayammum*.

If the prayer becomes due while you are travelling and you cannot find anywhere to pray because of mud, you should get off your riding animal and do the prayer standing up, making the motion you do for *sajdah* lower than the one for *rukū'*. If there is so much mud that you cannot even dismount you should do the prayer on your riding animal facing *qiblah*. A traveller may do *nāfilah* prayers on the move while seated on his riding animal no matter what direction the animal is going in, provided that he is on a journey for which the prayer can be shortened. However *farḍ* prayers, even in the case of illness, should only be done on the ground unless the illness is such that getting off

ومن صلى على موضع طاهر من حصير وبموضع آخر منه نجاسة فلا شيء عليه. والمريض إذا كان على فراش نجس فلا بأس أن يبسط عليه ثوبا طاهرا كثيفا ويصلي عليه. وصلاة المريض إن لم يقدر على القيام صلى جالسا إن قدر على التربع، وإلا فبقدر طاقته، وإن لم يقدر على السجود فليومئ بالركوع والسجود، ويكون سجوده أخفض من ركوعه، وإن لم يقدر صلى على جنبه الأيمن إيماء، وإن لم يقدر إلا على ظهره فعل ذلك، ولا يؤخر الصلاة إذا كان في عقله، وليصلها بقدر ما يطيق.

وإن لم يقدر على مس الماء لضرر به أو لأنه لا يجد من يناوله إياه تيمم، فإن لم يجد من يناوله ترابا تيمم بالحائط إلى جانبه إن كان طينا أو عليه طين، فإن كان عليه جص أو جير فلا يتيمم به.

والمسافر يأخذه الوقت في طين خضخاض لا يجد أين يصلي فلينزل عن دابته ويصلي فيه قائما يومئ بالسجود أخفض من الركوع، فإن لم يقدر أن ينزل فيه صلى على دابته إلى القبلة. وللمسافر أن يتنفل على دابته في سفره حيثما توجهت به إن كان سفرا تقصر فيه الصلاة، وليوتر على دابته إن شاء، ولا يصلي الفريضة، وإن كان مريضا إلا بالأرض،إلا أن يكون إن نزل صلى جالسا إيماء لمرضه فليصل على الدابة بعد أن توقف له ويستقبل بها القبلة.

the animal would mean that the sick person was forced by his illness to do the prayer sitting down using gestures. In this case he should pray on his animal after it has been brought to a halt and made to face *qiblah*.

If you have a nosebleed when you are praying behind an imam you should go out and wash off the blood and then return and complete the prayer as long as you have not spoken or stepped on any impurity. You should discount any partial *rak'at* you have already prayed unless you completed its two *sajdahs*. If there is only a little blood you should not leave the prayer but staunch the blood with your fingers except if it is pouring out or dripping. You may not, however, complete a prayer in this way if you have to leave it because of vomiting or breaking *wuḍū'*. If your nosebleed starts after the imam has said the *salām*, you say the *salām* and then leave the prayer-line, but if it starts just before the imam says the *salām* you should go out, wash off the blood, come back, sit down, and then say the *salām*. If there is no chance of catching the end of the prayer with the imam, you can complete the prayer in your house, except in the case of *Jumu'ah* when you must complete it in the mosque.

If there is a small amount of blood on your clothes you should wash it off but you do not have to repeat the prayer. If there is a large amount of blood you have to repeat the prayer. With any other impurity it is immaterial whether the amount is small or large, you have to repeat the prayer in any case. You do not have to wash off the blood which comes from insects bites except if it is excessive.

ومن رعف مع الإمام خرج فغسل الدم ثم بنى ما لم يتكلم أو يمش على نجاسة، ولا يبني على ركعة لم تتم بسجدتيها وليلغها، ولا ينصرف لدم خفيف، وليفتله بأصابعه إلا أن يسيل أو يقطر، ولا يبني في قيء ولا حدث. ومن رعف بعد سلام الإمام سلم وانصرف، وإن رعف قبل سلامه انصرف وغسل الدم ثم رجع فجلس وسلم، وللراعف أن يبني في منزله إذا يئس أن يدرك بقية صلاة الإمام، إلا في الجمعة فلا يبني إلا في الجامع،

يغسل قليل الدم من الثوب، ولا تعاد الصلاة إلا من كثيره. وقليل كل نجاسة غيره وكثيرها سواء. ودم البراغيث ليس عليه غسله إلا أن يتفاحش.

13. On the *Sajdahs* of the Qur'an

There are eleven places of *sajdah* in the Qur'an, these being the places where you are commanded to go into *sujūd*. None of these are in the *Mufaṣṣal*. They are:

1. In *Sūrat al-A'rāf*, (7:206) where Allah *ta'ālā* says:

"*They glorify His praise and they prostrate to Him*" which is the end of the *sūrah*.

If you are doing the prayer you should go into *sujūd* when you reach this point and then, after getting up again, recite what is easy for you from *Sūrat al-Anfāl* or some other *sūrah* and then go into *rukū'* and *sujūd*.

2. In *Sūrat ar-Ra'd* (13:15) where Allah *ta'ālā* says:

"*...as do their shadows in the morning and in the evening*".

3. In *Sūrat an-Naḥl* (16:50) where Allah *ta'ālā* says:

"*They fear their Lord above them and do everything they are ordered to do.*"

4. In *Sūrat al-Isrā'* (17:109) where Allah *ta'ālā* says:

"*Weeping, they fall to the ground in prostration,*
and it increases them in humility."

5. In *Sūrah Maryam* (19:58) where Allah *ta'ālā* says:

"*When the Signs of the All-Merciful were recited to them*
they fell on their faces, weeping, in prostration."

6. In *Sūrat al-Ḥajj* (22:18) where Allah *ta'ālā* says:

"*Those Allah humiliates will have no one to honour them.*
Allah does whatever He wills."

١٣ - باب في سجود القرءان

وسجود القرآن إحدى عشرة سجدة، وهي العزائم. ليس في المفصل منها شيء.

في المص عند قوله تعالى:

يُسَبِّحُونَهُۥ وَلَهُۥ يَسْجُدُونَ ۩ ﴿٢٠٦﴾ وهو آخرها،

فمن كان في صلاة، فإذا سجدها قام فقرأ من الأنفال أو من غيرها ما تيسر عليه، ثم ركع وسجد.

وفي الرعد عند قوله:

وَظِلَٰلُهُم بِٱلْغُدُوِّ وَٱلْءَاصَالِ ۩ ﴿١٥﴾

وفي النحل:

يَخَافُونَ رَبَّهُم مِّن فَوْقِهِمْ وَيَفْعَلُونَ مَا يُؤْمَرُونَ ۩ ﴿٥٠﴾

وفي بني إسرائيل:

وَيَخِرُّونَ لِلْأَذْقَانِ يَبْكُونَ وَيَزِيدُهُمْ خُشُوعًا ۩ ﴿١٠٩﴾

وفي مريم:

إِذَا تُتْلَىٰ عَلَيْهِمْ ءَايَٰتُ ٱلرَّحْمَٰنِ خَرُّوا سُجَّدًا وَبُكِيًّا ۩ ﴿٥٨﴾

وفي الحج أولها:

وَمَن يُهِنِ ٱللَّهُ فَمَا لَهُۥ مِن مُّكْرِمٍ إِنَّ ٱللَّهَ يَفْعَلُ مَا يَشَآءُ ۩ ﴿١٨﴾

7. In *Sūrat al-Furqān* (25:60) where Allah *ta'ālā* says:

"'Are we to prostrate to something you command us to?'
And it merely makes them run away all the more."

8. In *Sūrat an-Naml* (27:26) where Allah *ta'ālā* says:

"There is no god except Him, the Lord of the Mighty Throne."

9. In *Sūrat as-Sajdah* (32:15) where Allah *ta'ālā* says:

"They glorify their Lord with praise, and are not arrogant."

10. In *Sūrat Sād* (38:24) where Allah *ta'ālā* says:

"He begged forgiveness from His Lord
and fell down prone, prostrating, and repented."

It is also said that this *sajdah* is done after the words:

"...nearness to Us and a good Homecoming." (38:25)

11. In *Sūrat Fuṣṣilat* (41:37) where Allah *ta'ālā* says:

"Prostrate to Allah who created them, if you worship Him."

You should not perform these *sajdahs* in the Qur'an unless you are in *wuḍū'*. You say a *takbīr* for them but do not say the *salām*. There is leeway as to whether you say '*Allāhu akbar*' as you come up from the *sajdah* although we consider it preferable to do so. You should do these *sajdahs*, if you recite the *āyats* where they appear, in both the *farḍ* and *nāfilah* prayers. You should also do them if you recite any of these *āyats* after praying *Ṣubḥ*, provided the light is not yet bright, and after *'Aṣr* provided the sun has not turned yellow.

وفي الفرقان:

أَنَسْجُدُ لِمَا تَأْمُرُنَا وَزَادَهُمْ نُفُورًا ۩ ﴿٦٠﴾

وفي الهدهد:

ٱللَّهُ لَآ إِلَٰهَ إِلَّا هُوَ رَبُّ ٱلْعَرْشِ ٱلْعَظِيمِ ۩ ﴿٢٦﴾

وفي ألم تنزيل:

وَسَبَّحُوا۟ بِحَمْدِ رَبِّهِمْ وَهُمْ لَا يَسْتَكْبِرُونَ ۩ ﴿١٥﴾

وفي ص:

فَٱسْتَغْفَرَ رَبَّهُۥ وَخَرَّ رَاكِعًا وَأَنَابَ ۩ ﴿٢٤﴾

وقيل عند قوله:

وَإِنَّ لَهُۥ عِندَنَا لَزُلْفَىٰ وَحُسْنَ مَـَٔابٍ ﴿٢٥﴾

وفي حم تنزيل:

وَٱسْجُدُوا۟ لِلَّهِ ٱلَّذِى خَلَقَهُنَّ إِن كُنتُمْ إِيَّاهُ تَعْبُدُونَ ۩ ﴿٣٧﴾

ولا يسجد السجدة في التلاوة إلا على وضوء، ويكبر لها ولا يسلم منها. وفي التكبير في الرفع منها سعة، وإن كبر فهو أحب إلينا. ويسجدها من قرأها في الفريضة والنافلة، ويسجدها من قرأها بعد الصبح ما لم يسفر، وبعد العصر ما لم تصفر الشمس.

14. TRAVELLING PRAYERS

If you travel a distance of four mail stages, which is forty-eight miles, you should shorten the prayer, doing only two *rak'at*s for each, except in the case of *Maghrib* which is not shortened. You are not permitted to shorten the prayer until you have passed beyond the houses of the town you are in so they are all behind you, leaving none in front of you or level with you. You do not leave off shortening the prayers until you return to the place you set out from or come within a mile of it.

If a traveller intends to stay in a place for four days or twenty prayers he should do the complete prayer until he moves from that place. If you leave a place before you have prayed *Ẓuhr* and *'Aṣr* and there is still enough daytime left to pray three *rak'at*s you should pray them both as travelling prayers. If there is only enough time to pray two *rak'at*s or one you should pray *Ẓuhr* in full and *'Aṣr* as a travelling prayer. If you return from a journey without having prayed these two prayers and there is still time for five *rak'at*s you perform them both as full prayers but if there is time for four *rak'at*s or less down to one *rak'at* you perform *Ẓuhr* as a travelling prayer and *'Aṣr* in full.

If you return during the night without having prayed *Maghrib* and *'Ishā'* and there is still time enough before *Fajr* for one or more *rak'at*s you pray both *Maghrib* and *'Ishā'* in full. If you set out on a journey and there is enough of the night left to pray one *rak'at* or more you do *Maghrib* in full and pray *'Ishā'* as a travelling prayer.

١٤ - باب في صلاة السفر

ومن سافر مسافة أربعة برد وهي ثمانية وأربعون ميلا فعليه أن يقصر الصلاة فيصليها ركعتين إلا المغرب. فلا يقصرها حتى يجاوز بيوت المصر، وتصير خلفه ليس بين يديه ولا بحذائه منها شئ، ثم لا يتم حتى يرجع إليها أو يقاربها بأقل من الميل.

وإن نوى المسافر إقامة أربعة أيام بموضع أو ما يصلي فيه عشرين صلاة أتم الصلاة حتى يظعن من مكانه ذلك. ومن خرج ولم يصل الظهر والعصر وقد بقي من النهار قدر ثلاث ركعات صلاهما سفريتين، فإن بقي قدر ما يصلي فيه ركعتين أو ركعة صلى الظهر حضرية والعصر سفرية، ولو دخل لخمس ركعات ناسيا لهما صلاهما حضريتين، فإن كان بقدر أربع ركعات فأقل إلى ركعة صلى الظهر سفريه والعصر حضرية.

وإن قدم في ليل وقد بقي للفجر ركعة فأكثر، ولم يكن صلى المغرب والعشاء صلى المغرب ثلاثا والعشاء حضرية، ولو خرج وقد بقي من الليل ركعة فأكثر صلى المغرب ثم صلى العشاء سفرية.

15. The *Jumu'ah* prayer

Hastening to *Jumu'ah* is obligatory. It becomes obligatory when the imam sits on the minbar and the *mu'adhdhins* begin the *adhān*. The early *sunnah* was for the *mu'adhdhins* to climb the minaret. At that point selling or doing anything else which might distract you from going to *Jumu'ah* becomes *ḥarām*. The calling of an earlier *adhān* is a practice which was introduced by the Banū Umayyah.

Jumu'ah is obligatory if there is a large enough town and a large enough group of people in it. There must be a *khuṭbah* before the prayer. During the *khuṭbah* the imam should lean on a bow shaft or a staff. He should sit before the start of the *khuṭbah* and in the middle of it. The prayer is performed when the *khuṭbah* is finished. The imam prays two *rak'ats* in which the recitation is done out loud. In the first *rak'at* he should recite *Sūrat al-Jumu'ah* or something similar, and in the second *Sūrat al-Ghāshiyah* or something similar.

Going to *Jumu'ah* is obligatory for anyone in the town or within three miles of it. It is not obligatory for travellers nor is it obligatory for the people at Minā nor for slaves, women or children. If a slave or a woman does attend they should do the *Jumu'ah* prayer. Women should stand behind the rows of the men. Young women should not go to *Jumu'ah*.

It is obligatory to listen to the imam while he is giving the *khuṭbah* and you should sit facing him. It is also necessary to have a *ghusl* before going to *Jumu'ah*. It is recommended to get to the mosque early, but not right at the beginning of the day. It is also good to put on perfume and dress in your best clothes.

With us it is preferred that you should leave after finishing the

١٥ - باب في صلاة الجمعة

والسعي إلى الجمعة فريضة، وذلك عند جلوس الإمام على المنبر، وأخذ المؤذنون في الأذان، والسنة المتقدمة أن يصعدوا حينئذ على المنار فيؤذنون، ويحرم حينئذ البيع وكل ما يشغل عن السعي إليها، وهذا الأذان الثاني أحدثه بنو أمية.

والجمعة تجب بالمصر والجماعة، والخطبة فيها واجبة قبل الصلاة، ويتوكأ الإمام على قوس أو عصا، ويجلس في أولها وفي وسطها، وتقام الصلاة عند فراغها، ويصلي الإمام ركعتين، يجهر فيهما بالقراءة، يقرأ في الأولى بالجمعة ونحوها، وفي الثانية ب﴿هل أتاك حديث الغاشية﴾ ونحوها.

ويجب السعي إليها على من في المصر ومن على ثلاثة أميال منه فأقل، ولا تجب على مسافر، ولا على أهل منى، ولا على عبد، ولا امرأة ولا صبي، وإن حضرها عبد أو امرأة فليصلها، وتكون النساء خلف صفوف الرجال، ولا تخرج إليها الشابة.

وينصت للإمام في خطبته، ويستقبله الناس. والغسل لها واجب، والتهجير حسن، وليس ذلك في أول النهار، وليتطيب لها، ويلبس أحسن ثيابه.

وأحب إلينا أن ينصرف بعد فراغها، ولا يتنفل في المسجد، وليتنفل

prayer without doing any *nāfilah rak'at*s in the mosque but you may do *nāfilah rak'at*s before *Jumu'ah*. The imam should not perform any *nāfilah rak'at*s before the prayer but should go straight to the minbar when he comes in.

إن شاء قبلها، ولا يفعل ذلك الإمام، وليرق المنبر كما يدخل.

16. The Fear Prayer

The fear prayer is performed when travelling if there is fear of trouble from an enemy. The imam steps forward with one group leaving the other group to face the enemy. He prays one *rak'at* with this group and then remains standing while they pray a second *rak'at* by themselves. They then say the *salām* and go and stand where their companions were standing. This second group then come and do the *takbīr al-iḥrām*. The imam prays his second *rak'at* with them and then does the *tashahhud* and says the *salām* whereupon they pray their second *rak'at* and finish their prayer. This is what is done for all the *farḍ* prayers except *Maghrib* when the imam prays two *rak'at*s with the first group and one with the second.

If an imam is leading the prayer in a situation of great danger for a group of people who are not travelling, he prays two *rak'ats* with each group for *Ẓuhr*, *'Aṣr*, and *'Ishā'*. The *adhān* and the *iqāmah* are done for each prayer.

If the situation is too dangerous for even this, then everyone should pray individually as best they can, either on foot or horseback, walking or running, and whether facing the *qiblah* or not.

١٦ - باب في صلاة الخوف

صلاة الخوف في السفر إذا خافوا العدو: أن يتقدم الإمام بطائفة ويدع طائفة مواجهة العدو، فيصلي الإمام بطائفة ركعة ثم يثبت قائما، ويصلون لأنفسهم ركعة، ثم يسلمون فيقفون مكان أصحابهم، ثم يأتي أصحابهم فيحرمون خلف الإمام، فيصلي بهم الركعة الثانية، ثم يتشهد ويسلم، ثم يقضون الركعة التي فاتتهم وينصرفون، هكذا يفعل فقي صلاة الفرائض كلها إلا المغرب، فإنه يصلي بالطائفة الأولى ركعتين وبالثانية ركعة.

وإن صلى بهم الحضر لشدة خوف صلى في الظهر والعصر والعشاء لكل طائفة ركعتين، ولكل صلاة أذان وإقامة.

وإذا اشتد الخوف عن ذلك صلوا وحدانا بقدر طاقتهم، مشاة أو ركبانا، ماشين أو ساعين، مستقبلي القبلة وغير مستقبليها.

17. The two *'Īd* prayers
and the *takbīr*s on the days of Minā

Praying the two *'Īd* prayers is an obligatory *sunnah*. The imam and the people should leave for the prayer early in the morning, so that by the time they arrive at the prayer place the time for the prayer has come. There is no *adhān* or *iqāmah* for the *'Id* prayers.

The imam leads the prayer in two *rak'at*s, reciting out loud in each of them. In both he recites the *Fātiḥah* and a *sūrah* such as *Sūrat al-A'lā* (87) or *Sūrat ash-Shams* (91). In the first *rak'at* he says seven *takbīr*s including the *takbīr al-iḥrām*. In the second he says five *takbīr*s not including the *takbīr* for standing up from *sajdah*. There are two *sajdah*s in each *rak'at* and the prayer is completed with the *tashahhud* followed the *salām*. The imam then gets up onto the minbar and gives a *khuṭbah*. He sits before it begins and sits again in the middle. When it is finished he leaves. It is recommended for him to return by a different route from the one he came by and this applies to everyone else as well.

If it is the *'Īd al-Aḍḥā* (sacrifice) the imam should bring his sacrificial animal to the prayer-place and slaughter it there so that everyone else can slaughter their animals after him. On both the *'Īd al-Fiṭr* and the *'Īd al-Aḍḥā* the imam should do *dhikr* of Allah out loud from the time he leaves his house until he arrives at the prayer-place. Everyone else does the same continuing until the arrival of the imam when they stop. Every time the imam says the *takbīr* during his *khuṭbah* everyone else should repeat it. Otherwise they should remain silent and pay attention.

During the 'Days of Sacrifice' you should say the *takbīr* straight after each *farḍ* prayer starting with *Ẓuhr* on the day of the *'Īd* and ending with

١٧ - باب في صلاة العيدين والتكبير أيام منى

وصلاة العيدين سنة واجبة، يخرج لها الإمام والناس ضحوة بقدر ما إذا و صل حانت الصلاة، وليس فيهما أذان ولا إقامة.

فيصلي بهم ركعتين، يقرأ فيهما جهرا بأم القرآن (وسبح اسم ربك الأعلى) و(الشمس وضحاها) ونحوهما، ويكبر في الأولى سبعا قبل القراءة، يعد فيهما تكبيرة الإحرام وفي الثانية خمس تكبيرات القيام، وفي كل ركعة سجدتان، ثم يتشهد ويسلم، ثم يرقى المنبر ويخطب ويجلس في أول خطبته ووسطها، ثم ينصرف. ويستحب أن يرجع من طريق غير الطريق التي أتى منها، والناس كذلك.

وإن كان في الأضحى خرج بأضحيته إلى ا لمصلى فذبحها أو نحرها ليعلم ذلك الناس فيذبحون بعده. وليذكر الله في خروجه من بيته في الفطر والأضحى جهرا، حتى يأتي المصلى الإمام والناس كذلك، فإذا دخل الإمام للصلاة قطعوا ذلك ويكبرون بتكبير الإمام في خطبته، وينصتون له فيما سوى ذلك.

فإن كانت أيام النحر فليكبر الناس دبر الصلوات من صلاة الظهر

Ṣubḥ on the fourth day, this being the last of the days of Minā. The form of this *takbīr*, which is done after the prayers, is: *'Allāhu akbar, Allāhu akbar, Allāhu akbar.'* If you do *taḥlīl "Lā ilāha illa-llāh* – There is no god but Allah" and *taḥmīd "Al-ḥamdulillāh* – Praise be to Allah" as well, that is good. If you want to do that you say:

> *Allāhu akbar, Allāhu akbar, lā ilāha illa-llāhu wa-llāhu akbar, Allāhu akbar, wa lillāhi-l-ḥamd.'*
> "Allah is greater, Allah is greater, Allah is greater. There is no god but Allah and Allah is greater, Allah is greater, and to Allah belongs praise."

This and the former have been related from Mālik. Both are equally acceptable. The "specific days (*al-ayyām al-ma'lūmāt*)" (22:28) are the three days of sacrifice. The "designated days (*ayyām ma'dūdāt*)" (2:203) are the days of Minā, namely the three days after the *'Īd*.

It is good to perform a *ghusl* for both the *'Īd*s, but it is not mandatory, and it is recommended to use perfume and to wear your best clothes.

من يوم النحر إلى صلاة الصبح من اليوم الرابع منه، وهو آخر أيام منى، يكبر إذا صلى الصبح ثم يقطع. والتكبير دبر الصلوات: الله أكبر،الله أكبر، الله اكبر، وإن جمع مع التكبير تهليلا وتحميدا فحسن. يقول إن شاء ذلك:

اَللهُ أَكْبَرُ اَللهُ أَكْبَرُ لاَ إِلَهَ إِلاَّ اللهُ وَاللهُ أَكْبَرُ اَللهُ أَكْبَرُ وَلِلهِ الْحَمْدُ

وقد روي عن مالك هذا والأول. والكل واسع. والأيام المعلومات أيام النحر الثلاثة، والأيام المعدودات أيام منى، وهي ثلاثة أيام بعد يوم النحر.

والغسل للعيدين حسن وليس بلازم، ويستحب فيهما الطيب والحسن من الثياب .

18. The eclipse prayer

The eclipse prayer is an obligatory *sunnah* whenever there is an eclipse of the sun. The imam goes to the mosque and begins to lead the people in prayer without either an *adhān* or an *iqāmah*. He recites silently a very long piece of Qur'an such as *Sūrat al-Baqarah*. Then he goes into *rukū'* for the same amount of time. Then he stands upright again saying *'sami'a-llāhu liman ḥamidah.'* Then he recites another piece of Qur'an slightly shorter than the first. Then he goes into *rukū'* again for the same amount of time as he spent reciting. Then he once more stands upright saying, *'sami'a-llāhu liman ḥamidah.'* Then he does two full *sajdah*s. After this he stands up again and recites another piece of Qur'an slightly shorter than the previous one and then goes into *rukū'* for the same length of time. Then, as before, he stands upright again and recites one more slightly shorter piece of Qur'an which is followed by *rukū'* for the same amount of time as the recitation. He stands back upright again and then does two *sajdah*s as before. Finally he says the *tashahhud* and then the *salām*. If you like, the prayer can be done in this way in your own house.

If there is an eclipse of the moon there is no group prayer. When it happens people should pray individually, reciting out loud as for any other *nāfilah* prayer at night. There is no formal *khuṭbah* after the prayer for the eclipse of the sun but there is no harm in the imam taking the opportunity to admonish and remind people.

١٨ - باب في صلاة خسوف

وصلاة الخسوف سنة واجبة، إذا خسفت الشمس خرج الإمام إلى المسجد فافتتح الصلاة بالناس بغير أذان ولا إقامة، ثم قرأ قراءة طويلة سرا بنحو سورة البقرة، ثم يركع ركوعا طويلا نحو ذلك، ثم يرفع رأسه يقول: سمع الله لمن حمده، ثم يقرأ دون قراءته الأولى ثم يركع نحو قراءته الثانية، ثم يرفع رأسه يقول سمع الله لمن حمده، ثم يسجد سجدتين تامتين، ثم يقوم فيقرأ دون قراءته التي تلي ذلك، ثم يركع نحو قراءته، ثم، يرفع كما ذكرنا، ثم يقرأ دون قراءته هذه، ثم يركع نحو ذلك، ثم يرفع كما ذكرنا، ثم يسجد كما ذكرنا، ثم يتشهد ويسلم، ولمن شاء أن يصلي في بيته مثل ذلك أن يفعل.

وليس في صلاة خسوف القمر جماعة، وليصل الناس عند ذلك أفذاذا، والقراءة فيها جهرا كسائر ركوع النوافل. وليس في إثر صلاة خسوف الشمس خطبة مرتبة، ولا بأس أن يعظ الناس ويذكرهم.

19. The rain prayer

The rain prayer is a *sunnah* which is acted upon. The imam goes out for the prayer in the early morning as for the *'Īd* prayers. He leads the people in two *rak'at*s in which the recitation is done out loud. He recites *Sūrat al-A'lā* in the first *rak'at* and *Sūrat ash-Shams* in the second. He does two *sajdah*s and one *rukū'* in each *rak'at* and finishes with the *tashahhud* and the *salām*. He then turns and faces the people. When everyone is quiet he stands and, leaning on a bow-shaft or staff, gives two *khuṭbah*s sitting down between them. When he finishes, he faces the *qiblah* and then turns his cloak back to front, putting what was on his right shoulder on his left shoulder and vice versa. He does not turn it upside down. Everyone else does the same except that he is standing and they remain seated. Then, while like this, the imam makes *du'ā'* after which he and everyone else leave.

There are no special *takbīr*s in this prayer or in the eclipse prayer. There is just the *takbīr al-iḥrām* and the normal *takbīr*s for going into *rukū'* and for going into *sujūd* and coming back out of it. There is no *adhān* or *iqāmah* for the rain prayer.

١٩ - باب في صلاة الاستسقاء

وصلاة الاستسقاء سنة، تقام، يخرج لها الإمام كما يخرج للعيدين ضحوة، فيصلي بالناس ركعتين يجهر فيهما بالقراءة، يقرأ ب﴿سبح اسم ربك الأعلى﴾ و﴿والشمس وضحاها﴾ وفي كل ركعة سجدتان وركعة واحدة، ويتشهد ويسلم، ثم يستقبل الناس بوجهه فيجلس جلسة، فإذا اطمأن الناس، قام متوكئا على قوس أو عصا، فخطب ثم جلس، ثم قام فخطب، فإذا فرغ استقبل القبلة فحول رداءه: يجعل ما على منكبه الأيمن على الأيسر، وما على الأيسر على الأيمن،ولا يقلب ذلك، وليفعل الناس مثله وهو قائم وهم قعود، ثم يدعو كذلك. ثم ينصرف وينصرفون.

ولا يكبر فيها ولا في الخسوف غير تكبيرة الإحرام والخفض والرفع.

ولا أذان فيهما ولا إقامة.

20. On what to do when someone is at the point of death and on washing the dead, shrouding them, embalming them, carrying them and burying them

When someone is at the point of death, it is recommended to turn them so that they face the *qiblah* and to close their eyes after they have died. *Lā ilāha illa-llāh* should be said in the presence of the dying person so they will be reminded of it. It is better that the body and what it is on should be free of any impurity. It is also better that menstruating women or anyone in a state of *janābah* do not come near someone who is dying. Some scholars recommend reciting *Sūrah Yāsīn* at the bedside of the dying person although according to Mālik this was not the usual practice. There is no harm in weeping when someone dies, although self-control and patient endurance are better if that is possible. But shouting out and wailing are forbidden.

There is no fixed limit to the number of times you wash a dead body. The body should be thoroughly cleaned and the number of times it is washed should be odd. It should be washed with water and *sidr* (lote tree leaves) and in the last washing camphor should be added to the water. During the washing the body's private parts should be kept covered. The nails should not be cut nor should the hair be shaved off. The stomach should be gently squeezed. It is good if *wuḍū'* is done for the dead person although this is not obligatory. It is better if the body is turned on its side for washing although it is acceptable to wash it in a sitting position. It is also good for a husband or wife to wash their dead partner, although it does not necessarily have to be them who do it.

If a woman dies on a journey and there are no other women present

٢٠ - باب ما يفعل بالمحتضر في غسل الميت وكفنه وتحنيطه وحمله ودفنه

ويستحب استقبال القبلة بالمحتضر، وإغماضه إذا قضى، ويلقن لا اله إلا الله عند الموت، وإن قدر على أن يكون طاهرا وما عليه طاهر فهو أحسن، ويستحب أن لا يقربه حائض ولا جنب. وأرخص بعض العلماء في القراءة عند رأسه بسورة يس، ولم يكن ذلك عند مالك أمرا معمولا به. ولا بأس بالبكاء بالدموع حينئذ، وحسن التعزي والتصبر أجمل لمن استطاع. وينهى عن الصراخ والنياحة.

كيفية غسل الميت ومن يقوم به:

وليس في غسل الميت حد، ولكن ينقى، ويغسل وترا بماء وسدر، ويجعل في الأخيرة كافورا، وتستر عورته، ولا تقلم أظفاره، ولا يحلق شعره، يعصر بطنه عصرا رفيقا، وإن وضئ وضوء الصلاة فحسن، وليس بواجب، ويقلب لجنبه في الغسل أحسن، وإن أجلس فذلك واسع. لا بأس بغسل أحد الزوجين صاحبه من غير ضرورة.

والمرأة تموت في السفر لا نساء معها ولا محرم من الرجال فلييمم

nor any men of *maḥram* status then a man should do *tayammum* for her, wiping her face and hands. Similarly if the dead person is a man and there are no other men present nor a woman of *maḥram* status, then a woman should do *tayammum* for him, wiping his face and his hands and arms to the elbows. If there is a woman of *maḥram* status present she should wash his body, keeping his *'awrah* covered. If a woman has died and there is a man of *maḥram* status present he should wash her through a cloth covering her whole body.

It is recommended for the body to be shrouded in an odd number of lengths of cloth, either three, five or seven. Any waist-wrapper, shirt or turban that is put on the body is counted as one piece of cloth. The Prophet ﷺ was shrouded in three lengths of white *saḥūlī* cloth, each layer being well wrapped round him ﷺ. There is no harm in a dead man being dressed in a shirt and a turban. The body should be perfumed, with the perfume being put between the layers of cloth that make up the shroud and also directly onto the body and the places which touch the ground in prostration. A martyr on the battlefield is not washed nor is the prayer done for him. He is buried in his clothes.

If someone kills himself, the prayer is done for him. The prayer is also done for someone killed by the ruler as a *ḥadd* punishment or because they have killed someone. The ruler himself does not participate in the prayer. Incense should not be burned during funeral processions and it is better to walk in front of the bier.

The body should be placed in the grave on its right side and slabs made of clay and straw should be laid over it. When this is done you should say:

Allāhumma inna ṣāḥibanā qad nazala bika, wa khallafa-d-dunyā warā'a ẓahrihi, wa-ftaqara ilā mā 'indak. Allāhumma thabbit 'inda-l-mas'alati manṭiqahu walā tabtalihi fī qabrihi bimā lā ṭāqata lahu bihi, wa alḥiqhu binabīyihi Muḥammadin ﷺ

رجل وجهها وكفيها، ولو كانت الميت رجلا يمم النساء وجهه ويديه إلى المرفقين إن لم يكن معهن رجل يغسله، ولا امرأة من محارمه، فإن كانت امرأة من محارمه غسلته وسترت عورته، وإن كان مع الميتة ذو محرم غسلها من فوق ثوب يستر جميع جسدها.

ويستحب أن يكفن الميت في وتر: ثلاث أثواب أو خمسة أو سبعة، وما جعل له من أزرة وقميص وعمامة فذلك محسوب في عدد أثواب الوتر. وقد كفن النبي صلى الله عليه وسلم في ثلاثة أثواب بيض سحولية، أدرج فيها إدراجا صلى الله عليه وسلم. ولا بأس أن يقمص الميت ويعمم، وينبغي أن يحنط، ويجعل الحنوط بين أكفانه وفي جسده ومواضع السجود منه. ولا يغسل الشهيد في المعترك، ولا يصلى عليه، ويدفن بثيابه.

ويصلى على قاتل نفسه، ويصلى على من قتله الإمام في حد أو قود، ولا يصلى عليه الإمام. ولا يتبع الميت بمجمر، والمشي أمام الجنازة أفضل.

ويجعل الميت في قبره على شقه الأيمن، وينصب عليه اللبن، ويقول حينئذ:

اَللَّهُمَّ إِنَّ صَاحِبَنَا قَدْ نَزَلَ بِكَ، وَخَلَّفَ الدُّنْيَا وَرَاءَ ظَهْرِهِ، وَافْتَقَرَ إِلَى مَا عِنْدَكَ. اَللَّهُمَّ ثَبِّتْ عِنْدَ الْمَسْأَلَةِ مَنْطِقَهُ وَلَا تَبْتَلِهِ فِي قَبْرِهِ بِمَا لَا طَاقَةَ لَهُ بِهِ، وَأَلْحِقْهُ بِنَبِيِّهِ مُحَمَّدٍ ﷺ.

"O Allah, our companion is now with You. He has left this world behind him and is in need of what is with You. O Allah, make his speech firm when he is questioned and do not test him in his grave beyond what he can bear. Grant that he may be in the company of his Prophet Muḥammad ﷺ."

It is disliked to build anything on graves or to whitewash them. A Muslim should not wash his father if he is not a Muslim nor should he put him in his grave unless it is feared that his body will remain unburied, in which case he should cover the body and then bury it.

According to the people of knowledge the *laḥd*-type (niche) grave is better than the *shaqq*-type (a simple trench). A *laḥd*-type grave is one in which, after having dug the basic trench, you dig out a place for the body at the bottom of the side which faces *qiblah* so that the body is protected by an overhang. This should be done provided that the earth is firm enough and will not crumble or cave in. This was how the grave of the Prophet ﷺ was.

ويكره البناء على القبور وتجصيصها، ولا يغسل المسلم أباه الكافر، ولا يدخله قبره إلا أن يخاف أ ن يضيع فليواره.

واللحد أحب إلى أهل العلم من الشق، وهو أن يحفر للميت تحت الجرف في حائط قبلة القبر، وذلك إذا كانت تربته صلبة لا تتهيل ولا تتقطع، وكذلك فعل برسول الله صلى الله عليه وسلم.

21. THE FUNERAL PRAYER
AND THE SUPPLICATION FOR THE DEAD

The *janāzah* (funeral) prayer contains four *takbīrs*. You raise your hands for the first *takbīr* and there is no harm in doing so for each of the others. If you like, you can make a *du'ā'* after the fourth *takbīr* before the *salām* or if you like, you can say the *salām* directly after the *takbīr*. The imam stands opposite the middle of the body if the dead person is a man and opposite the shoulders if it is a woman. The *salām* for this prayer is said once quietly both by the imam and those following him. There is a great reward to be gained from performing the prayer and for being present at the burial. This reward is equivalent in size to Mount Uḥud.

There is no specific formula for the supplication to be made when performing the funeral prayer. All the things which have come down are acceptable. One good thing to say after doing the *takbīr* is:

Al-ḥamdu lillāhi-lladhī amāta wa aḥyā, wa-l-ḥamdu lillāhi-lladhī yuḥyi-l-mawtā, lahu-l-'aẓamatu wa-l-kibriyā'u wa-l-mulku wa-l-qudratu wa-s-sanā'u wahuwa 'alā kulli shay'in qadīr. Allāhumma ṣalli 'alā Muḥammadin wa 'alā āli Muḥammadin, kamā ṣallayta waraḥimta wabārakta 'alā Ibrāhīma wa 'alā āli Ibrāhīma fi-l-'ālamīna inna-ka ḥamīdun majīd. Allāhumma inna-hu 'abduka wa-bnu 'abdika wa-bnu amatika, anta khalaqtahu wa razaqtahu, wa anta amattahu wa anta tuḥyīhi wa anta a'lamu bisirrihi wa 'alāniyatihi, ji'nāka shufa'ā'a lahu fashaffi'nā fīh. Allāhumma innā nastajīru biḥabli jiwārika lahu inna-ka dhū wafā'in wa dhimmah. Allāhumma qihi min fitnati-l-qabri wa min 'adhābi Jahannam. Allāhumma-ghfir lahu wa-rḥamhu wa-'fu 'anhu wa 'āfihi wa akrim nuzulahu wawassi' madkhalahu wa-ghsilhu bimā'in wa thaljin wa baradin

٢١ - باب في الصلاة على الجنائز والدعاء للميت

والتكبير على الجنازة أربع تكبيرات يرفع يديه في أولاهن، وإن رفع في كل تكبيرة فلا بأس. وإن شاء سلم بعد الرابعة مكانه، ويقف الإمام في الرجل عند وسطه، وفي المرأة عند منكبيها، والسلام من الصلاة على الجنائز تسليمة واحدة خفية للإمام والمأموم، وفي الصلاة على الميت قيراط من الأجر، وقيراط في حضور دفنه، وذلك في التمثيل مثل جبل أحد ثوابا.

ويقال في الدعاء على الميت شئ غير محدود، وذلك كله واسع. ومن مستحسن ما قيل في ذلك أن يكبر، ثم يقول:
اَلْحَمْدُ لِلهِ الَّذِي أَمَاتَ وَأَحيَا، وَالْحَمْدُ لِلهِ الَّذِي يُحْيِي الْمَوْتَى، لَهُ الْعَظَمَةُ وَالْكِبْرِيَاءُ وَالْمُلْكُ وَالْقُدْرَةُ وَالسَّنَاءُ وَهُوَ عَلَى كُلِّ شَيْءٍ قَدِيرٌ. اَللَّهُمَّ صَلِّ عَلَى مُحَمَّدٍ وَعَلَى ءَالِ مُحَمَّدٍ، كَمَا صَلَّيْتَ وَرَحِمْتَ وَبَارَكْتَ عَلَى إِبْرَاهِيمَ وَعَلَى آلِ إِبْرَاهِيمَ فِي الْعَالَمِينَ إِنَّكَ حَمِيدٌ مَجِيدٌ. اَللَّهُمَّ إِنَّهُ عَبْدُكَ وَابْنُ عَبْدِكَ وَابْنُ أَمَتِكَ، أَنْتَ خَلَقْتَهُ وَرَزَقْتَهُ، وَأَنْتَ أَمَتَّهُ وَأَنْتَ تُحْيِيهِ وَأَنْتَ أَعْلَمُ بِسِرِّهِ وَعَلَانِيَتِهِ، جِئْنَاكَ شُفَعَاءَ لَهُ فَشَفِّعْنَا فِيهِ. اَللَّهُمَّ إِنَّا نَسْتَجِيرُ بِحَبْلِ جِوَارِكَ لَهُ إِنَّكَ ذُو وَفَاءٍ وَذِمَّةٍ. اَللَّهُمَّ قِهِ مِنْ فِتْنَةِ الْقَبْرِ وَمِنْ عَذَابِ جَهَنَّمَ. اَللَّهُمَّ اغْفِرْ لَهُ وَارْحَمْهُ وَاعْفُ عَنْهُ وَعَافِهِ وَأَكْرِمْ نُزُلَهُ وَوَسِّعْ مَدْخَلَهُ وَاغْسِلْهُ بِمَاءٍ

wanaqqihi mina-l-khaṭāyā kamā yunaqqa-th-thawbu-l-abyaḍu mina-d-danasi, wa abdilhu dāran khayran min dārihi, wa ahlan khayran min ahlihi, wa zawjan khayran min zawjih. Allāhumma in kāna muḥsinan fazid fī iḥsānihi wa in kāna musī'an fatajāwaz 'anhu. Allāhumma inna-hu qad nazala bika – wa anta khayru manzūlin bihi – faqīrun ilā raḥmatika wa anta ghanīyun 'an 'adhābih. Allāhumma thabbit 'inda-l-mas'alati manṭiqahu walā tabtalihi fī qabrihi bimā lā ṭāqata lahu bih. Allāhumma lā taḥrimnā ajrahu walā taftinnā ba'dah.

"Praise be to Allah who makes die and brings to life and praise be to Allah who brings the dead to life. To Him belong Greatness, Sovereignty, Power, Exaltedness and He has power over all things. O Allah, bless Muḥammad and the family of Muḥammad as You blessed and were merciful to and poured goodness on Ibrāhīm and the family of Ibrāhīm. In all the worlds, You are Praiseworthy, Glorious. O Allah, he is your slave and the son of Your slaves. You created him and provided for him. You made him die and You will bring him to life and You know best about his outward and his inward. We have come to You as intercessors on his behalf so please accept our intercession. O Allah, we seek safety for him by Your bond of protection with him. Certainly You keep Your word and promise. O Allah, protect him from the trials of the grave and from the torment of Jahannam. O Allah, forgive him, have mercy on him, pardon him and grant him well-being. Be generous to him when he arrives and open the way wide for him to come in. Wash him with water, snow and ice and cleanse him from his wrong actions as a white garment is cleansed of dirt. Give him a home better than the home he had, a family better than the family he had and a wife better than the wife he had. O Allah, if he was right-acting, increase him in right actions and if he was wrongdoing, then overlook his wrong actions. O Allah, he has come to You and

وَثَلْجٍ وَبَرَدٍ وَنَقِّهِ مِنَ الْخَطَايَا كَمَا يُنَقَّى الثَّوْبُ الأَبْيَضُ مِنَ الدَّنَسِ، وَأَبْدِلْهُ دَارًا خَيْرًا مِنْ دَارِهِ، وَأَهْلاً خَيْرًا مِنْ أَهْلِهِ، وَزَوْجًا خَيْرًا مِنْ زَوْجِهِ. اَللَّهُمَّ إِنْ كَانَ مُحْسِنًا فَزِدْ فِي إِحْسَانِهِ وَإِنْ كَانَ مُسِيئًا فَتَجَاوَزْ عَنْهُ. اَللَّهُمَّ إِنَّهُ قَدْ نَزَلَ بِكَ وَأَنْتَ خَيْرُ مَنْزُولٍ بِهِ فَقِيرٌ إِلَى رَحْمَتِكَ وَأَنْتَ غَنِيٌّ عَنْ عَذَابِهِ. اَللَّهُمَّ ثَبِّتْ عِنْدَ الْمَسْأَلَةِ مَنْطِقَهُ وَلَا تَبْتَلِهِ فِي قَبْرِهِ بِمَا لاَ طَاقَةَ لَهُ بِهِ. اَللَّهُمَّ لاَ تَحْرِمْنَا أَجْرَهُ وَلَا تَفْتِنَّا بَعْدَهُ.

You are the Best that anyone can come to. He is in need of Your mercy and You have no need to punish him. O Allah, make his speech firm when he is questioned and do not test him in his grave beyond what he can bear. Do not deprive us of our reward for doing this on his behalf and do not test us after him."

You say this after each *takbīr* and then after the fourth *takbīr*:

Allāhumma-ghfir liḥayyinā wa mayyitinā wa ḥāḍirinā wa ghā'ibinā wa ṣaghīrinā wa kabīrinā wa dhakarinā wa unthānā, inna-ka ta'lamu mutaqallabanā wamathwana, wa liwālidīnā wa liman sabaqanā bi-l-īmāni wa li-l-muslimīna wa-l-muslimāti wa-l-mu'minīna wa-l-mu'mināti-l-aḥyā'i minhum wa-l-amwāt. Allāhumma man aḥyaytahu minnā fa aḥyihi 'ala-l-īmāni, wa man tawaffaytahu minnā fa tawaffahu 'ala-l-islāmi, wa as'idnā biliqā'ika wa ṭayyibnā li-l-mawti wa ṭayyibhu lanā wa-j'al fīhi rāḥatanā wamasarratanā.

"O Allah, forgive those who are alive and those who are dead, those present with us and those absent, those who are young and those who are old, those who are male and those who are female. You know everything that we do and where we will end up – and forgive our parents and those who have gone before us with faith and all the Muslims, both men and women and all the believers, both men and women, the living and the dead. O Allah whoever of us You keep alive, keep him alive in faith and whoever You take back to Yourself, take him back as a Muslim. Make us glad when we meet You. Make us pleasing at the time of our death and make death pleasant for us. Make it a source of rest and happiness for us."

After this you say the *salām*.

If the dead person is a woman you say:

Allāhumma innahā amatuka...

"O Allah, she is your slave and the daughter of Your slaves...." and you go on making the object of the supplication feminine rather than

تقول هذا بإثر كل تكبيرة. وتقول بعد الرابعة:

اَللَّهُمَّ اغْفِرْ لِحَيِّنَا وَمَيِّتِنَا وَحَاضِرِنَا وَغَائِبِنَا وَصَغِيرِنَا وَكَبِيرِنَا وَذَكَرِنَا وَأُنْثَانَا، إِنَّكَ تَعْلَمُ مُتَقَلَّبَنَا وَمَثْوَانَا، وَلِوَالِدِينَا وَلِمَنْ سَبَقَنَا بِالْإِيمَانِ وَلِلْمُسْلِمِينَ وَالْمُسْلِمَاتِ وَالْمُؤْمِنِينَ وَالْمُؤْمِنَاتِ الْأَحْيَاءِ مِنْهُمْ وَالْأَمْوَاتِ. اَللَّهُمَّ مَنْ أَحْيَيْتَهُ مِنَّا فَأَحْيِهِ عَلَى الْإِيمَانِ، وَمَنْ تَوَفَّيْتَهُ مِنَّا فَتَوَفَّهُ عَلَى الْإِسْلَامِ، وَأَسْعِدْنَا بِلِقَائِكَ وَطَيِّبْنَا لِلْمَوْتِ وَطَيِّبْهُ لَنَا وَاجْعَلْ فِيهِ رَاحَتَنَا وَمَسَرَّتَنَا.

ثم تسلم.

وإن كانت امرأة قلت:

اَللَّهُمَّ إِنَّهَا أَمَتُكَ... ثم تمادى بذكرها على التأنيث، غير أنك لا تقول: وأبدلها زوجا خيرا من زوجها، لأنها قد تكون زوجا في الجنة

masculine. The only difference is that you do not say, "Give her a husband better than her husband…" because in the Garden she can be the wife of the man who was her husband in this world and the women of the Garden are attached only to their husbands and have no desire for anyone else. A man may have many wives in the Garden whereas women only have one husband.

There is no harm in having one funeral prayer for several dead people. If there are both men and women among the dead, the men are placed next to the imam. If there are only men, the best of them is placed next to the imam. If there are women and children as well, they are placed behind the men in the direction of the *qiblah*. There is no harm in a number of bodies being placed in a row, and in such a case the one nearest the imam should be the best of them. If a number of people are being buried in one grave the best should be nearest the *qiblah*.

If someone has been buried without the funeral prayer having been done for him and the grave has already been filled in, then the prayer should be done over his grave. You do not perform the funeral prayer a second time if it has already been performed once. The funeral prayer is done for a person as long as the majority of the body remains. There is a difference of opinion about whether you do the funeral prayer for, for example, someone's hand or foot.

لزوجها في الدنيا، ونساء الجنة مقصورات على أزواجهن لا يبغين بهم بدلا. والرجل له زوجات كثيرات في الجنة، ولا يكون للمرأة أزواج.

ولا بأس أن تجمع الجنائز في صلاة واحدة. ويلي الإمام الرجال إن كان فيهم نساء، وإن كانوا رجالا جعل أفضلهم مما يلي الإمام، وجعل من دونه النساء، والصبيان من وراء ذلك إلى القبلة. ولا باس أن يجعلوا صفا واحدا، ويقرب إلى الإمام أفضلهم. وأما دفن الجماعة في قبر واحد فيجعل أفضلهم مما يلي القبلة.

ومن دفن ولم يصل عليه ووري فإنه يصلي على قبره. ولا يصلى على من قد صلي عليه. ويصلى على أكثر الجسد. واختلف في الصلاة على مثل اليد والرجل.

22. The supplication for a dead child, how the funeral prayer is done for children and how they are washed

You praise Allah ﷻ and ask for blessing on His Prophet Muḥammad ﷺ and then you say:

Allāhumma inna-hu 'abduka wa-bnu 'abdika wa-bnu amatika, anta khalaqtahu wa razaqtahu, wa anta amattahu wa anta tuḥyīh. Allāhumma fa-j'alhu li wālidayhi salafan wa dhukhran wa faraṭan wa ajran, wa thaqqil bihi mawāzīnahum, wa a'ẓim bihi ujūrahum, walā taḥrimnā wa iyyāhum ajrahu, wa lā taftinnā wa iyyāhum ba'dah. Allāhumma alḥiqhu biṣāliḥi salafi-l-mu'minīna fī kafālati Ibrāhīma, wa abdilhu dāran khayran min dārihi, wa ahlan khayran min ahlihi, wa 'āfihi min fitnati-l-qabri wa min 'adhābi jahannam.

"O Allah, he is Your slave and the son of Your slaves. You created him and provided for him. You made him die and will bring him to life. Make him a forerunner and a stored-up treasure and a reward for his parents. Make their balances weigh heavy through him, make their reward greater because of him, do not deprive either us or them of their reward through him, and do not test either us or them after him. O Allah, give him the company of the right-acting believers who have gone ahead under the guardianship of Ibrāhīm. Give him a house better than the one he had and a family better than the one he had. Save him from the trial of the grave and the torment of Hell."

You say this after each *takbīr* and after the fourth you say:

Allāhumma-ghfir li aslāfinā wa afrāṭinā wa liman sabaqanā bi-l-īmān. Allāhumma man aḥyaytahu minnā fa aḥyihi 'ala-l-īmāni, waman

٢٢ - غسل في الدعاء للطفل والصلاة عليه وغسله

تثني على الله تبارك وتعالى، وتصلي على نبيه محمد صلى الله عليه وسلم. ثم تقول:

اَللَّهُمَّ إِنَّهُ عَبْدُكَ وَابْنُ عَبْدِكَ وَابْنُ أَمَتِكَ، أَنْتَ خَلَقْتَهُ وَرَزَقْتَهُ، وَأَنْتَ أَمَتَّهُ وَأَنْتَ تُحْيِيهِ. اَللَّهُمَّ فَاجْعَلْهُ لِوَالِدَيْهِ سَلَفًا وَذُخْرًا وَفَرَطًا وَأَجْرًا، وَثَقِّلْ بِهِ مَوَازِينَهُمْ، وَأَعْظِمْ بِهِ أُجُورَهُمْ، وَلاَ تَحْرِمْنَا وَإِيَّاهُمْ أَجْرَهُ، وَلاَ تَفْتِنَّا وَإِيَّاهُمْ بَعْدَهُ. اَللَّهُمَّ أَلْحِقْهُ بِصَالِحِ سَلَفِ الْمُؤْمِنِينَ فِي كَفَالَةِ إِبْرَاهِيمَ، وَأَبْدِلْهُ دَارًا خَيْرًا مِنْ دَارِهِ، وَأَهْلاً خَيْرًا مِنْ أَهْلِهِ، وَعَافِهِ مِنْ فِتْنَةِ الْقَبْرِ وَمِنْ عَذَابِ جَهَنَّمَ.

تقول ذلك في كل تكبيرة. وتقول بعد الرابعة:

اَللَّهُمَّ اغْفِرْ لِأَسْلاَفِنَا وَأَفْرَاطِنَا وَلِمَنْ سَبَقَنَا بِالْإِيمَانِ. اَللَّهُمَّ مَنْ أَحْيَيْتَهُ مِنَّا

tawaffaytahu minnā fatawaffahu 'ala-l-islāmi, wa-ghfir li-l-muslimīna wa-l-muslimāti wa-l-mu'minīna wa-l-mu'mināti-l-aḥyā'i minhum wa-l-amwāt.

"O Allah, forgive our forbears and predecessors and those who have gone before us. O Allah, whoever among us You make live make him live in *īmān* and whoever You take back to Yourself take him back as a Muslim. Forgive all the Muslims, both men and women, and all the believers, both men and women, the living and the dead."

Then you say the *salām*.

You do not do the funeral prayer for a stillborn baby. Such a baby does not inherit and cannot be inherited from. If a baby is prematurely stillborn, it is disliked for its body to be buried inside a house. There is no harm in women washing the body of a young boy of six or seven years old, but men do not wash the bodies of young girls. There is a difference of opinion regarding young girls who have not reached an age when they might be desired but the former ruling is the one preferred by us.

فَأَحْيِهِ عَلَى الْإِيمَانِ، وَمَنْ تَوَفَّيْتَهُ مِنَّا فَتَوَفَّهُ عَلَى الْإِسْلَامِ، وَاغْفِرْ لِلْمُسْلِمِينَ وَالْمُسْلِمَاتِ وَالْمُؤْمِنِينَ وَالْمُؤْمِنَاتِ الْأَحْيَاءِ مِنْهُمْ وَالْأَمْوَاتِ.

ثم تسلم.

ولا يصلى على من لم يستهل صارخا، ولا يرث ولا يورث، ويكره أن يدفن السقط في الدور، ولا بأس أن يغتسل النساء الصبي الصغير ابن ست سنين أو سبع، ولا يغسل الرجال الصبية، واختلف فيها إن كانت لم تبلغ أن تشتهى، والأول أحب إلينا.

23. Fasting

Fasting the month of Ramadan is obligatory. You start fasting when the new moon is sighted and you stop fasting when the new moon is sighted, whether this is after thirty or twenty-nine days. If the new moon cannot be seen because of clouds you count thirty days from the beginning of the preceding month and then begin fasting. The same applies to ending the fast. You should make an intention to fast the whole month at the beginning of the month and it is not necessary to make a new intention every night for the rest of the month.

You fast until night comes and it is *sunnah* to break the fast as soon as possible and to delay your *suḥūr* – the before dawn meal. If you are not sure if the time of *Fajr* has come or not you should not eat. You do not fast the 'Day of Doubt', fasting on the grounds that it might be part of Ramadan. If you do this it is not counted even if it turns out to have been Ramadan. If you want to fast that day as a voluntary fast, however, you can do so. If you get up in the morning and discover, before having eaten or drunk anything, that Ramadan has begun you must fast the rest of the day but you cannot count it as one of the days of your Ramadan and you have to make up a day. If someone returns from a journey and they are not fasting or if a woman finishes menstruating during the day then in both these cases it is all right for them to eat and drink during the remainder of that day.

If you are doing a voluntary fast and break your fast intentionally, or if you start off on a journey and break your fast because of it, you must make up that day. If, in a voluntary fast, you break your fast unintentionally you do not have to make up a day but if this happens in the obligatory fast you have to make up a day.

٢٣ - باب في الصيام

وصوم شهر رمضان فريضة، يصام لرؤية الهلال ويفطر لرؤيته، كان ثلاثين يوما أو تسعة وعشرين يوما، فإن غم الهلال فيعد ثلاثين يوما من غرة الشهر الذي قبله، ثم يصام وكذلك في الفطر. ويبيت الصيام في أوله، وليس عليه البيات في بقيته.

ويتم الصيام إلى الليل. ومن السنة تعجيل الفطر وتأخير السحور. وإن شك في الفجر فلا يأكل، ولا يصام يوم الشك ليحتاط به من رمضان، ومن صامه كذلك لم يجزه إن وافقه من رمضان، ولمن شاء تطوعا أن يفعل. ومن أصبح فلم يأكل ولم يشرب ثم تبين له أن ذلك اليوم من رمضان لم يجزه، وليمسك عن الأكل في بقيته ويقضيه. وإذا قدم المسافر مفطرا أو طهرت الحائض نهارا فلهما الأكل في بقية يومهما.

ومن أفطر في تطوعه عامدا أو سافر فيه فأفطر لسفره فعليه القضاء، وإن أفطر ساهيا فلا قضاء عليه، بخلاف الفريضة.

There is no harm in using a *siwāk* – toothstick – at any time during the day while you are fasting, and blood-letting is not disliked except if doing it will cause over-exhaustion. If you vomit involuntarily while fasting in Ramadan you do not have to make up a day but if you make yourself vomit you have to make up a day.

If a pregnant woman is afraid on account of the child in her womb she should break the fast. She does not have to feed anyone in expiation. It has also been said that she should feed people. Similarly, if a nursing mother fears for her child and cannot find a wet-nurse, or if the child will not accept to be fed by anyone else, she can break the fast but she must feed people in expiation. If an old man cannot fast, it is recommended for him to feed people. Feeding people in this context consists of giving away one *mudd* for each day which has to be made up. Someone who fails to make up missed days before the following Ramadan should also feed a poor person for each day they still owe.

Children are not obliged to fast until such time as a boy has his first wet dream or a girl her first menstrual period, because it is when children reach physical maturity that all the physical acts of worship become obligatory for them. Allah Almighty says, "*Once your children have reached puberty, they should ask your permission (to enter).*" (24:59)

If someone who has not done *ghusl* wakes up after *Fajr* in a state of *janābah* or if the period of a woman who has been menstruating finishes before *Fajr* and she does not do *ghusl* till after *Fajr*, then fasting that day is valid in both these cases.

Fasting is not permitted on the day of *'Īd al-Fiṭr* or the day of the *'Īd al-Aḍḥā* nor should anyone fast the two days after the *'Īd al-Aḍḥā* unless he is performing *ḥajj tamattu'* and does not have an animal to sacrifice. There should be no voluntary fasting on the fourth day either but if someone has vowed to fast or has previously broken off a consecutive fast, they should fast that day.

ولا بأس بالسواك للصائم في جميع نهاره. ولا تكره له الحجامة إلا خيفة التغرير. ومن ذرعه القيء في رمضان فلا قضاء عليه، وإن استقاء فقاء فعليه القضاء.

وإذا خافت الحامل على ما في بطنها أفطرت ولم تطعم، وقد قيل : تطعم. وللمرضع إن خافت على ولدها ولم تجد من تستأجر له أو لم يقبل غيرها أن تفطر وتطعم، ويستحب للشيخ الكبير إذا أفطر أن يطعم. والإطعام في هذا كله مد عن كل يوم يقضيه، وكذلك يطعم من فرط في قضاء رمضان حتى يدخل عليه رمضان آخر.

ولا صيام على الصبيان حتى يحتلم الغلام وتحيض الجارية. وبالبلوغ لزمتهم أعمال الأبدان فريضة.قال الله سبحانه وتعالى:﴿ وإذا بلغ الأطفال منكم الحلم فليستأذنوا﴾ .

ومن أصبح جنبا ولم يتطهر أو امرأة حائض طهرت قبل الفجر فلم يغتسلا إلا بعد الفجر أجزأهما صوم ذلك اليوم.

ولا يجوز صيام يوم الفطر ولا يوم النحر، ولا يصوم اليومين اللذين بعد النحر إلا المتمتع الذي لا يجد هديا، واليوم الرابع لا يصومه متطوع، ويصومه من نذره أو من كان في صيام متتابع قبل ذلك.

If you break the fast in Ramadan out of forgetfulness you only have to make up that day. The same applies if you are forced to break the fast due to illness. If you are on a journey for which you can shorten the prayer you are permitted to break the fast even if there is no particular need to do so, making up any days missed later, but according to us it is better to fast. If someone travels less than four mail stages (48 miles) and breaks the fast thinking it is permissible to do so, he does not have to do *kaffārah* although he must make up the day.

Whoever breaks the fast because of a reasonable interpretation does not have to do *kaffārah*. *Kaffārah* only applies to people who break the fast deliberately either by eating, drinking, or sexual intercourse. The actual day when the *kaffārah* was incurred must also be made up on top of the *kaffārah* itself. The *kaffārah* for breaking the fast consists of feeding sixty poor people with one *mudd* for each person using the *mudd* of the Prophet ﷺ. This is the preferred way of doing *kaffārah* according to us. However, it is also possible to carry out *kaffārah* by freeing a slave or fasting for two consecutive months. Someone who breaks the fast deliberately while making up a day of Ramadan does not have to do *kaffārah*.

If someone becomes unconscious during the night and recovers consciousness after *Fajr* he should make up a day. He only has to make up a missed prayer if he regains consciousness during the time it is due.

When you are fasting you should guard your tongue and limbs and honour the month of Ramadan as Allah has honoured it.

A fasting man may not have sexual intercourse during the daytime in Ramadan nor may he touch a woman or kiss her to gain pleasure. None of these things, however, is unlawful for him during the night.

ومن أفطر في نهار رمضان ناسيا فعليه القضاء فقط. وكذلك من أفطر فيه لضرورة من مرض. ومن سافر سفرا تقصر فيه الصلاة فله أن يفطر، وإن لم تنله ضرورة، وعليه القضاء، والصوم أحب إلينا. ومن سافر أقل من أربعة برد فظن أن الفطر مباح له فأفطر فلا كفارة عليه وعليه القضاء.

وكل من أفطر متأولا فلا كفارة عليه، وإنما الكفارة على من أفطر متعمدا بأكل أو شرب أو جماع أو شرب مع القضاء. والكفارة في ذلك إطعام ستين مسكينا، لكل مسكين مد بمد النبي صلى الله عليه وسلم، فذلك أحب إلينا، وله أن يكفر بعتق رقبة أو صيام شهريين متتابعين. وليس على من أفطر في قضاء رمضان متعمدا كفارة.

ومن أغمي عليه ليلا فأفاق بعد طلوع الفجر فعليه قضاء الصوم، ولا يقضي من الصلوات إلا ما أفاق في وقته.

وينبغي للصائم أن يحفظ لسانه وجوارحه، ويعظم من شهر رمضان ما عظم الله سبحانه وتعالى.

ولا يقرب الصائم النساء بوطء ولا مباشرة ولا قبلة للذة في نهار رمضان، ولا يحرم ذلك عليه في ليلة. ولا بأس أن يصبح جنبا من

It does not matter if you wake up in the morning in a state of *janābah* because of having had sexual intercourse. If you do get sexual pleasure during the daytime by touching or kissing and this results in the emission of *madhy* (prostatic fluid), then you must make up that day. If you do it deliberately and the result is the ejaculation of *many* (semen) you have to do *kaffārah*.

Anyone who stands in prayer in Ramadan with belief and with awareness of the reward for doing it is forgiven all his previous wrong actions. If you stand up in prayer during the night, to the extent that you able to do so, you can expect great good from it and pardon for your wrong actions. These night prayers are done behind an imam in mosques where the prayer is normally done in congregation. But if you want to you can do these night prayers at home. Indeed this is considered better if your intention is strong enough for you to do them by yourself.

The righteous people of the first community used to perform these prayers in the mosque. They did twenty *rak'at*s followed by three *rak'at*s – two for *shaf'* and one for *witr* with a *salām* in between. Later they began praying thirty-six *rak'at*s not including the *shaf'* and *witr*. Both of these are acceptable. You say the *salām* after each two *rak'at*s. 'A'isha ﷺ said that the Messenger of Allah ﷺ never did more than twelve *rak'at*s followed by a single *rak'at* of *witr*, either in Ramadan or out of it.

الوطء. ومن التذ في نهار رمضان بمباشرة أو قبله فأمذى لذلك فعليه القضاء، وإن تعمد ذلك حتى أمنى فعليه الكفارة.

ومن قام رمضان إيمانا واحتسابا غفر له ما تقدم من ذنبه، وإن قمت فيه بما تيسر فذلك مرجو فضله، وتكفير الذنوب به، والقيام فيه في مساجد الجماعات بإمام، ومن شاء قام في بيته، وهو أحسن لمن قويت نيته وحده.

وكان السلف الصالح يقومون فيه في المساجد بعشرين ركعة ثم يوترون بثلاث، ويفصلون بين الشفع والوتر بسلام، ثم صلوا بعد ذلك ستا وثلاثين ركعة غير الشفع والوتر، وكل ذلك واسع، ويسلم من كل ركعتين. وقالت عائشة رضي الله عنها: ما زاد رسول الله صلى الله عليه وسلم في رمضان ولا في غيره على اثنتي عشرة ركعة بعدها الوتر.

24. *I'tikāf*

I'tikāf is a meritorious voluntary act. It derives from a word meaning 'to stay in one place'. You can only do *i'tikāf* if you are fasting and if it is consecutive and in a mosque, as in the words of Allah Almighty, '*While you are doing i'tikāf in the mosques.*' (2:187) If the town is one where there is a *Jumu'ah*, then *i'tikāf* must be done in the *Jumu'ah* mosque, unless you are fulfilling a vow to do a certain number of days in *i'tikāf* and these do not include the day of *Jumu'ah*. According to us it best to do at least ten days. However, if someone makes a vow to do *i'tikāf* for one day or more, they must fulfil their vow. If the vow was just for one night, they must do *i'tikāf* for a day and a night.

If someone in *i'tikāf* deliberately breaks their fast, they have to begin their *i'tikāf* all over again, and the same applies to someone who has sexual intercourse while in *i'tikāf* whether during the day or the night and whether it is through forgetfulness or is deliberate. If you fall ill in *i'tikāf* you can return home, but you should complete your *i'tikāf* when you are well again. The same applies to a woman who starts to menstruate while in *i'tikāf*. The restrictions of *i'tikāf* continue to apply to both sick people and women who are menstruating during the time they are away from the mosque. When the woman regains her purity she should return immediately to the mosque whether this happens by night or by day. People doing *i'tikāf* should not leave the mosque except for essential needs.

You should enter the mosque where you are intending to do your *i'tikāf* before sunset on the night you intend to start. While in *i'tikāf* you should not visit the sick, follow funeral processions or go out to transact any business. You cannot make your *i'tikāf* conditional in

٢٤ - باب في الاعتكاف

والاعتكاف من نوافل الخير، والعكوف الملازمة، ولا اعتكاف إلا بصيام، ولا يكون إلا متتابعا، ولا يكون إلا في المساجد كما قال سبحانه وتعالى ﴿وأنتم عاكفون في المساجد﴾. فإن كان بلد فيه الجمعة فلا يكون إلا في الجامع إلا أن ينذر أياما لا تأخذه فيها الجمعة، وأقل ما هو أحب إلينا من الاعتكاف عشرة أيام. ومن نذر اعتكاف يوم فأكثر لزمه، وإن نذر ليلة لزمه يوم وليلة.

ومن أفطر فيه متعمدا فليبتدئ اعتكافه، وكذلك من جامع فيه ليلا أو نهارا ناسيا أو متعمدا، وإن مرض خرج إلى بيته، فإذا صح بنى على ما تقدم، وكذلك إن حاضت المعتكفة وحرمة الاعتكاف عليهما في المرض، وعلى الحائض في الحيض، فإذا طهرت الحائض أو أفاق المريض في ليل أو نهار رجعا ساعتئذ إلى المسجد، ولا يخرج المعتكف من معتكفه إلا لحاجة الإنسان.

وليدخل معتكفة قبل غروب الشمس من الليلة التي يريد أن يبتدئ فيهما اعتكافه. ولا يعود مريضا، ولا يصلي على جنازة، ولا يخرج لتجارة، ولا شرط في الاعتكاف. ولا بأس أن يكون إمام المسجد،

any way. There is no harm in the imam of a mosque doing *i'tikāf*. It is permissible for someone in *i'tikāf* to get married and for him to officiate at someone else's marriage.

If you go into *i'tikāf* at the beginning of the month or in the middle of the month, when you leave from your *i'tikāf* you should do so after the *Maghrib* of its last day. However, if the period of your *i'tikāf* continues until the day of the *'Īd al-Fiṭr* then you should spend the night before the *'Īd* in the mosque and leave from it in the morning to go to the place where the *'Īd* prayer is going to be held.

وله أن يتزوج أو يعقد نكاح غيره.

ومن اعتكف أول الشهر أو وسطه خرج من اعتكافه بعد غروب الشمس من آخره وإن اعتكف بما يتصل فيه اعتكافه بيوم الفطر فليبت ليلة الفطر في المسجد حتى يغدو منه إلى المصلى.

25. The *Zakāt* of Money, Crops, and What Comes out of Mines; *Jizyah* and What Should Be Taken from *Dhimmī* Merchants and Mercants Who Come from the *Dār al-Ḥarb*

It is obligatory to pay *zakāt* on money, crops and livestock. *Zakāt* on crops must be paid on the day they are harvested. *Zakāt* on money and livestock is paid once a year.

No *zakāt* is due on any amount of dates or grain less than five *wasqs*. Five *wasqs* is the same as six and a quarter *qafīz*. One *wasq* is sixty *ṣā*'s measuring by the *ṣā*' of the Prophet ﷺ. One *ṣā*' is four *mudds*. Wheat, barley and ṣult barley are considered as one category for *zakāt* purposes so that if together they add up to five *wasqs* you have to pay *zakāt* on them. In the same way different kinds of pulses are added together. This also applies to different varieties of dates and raisins. However rice, sorghum and millet are each considered to be in a different category and are not added together when calculating *zakāt*.

If there are various types of dates in a date-garden you use the middle quality when paying *zakāt*. You pay *zakāt* on olives when the amount of them reaches five *wasqs*, paying the *zakāt* in oil. You also pay *zakāt* on sesame seeds and *seemga* (*raphanus oleifer*) in oil. If you sell this produce, it is possible to pay the *zakāt* owed using the money you have received, if Allah wills. You do not pay *zakāt* on fruit and vegetables.

There is no *zakāt* on gold if you have less than twenty dinars. If

٢٥ - باب في زكاة العين والحرث والماشية وما يخرج من المعدن وذكر الجزية وما يؤخذ من تجار الذمة والحربيين

وزكاة العين والحرث والماشية فريضة. فأما الحرث فيوم حصاده، والعين والماشية ففي كل حول مرة.

ولا زكاة من الحب والتمر في أقل من خمسة أوسق، وذلك ستة أقفزة وربع قفيز. والوسق ستون صاعا بصاع النبي صلى الله عليه وسلم، وهو أربعة أمداد بمده عليه الصلاة والسلام، ويجمع القمح الشعير والسلت في الزكاة، فإذا اجتمع من القمح والشعير والسلت في الزكاة، فإذا اجتمع من جميعها خمسة أوسق فليزك ذلك، وكذلك تجمع أصناف القطنية، وكذلك تجمع أصناف التمر، وكذلك أصناف الزبيب. والأرز والدخن والذرة، كل واحد منها صنف لا يضم إلى الآخر في الزكاة. وإذا كان في الحائط أصناف من التمر أدى الزكاة عن الجميع من وسطه. ويزكي الزيتون إذا بلغ حبه خمسة أوسق أخرج من زيته. ويخرج من الجلجلان وحب الفجل من زيته، فإن باع ذلك أجزأه أن يخرج من ثمنه إن شاء الله. ولا زكاة في الفواكه والخضر.

ولا زكاة من الذهب في أقل من عشرين دينارا، فإذا بلغت دينارا

the amount reaches twenty dinars you pay one half of a dinar, in other words, one-fortieth of the total amount. Any more than that is calculated on the same basis, however small the additional amount is. There is no *zakāt* on silver if you have less than two hundred dirhams, which is five *ūqiyyah*s – one *ūqiyyah* being forty dirhams. This is based on seven dinars being of the same weight as ten dirhams. If you have two hundred such dirhams you pay one-fortieth, that is five dirhams. Anything more than that is calculated on the same basis. Gold and silver are considered as one category for the purposes of *zakāt*. So if, for example, someone has one hundred dirhams and ten dinars they should pay one-fortieth of each.

There is no *zakāt* on goods unless they are for trading purposes. If you sell goods after one year or more from the day you bought them or paid *zakāt* on their price, then you only have to pay one year's *zakāt* on the proceeds of the goods, whether these goods were in your possession for one year or more than one year before you sold them. However, if you are a merchant with a constant turnover so that you never keep money or goods in your possession for any length of time then you should assess your goods every year and pay *zakāt* on them and on whatever cash you have in hand at that time. Similarly *zakāt* is due on the offspring of livestock if the mother animals have been in your possession for a year.

If you have wealth on which *zakāt* is due but you also have a debt of the same amount, or one which will reduce your wealth to less than the amount on which *zakāt* is due, then you do not have to pay *zakāt*. If, however, you have other assets on which *zakāt* is not due, such as personal effects or slaves or domestic animals or private property which could be used to pay off your debt, then you do pay *zakāt* on

ففيها نصف دينار ربع العشر، فما زاد فبحساب ذلك، وإن قل، ولا زكاة من الفضة في أقل من مائتي درهم، وذلك خمس أواق، والأوقية أربعون درهما من وزن سبعة، أعني أن السبعة دنانير وزنها عشرة دراهم، فإذا بلغت هذه الدراهم مائتي درهم ففيها ربع عشرة دراهم، فإذا بلغت هذه الدراهم مائتي درهم ففيها ربع عشرها خمسة دراهم، فما زاد فبحساب ذلك، ويجمع الذهب والفضة في الزكاة، فمن كان له مائة درهم وعشرة دنانير فليخرج من كل مال ربع عشره.

ولا زكاة في العروض حتى تكون للتجارة. فإذا بعتها بعد حول فأكثر من يوم أخذت ثمنها أو زكيته ففي ثمنها الزكاة لحول واحد، أقامت قبل البيع حولا أو أكثر، إلا أن تكون مديرا لا يستقر بيدك عين ولا عرض. فإنك تقوم عروضك كل عام وتزكي ذلك مع ما بيدك من العين. فإنك تقوم عروضك كل عام وتزكي ذلك مع ما بيد من العين. وحول ربح المال حول أصله، وكذلك حول نسل الأنعام حول الأمهات.

ومن له مال تجب فيه الزكاة وعليه دين مثله أو ينقصه عن مقدار مال الزكاة فلا زكاة عليه إلا أن يكون عنده مما لا يزكي من عروض مقتناة أو رقيق أو حيوان مقتناة أو عقار أو ربع ما فيه وفاء لدينه، فليزك ما بيده من المال، فإن لم تف عروضه بدينه حسب بقية دينه

your wealth. If your assets are not sufficient to pay your debt, then you calculate the difference between the debt and your assets and subtract the difference from the wealth on which *zakāt* is due. If there is still enough left for *zakāt* to be due you must pay the *zakāt*.

Debt does not, however, affect the obligation to pay *zakāt* on grain, dates or livestock. You do not have to pay *zakāt* on money owed to you until after you have received it and if the debt has been outstanding for a number of years you only pay one year's *zakāt* on it after it is repaid. This is the same as when you own goods. You only pay *zakāt* on them after you have sold them. If the debt owing to you on the goods has been inherited by you, you wait for one year after receiving payment before paying the *zakāt* due.

Zakāt must be paid on wealth belonging to minors whether it is in the form of money, crops or livestock. *Zakāt al-fiṭr* must also be paid on their behalf. Slaves, including those who are partially but not completely freed, do not have to pay *zakāt* on any of these categories. If they have been completely freed they do not pay *zakāt* on any wealth in their possession until a whole year has passed from the day when they were freed.

No *zakāt* is payable on slaves, servants, horses, your house nor on any private property or goods which are for your own personal use nor on jewellery which is in regular use. If you inherit or are given any goods or take any produce from your land, on which *zakāt* has already been paid, and then sell any of these things, no *zakāt* is due on the proceeds until a year has elapsed.

Zakāt is due on gold or silver extracted from mines as soon as the weight of gold amounts to twenty dinars or the weight of silver to five *ūqiyyahs*. One-fortieth must be paid on the day it is extracted. After this, *zakāt* is due on all gold and silver continuously extracted from the same deposit, however small the amount until such time as that

فيما بيده، فإن بقي بعد ذلك ما فيه الزكاة زكاة.

ولا يسقط الدين زكاة حب ولا تمر ولا ماشية، ولا زكاة عليه في دين حتى يقبضه، وإن أقام أعواما فإنما يزكيه لعام واحد بعد قبضه، وكذلك العرض حتى يبيعه. وإن كان الدين أو الأرض من ميراث فليستقبل حولا بما يقبض منه.

وعلى الأصاغر الزكاة في أموالهم في العين والحرث والماشية وزكاة الفطر، ولا زكاة على عبد ولا على من فيه بقية رق في ذلك كله، فإذا أعتق فليأتنف حولا من يومئذ بما يملك من ماله.

ولا زكاة على أحد في عبده وخادمه وفرسه وداره، ولا ما يتخذ للقنية من الرباع والعروض، ولا فيما يتخذ للباس من الحلي، ومن ورث عرضا أو وهب له أو رفع من أرضه زرعا فزكاه فلا زكاة عليه في شيء من ذلك حتى يباع ويستقبل به حولا من يوم يقبض ثمنه.
وفيما يخرج من المعدن من ذهب أو فضة الزكاة إذا بلغ وزن عشرين دينارا أو خمس أواق فضة، ففي ذلك ربع العشر يوم خروجه، وكذلك فيما يخرج بعد ذلك متصلا به وإن قل، فإن

deposit has been worked dry. If work is begun on another deposit, no *zakāt* is due until the amount extracted reaches the amount on which *zakāt* is due.

Jizyah is taken from the men of the people of *dhimmah* status, provided that they are both free and adult. It is not taken from their women, their children, or their slaves. It is taken from Magians and from Christian Arabs. For people who use gold the *jizyah* is four dinars and for people who use silver it is forty dirhams. It can be made less for people who are poor. Those among them who are engaged in long-distance trading should pay one tenth of what they receive when they sell their goods even if they come and go several times in one year. If they are carrying food destined specifically for Makkah or Madīnah only one-twentieth of what they sell it for should be taken. A tenth is also levied from traders who come from *Dār al-Ḥarb* (the land of war – beyond the frontiers of Islam) unless they have agreed to terms demanding more than that. If someone comes upon treasure (*rikāz*) that was buried in the time of the *Jāhiliyyah* (before Islam) he must pay the fifth.

انقطع نيله بيده وابتدأ غيره لم يخرج شيئا حتى يبلغ ما فيه الزكاة.

وتؤخذ الجزية من رجال أهل الذمة الأحرار البالغين، ولا تؤخذ من نسائهم وصبيانهم وعبيدهم، وتؤخذ من المجوس ومن نصارى العرب. والجزية على أهل الذهب أربعة دنانير، وعلى أهل الورق أربعون درهما، ويخفف عن الفقير، ويؤخذ ممن تجر منهم من أفق عشر ثمن ما يبيعونه وإن اختلفوا في السنة مرارا، وإن حملوا الطعام خاصة إلى مكة والمدينة خاصة أخذ منهم نصف العشر من ثمنه، ويؤخذ من تجار الحربيين العشر إلا أن ينزلوا على أكثر من ذلك، وفي الركاز وهو دفن الجاهلية الخمس على من أصابه.

26. *ZAKĀT* DUE ON LIVESTOCK

Zakāt on camels, cows, sheep and goats is obligatory. There is no *zakāt* on less than five camels, but on five to nine camels you must give either a sheep or a goat which is in its second year, depending on which of the two animals is most commonly kept by the people of the area. You must give two sheep or goats for ten to fourteen camels, and three sheep or goats for fifteen to nineteen camels. For twenty to twenty-five camels you must give four sheep or goats. For twenty-five to thirty-five camels you must give a female camel in its second year (*bint makhāḍ*) or, if there is not one available, a male camel in its third year (*ibn labūn*). For forty-six to sixty camels you must give a female camel in its fourth year capable of carrying loads and bearing children (*ḥiqqah*). For sixty-one to seventy-five camels you must give a female camel in its fifth year (*jadha'ah*). For seventy-six to ninety camels you must give two female camels in their third year (*bint labūn*). For ninety-one to one hundred and twenty camels you must give two *ḥiqqah*s. For any more than this you give one *ḥiqqah* for every fifty camels and one *bint labūn* for every forty.

There is no *zakāt* on less than thirty cattle. If there are thirty, you must give a calf in its third year (*tabīʿ*). This applies up to forty. If there are forty you must give a cow in its fourth year (*musinnah* or *thaniyyah*) – only females are acceptable. If there are more than that you must give a *musinnah* for every forty and a *tabīʿ* for every thirty.

٢٦ - باب في زكاة الماشية

وزكاة الإبل والبقر والغنم فريضة. ولا زكاة من الإبل في أقل من خمس ذود، وهي خمس من الإبل، ففيها شاة جدعة أو ثنية من جل غنم أهل ذلك البلد من ضأن أو معز إلى تسع، ثم في العشر شاتان إلى أربعة عشر، ثم في خمسة عشر ثلاث شياه إلى تسعة عشر، فإذا كانت عشرين فأربع شياه إلى أربع وعشرين، ثم في خمس وعشرين فأربع شياه إلى أربع وعشرين، ثم في خمس وعشرين بنت مخاض، وهي بنت سنتين، فإن لم تكن فيها فابن لبون ذكر إلى خمس وثلاثين، ثم في ست وثلاثين بنت لبون، وهي بنت ثلاث سنين، إلى خمس وأربعين، ثم في ست وأربعين حقة وهي التي يصلح على ظهرها الحمل، ويطرقها الفحل، وهي بنت خمس سنين إلى خمس وسبعين، ثم في ست وسبعين بنتا لبون إلى تسعين، ثم في إحدى وتسعين حقتان إلى عشرين ومائة، فما زاد على ذلك ففي كل خمسين حقة وفي كل أربعين بنت لبون.

ولا زكاة من البقر في أقل من ثلاثين، فإذا بلغتها ففيها تبيع: عجل جذع قد أوفى سنتين، ثم كذلك حتى تبلغ أربعين فيكون فيها مسنة، ولا تؤخذ إلا أنثى وهي بنت أربع سنين، وهي ثنية، فما زاد ففي كل أربعين مسنة، وفي كل ثلاثين تبيع.

There is no *zakāt* on sheep and goats until their number reaches forty. If it passes forty, you must give one in its fifth year (*jadha'ah*) or one in its fourth year (*thaniyyah*). This applies up to one hundred and twenty animals. If you have between one hundred and twenty and two hundred sheep and/or goats you must give two. For two hundred and one to three hundred you must give three, and for every additional hundred you give one animal.

Zakāt is not required on any number of animals between the figures mentioned and this ruling applies to all the types of animals mentioned above. Sheep and goats are considered as one category for *zakāt* purposes as are cattle and buffaloes and as are also Bactrian and dromedary camels.

The owners of herds which are mixed together pay *zakāt* jointly and settle between themselves the share each must pay. There is no *zakāt* due from someone whose share does not reach the number subject to *zakāt*. When the *zakāt* of the year is due, animals which were mixed together are not to be separated, nor those which were separate to be mixed, out of fear of paying the *zakāt*. If the *zakāt* paid is less because the two herds were separated or mixed, the herds should be restored to their prior condition.

A baby sheep or goat is not taken to pay *zakāt*. However, it is counted in numbering the owner's flock. Baby calves or camels are not taken, but they are counted in numbering the herd. Similarly exempt from being taken as *zakāt* are young billy goats, thin old females, pregnant females, a ram used for stud, a sheep or goat fattened for slaughter, a female nursing its young, nor the best of a man's property. For *zakāt* on animals, one may not collect goods or the price of the animal in place of the animal. If the collector forces the owner into giving the price of the animal or something else, that satisfies it, Allah willing. A debt does not cancel one's obligation to pay *zakāt* on grain, fruit or animals.

ولا زكاة في الغنم حتى تبلغ أربعين شاة، فإذا بلغتها ففيها شاة جدعة أو ثنية إلى عشرين ومائة، فإذا بلغت إحدى وعشرين ومائة ففيها شاتان إلى مائتي شاة، فإذا زادت واحدة ففيها ثلاث شياه إلى ثلاثمائة، فما زاد ففي كل مائة شاة.

ولا زكاة في الأوقاص، وهي ما بين الفريضتين من كل الأنعام.

الجمع بين صنفين متقاربين في وجوب الزكاة وتكوين النصاب في الأنعام. ويجمع الضأن والمعز في الزكاة، والجوامس والبقر، والبخت والعراب.

وكل خليطين فإنهما يترادان بينهما بالسوية. ولا زكاة على من لم تبلغ حصته عدد الزكاة، ولا يفرق بين مجتمع ولا يجمع بين متفرق خشية الصدقة، وذلك إذا قرب الحول، فإذا كان ينقص أداؤها بافتراقهما أو باجتماعهما أخذا بما كانا عليه قبل ذلك.

ولا تؤخذ في الصدقة السخلة وتعد على رب الغنم، ولا تؤخذ العجاجيل في البقر ولا الفصلان في الإبل، وتعد عليهم، ولا يؤخذ تيس ولا هرمة ولا الماخض ولا فحل الغنم ولا شاة العلف ولا التي تربي ولدها، ولا خيار أموال الناس، ولا يؤخذ في ذلك عرض ثمن، فإن أجبره المصدق على أخذ الثمن في الأنعام وغيرها أجزأه إن شاء الله. ولا يسقط الدين زكاة حب ولا تمر ولا ماشية.

حكمها، ووقتها، ومقدارها:

27. *Zakāt al-Fiṭr*

Zakāt al-fiṭr is an obligatory *sunnah* which the Messenger of Allah ﷺ made compulsory for all Muslims, whether old or young, male or female, free or slave. Its amount is one *ṣāʿ* measuring by the *ṣāʿ* of the Prophet ﷺ. It should be paid in kind using the staple food of the people of the region, which might be wheat, barley, sult barley, dates, dried cheese, raisins, millet, sorghum or rice. It is also said that if the staple food of the people is *al-ʿalas*, which is a small grain similar to wheat, that the *zakāt al-fiṭr* can be paid with that.

The *zakāt al-fiṭr* of a slave is paid by his master and that of a young child who has no personal wealth by his father. A man has to pay the *zakāt al-fiṭr* of every Muslim for whose maintenance he is responsible and he should also pay for his *mukātab* (partially freed slave), because even if he is not responsible for his maintenance, the *mukātab* is nevertheless still his slave. It is recommended to pay the *zakāt al-fiṭr* at daybreak on the day of the *ʿĪd al-Fiṭr*.

On the morning of the *ʿĪd al-Fiṭr*, it is recommended to break your fast before leaving for the prayer-place, whereas on the morning of the *ʿĪd al-Aḍḥā* it is recommended not to do so. On both *ʿĪd*s, however, it is recommended to go to the prayer by one route and return from it by another.

٢٧ - باب في زكاة الفطر

وزكاة الفطر سنة واجبة فرضها رسول الله صلى الله عليه وسلم على كل كبير أو صغير، ذكر أو أنثى، حر أو عبد، من المسلمين، صاعا عن كل نفس بصاع النبي صلى الله عليه وسلم، وتؤدى من جل عيش أهل ذلك البلد من بر أو شعير أو سلت أو تمر أو أقط أو زبيب أو دخن أو ذرة أو أرز. وقيل: إن كان العلس قوت قوم أخرجت منه، وهو حب صغير يقرب من خلقه البر، ويخرج عن العبد سيده، والصغير لا مال له يخرج عنه والده، ويخرج الرجل زكاة الفطر عن كل مسلم تلزمه نفقته وعن مكاتبه، وإن كان لا ينفق عليه لأنه عبد له بعد. ويستحب إخراجها إذا طلع الفجر من يوم الفطر.

ويستحب الفطر فيه قبل الغدو إلى المصلى، وليس ذلك في الأضحى، ويستحب في العيدين أن يمضي من طريق ويرجع من أخرى.

28. Ḥajj and ʿUmrah

Going on *ḥajj* to the Sacred House of Allah, situated in Bakkah, is an obligation for every free adult Muslim, who is able to find a way to perform it, once during his lifetime. What is meant by "way" here is a safe route, sufficient provisions to reach Makkah, sufficient strength to be able to get to Makkah, whether mounted or walking, and a good state of health.

You should go into '*iḥrām*' at the appropriate *mīqāt*. The *mīqāt* for the people of Syria, Egypt and North Africa is Juḥfah, but if they come via Madīnah, it is better for them to go into *iḥrām* at the *mīqāt* of the people of Madīnah which is Dhū al-Ḥulayfah. The *mīqāt* of the people of Iraq is Dhat 'Irq and that of the people of Yemen, Yalamlam. The people of Najd go into *iḥrām* at Qarn. If any of these go via Madīnah they too should go into *iḥrām* at Dhū al-Ḥulayfah since they will not be passing their own *mīqāt* again.

When going into *iḥrām* you should do so straight after praying, whether that prayer is *farḍ* or supererogatory. You start by saying the *talbiyah*:

> *Labbayk-Allāhumma labbayk, labbayka lā sharīka laka labbayk, inna-l-ḥamda wa-n-niʿmata laka wa-l-mulk, lā sharīka lak.*
>
> "At Your service, O Allah, at Your service. At Your service, none can be associated with You, at Your service. All praise and blessing is due to You as is the kingdom. None can be associated with You."

You say this and make the intention to perform *ḥajj* or *'umrah* according to what you are intending to do. Then you should have a *ghusl* and remove any clothes containing stitching before actually

٢٨ - باب في الحج والعمرة

وحج بيت الله الحرام ببكة فريضة على كل من استطاع إلى ذلك سبيلا من المسلمين الأحرار البالغين مرة في عمره، والسبيل: الطريق السابلة، والزاد المبلغ إلى مكة، والقوة على الوصول إلى مكة إما راكبا أو راجلا مع صحة البدن.

وإنما يؤمر أن يحرم من الميقات. وميقات أهل الشام ومصر والمغرب الجحفة، فإن مروا بالمدينة فالأفضل لهم أن يحرموا من ميقات أهلها من ذي الحليفة. وميقات أهل العراق ذات عرق. وأهل اليمن يلملم، وأهل نجد من قرن، ومن مر من هؤلاء بالمدينة فواجب عليه أن يحرم من ذي الحليفة إذ لا يتعداه إلى ميقات له.

ويحرم الحاج أو المعتمر بإثر صلاة فريضة أو نافلة ، يقول:

لَبَّيْكَ اللَّهُمَّ لَبَّيْكَ، لَبَّيْكَ لاَ شَرِيكَ لَكَ لَبَّيْكَ، إِنَّ الْحَمْدَ وَالنِّعْمَةَ لَكَ وَالْمُلْكُ، لاَ شَرِيكَ لَكَ.

وينوي ما أراد من حج أو عمرة، ويؤمر أن يغتسل عند الإحرام قبل أن يحرم ويتجرد من مخيط الثياب. ويستحب له أن يغتسل

entering the state of *iḥrām*. It is also recommended to have a *ghusl* when you enter Makkah.

You should continue to recite the *talbiyah* after all prayers, at the summit of every rise and every time you rejoin your travelling companions. However, you should not go to excess in it. When you enter Makkah you stop reciting the *talbiyah* until after you have completed your *ṭawāf* and *sā*'y. Then you start doing it again until midday on the Day of 'Arafah, if you have reached the place of prayer on 'Arafah.

It is recommended to enter Makkah through the pass of Kadā' ath-Thaniyyah in upper Makkah and to leave it by Kudā, but it does not matter if you do not do this. Mālik said that all those entering Makkah should first of all go straight to the Masjid al-Ḥarām, which it is recommended to enter by the door of Banū Shaybah. You should greet the Black Stone by kissing it, if possible, or if you cannot then by touching it and putting your hand to your mouth without kissing it. Then you do *ṭawāf* keeping the House on your left, going round it seven times, three times at a fast pace between walking and running and four times at a normal walking pace. Every time you pass the Black Stone, you greet it in the way we have already mentioned and say '*Allāhu akbar*'. You do not kiss the Yemeni corner but you greet it by touching it with your hand, which you then raise to your mouth without kissing it.

When you have finished your *ṭawāf* you pray two *rak'at*s at the Maqām of Ibrāhīm. Then, if you are able to, you greet the Black Stone once more and then go off to Ṣafā where you stand and make supplication. From there you walk to Marwah going faster across the bottom of the valley. When you reach Marwah you stand for a time making supplication and then walk back to Ṣafā. You do this seven times, standing four times on Ṣafā and four times on Marwah.

لدخول مكة.

ولا يزال يلبي دبر الصلوات، وعند كل شرف، وعند ملاقاة الرفاق، وليس عليه كثرة الإلحاح بذلك، فإذا دخل مكة أمسك عن التلبية حتى يطوف ويسعى، ثم يعاودها حتى تزول الشمس من يوم عرفة ويروح إلى مصلاها.

ويستحب أن يدخل مكة من كداء الثنية التي بأعلى مكة، وإذا خرج ، خرج من كدا ، وإن لم يفعل في الوجهين فلا حرج. قال: فإذا دخل مكة فليدخل المسجد الحرام، ومستحسن أن يدخل من باب بني شيبة فيستلم الحجر الأسود بفيه إن قدر، وإلا وضع يده عليه، ثم وضعها على فيه من غير تقبيل، ثم يطوف والبيت على يساره سبعة أطواف ثلاثة خببا، ثم أربعة مشيا، ويستلم الركن كلما مر به كما ذكرنا، ويكبر، ولا يستلم الركن اليماني بفيه، ولكن بيده، ثم يضعها على فيه من غير تقبيل.

فإذا تم طوافه ركع عند المقام ركعتين، ثم استلم الحجر إن قدر، ثم يخرج إلى الصفا فيقف عليه للدعاء ، ثم يسعى إلى المروة ويخب في بطن المسيل، فإذا أتى المروة وقف عليها للدعاء، ثم يسعى إلى الصفا، يفعل ذلك سبع مرات فيقف بذالك أربع وقفات على الصفا، وأربعا على المروة.

On the Day of Tarwiyah (8th Dhu-l-Ḥijjah) you go to Minā where you pray *Ẓuhr*, *'Aṣr*, *Maghrib*, *'Ishā'* and *Subḥ*, and then you go to 'Arafāt. During this time you continue to recite the *talbiyah* ceasing when the sun has passed its zenith on the Day of 'Arafah and you have reached the place of prayer there. You should have a *ghusl* before going off to perform the prayer on 'Arafah where you join *Ẓuhr* and *'Aṣr* with the imam. Then you accompany him to the standing place at 'Arafah and stay there with him till the sun has set.

Then when he moves off to go to Muzdalifah you go after him, praying *Maghrib*, *'Ishā'* and *Ṣubḥ* with him at Muzdalifah. After that you stand there with him at the Mash'ar al-Ḥarām and, shortly after sunrise, you go to Minā hurrying your mount across the Valley of Muḥassir. When you get to Minā you stone the Jamrat al-'Aqabah using seven small pebbles and saying "*Allāhu akbar*" with each pebble as you throw it. Then, if you have a sacrificial animal with you, you make sacrifice. Then you shave your head. After that you go the House and perform the *Ṭawāf al-Ifāḍah* going round seven times and finishing with the prayer.

You then stay for three days at Minā. On each day after the sun has passed the zenith, you first stone the *jamrah* nearest Minā using seven small pebbles and saying, '*Allāhu akbar*' with each pebble thrown. You then stone the other two *jamrah*s with the same number of pebbles again saying "*Allāhu akbar*" as you throw each one. After stoning the first two *jamrah*s you stand and make supplication but after stoning the Jamrat al-'Aqabah you do not stand but move straight off. When you have finished stoning on the third day, making four days including the *'Īd*, you leave for Makkah and your *ḥajj* is complete. If you want, you can speed up your departure by staying only two days at Minā, leaving after finishing stoning on the second day. When you are about to leave Makkah you perform the *Ṭawāf* of Farewell and the two *rak'at*s after it and then leave.

ثم يخرج يوم التروية إلى منى، فيصلي بها الظهر والعصر والمغرب والعشاء والصبح. ثم يمضي إلى عرفات، ولا يدع التلبية في هذا كله حتى تزول الشمس من يوم عرفة ويروح إلى مصلاها، وليتطهر قبل رواحه، فيجمع بين الظهر والعصر مع الإمام، ثم يروح معه إلى موقف عرفة فيقف معه إلى غروب الشمس.

ثم يدفع بدفعه إلى المزدلفة فيصلي معه بالمزدلفة المغرب والعشاء والصبح، ثم يقف معه بالمشعر الحرام يومئذ بها، ثم يدفع بقرب طلوع الشمس إلى منى، ويحرك دابته ببطن محسر. فإذا وصل إلى منى رمى جمرة العقبة بسبع حصيات مثل حصى الخذف، ويكبر مع كل حصاة، ثم ينحر إن كان معه هدي، ثم يحلق، ثم يأتي البيت فيفيض ويطوف سبعا، ويركع.

ثم يقيم بمنى ثلاثة أيام. فإذا زالت الشمس من كل يوم منها رمى الجمرة التي تلي منى بسبع حصيات يكبر مع كل حصاة، ثم يرمي الجمرتين ، كل جمرة بمثل ذلك ، ويكبر مع كل حصاة، ويقف للدعاء بإثر الرمي في الجمرة الأولى والثانية، ولا يقف عند جمرة العقبة ولينصرف، فإذا رمى في اليوم الثالث وهو رابع يوم النحر، انصرف إلى مكة وقد تم حجه، وإن شاء تعجل في يومين من أيام منى فرمى وانصرف، فإذا خرج من مكة طاف للوداع وركع وانصرف.

For *'umrah* you do the same as we said at the beginning of this chapter up until you have completed the *ṣā'y* between Ṣafā and Marwah. You then shave your head, and your *'umrah* is complete. For both *ḥajj* and *'umrah* it is better to shave your head but shortening the hair is acceptable in which case the hair should be shortened all over the head. The *sunnah* for women is to shorten the hair.

There is no harm in someone in *iḥrām* killing a rat, snake, scorpion or such like, nor in killing a dangerous dog or any other dangerous animal such as a jackal or a lion. You can also kill birds whose harm is feared, like crows and kites, but not any other birds. When performing *ḥajj* or *'umrah* you should avoid women, perfume, stitched clothing, hunting, killing insects and removing any hair from your body. When you are in *iḥrām*, you should not cover your head nor should you shave it except in a case of necessity. If you do you must make expiation by fasting three days or feeding six destitute people with two *mudd*s each, using the *mudd* of the Prophet ﷺ, or sacrificing a sheep. This sacrifice does not have to be carried out in any particular place.

Women may wear *khuff*s and ordinary clothing while they are in *iḥrām* but in all other respects they must avoid the same things as men. A woman's *iḥrām* consists in her not covering her face and hands and man's *iḥrām* in his not covering his face and head. A man may not wear *khuff*s while he is in *iḥrām* unless he does not have any thonged sandals in which case he should cut his *khuff*s down to below the ankles.

According to us doing *Ḥajj* by itself (*ifrād*) is better than doing *tamattu'* (*'umrah* then *ḥajj* separately in the same season) or *qirān* (*ḥajj* and *'umrah* together). If someone who is not from Makkah does *qirān* or *tamattu'*, at Minā he must sacrifice an animal, which he had with him at 'Arafah. If he did not have it at 'Arafah he should sacrifice it in Makkah at Marwah, having brought it there from outside the Ḥaram. If you do not have a sacrificial animal you should fast three days during the *ḥajj*,

والعمرة يفعل فيها كما ذكرنا أولا إلى تمام السعي بين الصفا والمروة، ثم يحلق رأسه وقد تمت عمرته، والحلاق أفضل في الحج والعمرة، والتقصير يجزيء، وليقصر من جميع شعره، وسنة المرأة التقصير.

ولا بأس أن يقتل المحرم الفأرة والحية والعقرب وشبهها والكلب العقور وما يعدو من الذئاب و السباع ونحوها، ويقتل من الطير ما يتقى أذاه من الغربان والأحدية فقط. ويجتنب في حجه وعمرته النساء والطيب ومخيط الثياب والصيد وقتل الدواب وإلقاء التفث، ولا يغطي رأسه في الإحرام، ولا يحلقه إلا من ضرورة. ثم يفتدي بصيام ثلاثة أيام أو إطعام ستة مساكين مدين لكل مسكين، بمد النبي صلى الله عليه وسلم أو ينسك بشاة يذبحها حيث شاء من البلاد.

وتلبس المرأة الخفين والثياب في إحرامها، وتجتنب ما سوى ذلك مما يجتنبه الرجل، وإحرام المرأة في وجهها وكفيها، وإحرام الرجل في وجهه ورأسه، ولا يلبس الرجل الخفين في الإحرام إلا أن لا يجد نعلين فليقطعهما أسفل من الكعبين.

والإفراد بالحج أفضل عندنا من التمتع ومن القران. فمن قرن أو تمتع من غير أهل مكة فعليه هدي يذبحه أو ينحره بمنى إن أوقفه بعرفة، وإن لم يوقفه بعرفة فلينحره بمكة بالمروة بعد أن يدخل به من الحل، فإن لم يجد هديا فصيام ثلاثة أيام في الحج، يعني من الوقت الذي يحرم إلى يوم عرفة، فإن فاته ذلك صام أيام منى وسبعة إذا رجع.

that being between the time you go into *iḥrām* and the Day of 'Arafah. If you do not manage to do that you fast the days of Minā. Then when you return to your own country you fast seven more days.

To perform *tamattu'*, you go into *iḥrām* for *'umrah* alone during the months of *ḥajj*, then come out of *iḥrām*, then go back into it again for *ḥajj* that same year without having travelled back to your country or to anywhere else a similar distance away. If this is the case you are permitted to go back into *iḥrām* from Makkah, if that is where you are, but to do so you must go outside the Ḥaram territory.

To perform *qirān* you go into *iḥrām* for *ḥajj* and *'umrah* together, making the intention to perform *'umrah* first. If you decide to perform *ḥajj* as well as *'umrah* before you have done the *ṭawāf* and its following two *rak'at*s you are considered as performing *qirān*. The people of Makkah do not have to sacrifice if they are performing *tamattu'* or *qirān*. If you come out of *iḥrām* after an *'umrah* before the months of *ḥajj* and then stay on for *ḥajj* during the same year, you are not considered as doing *tamattu'*.

If you kill any game while in *iḥrām* you have to make expiation for it by sacrificing a domestic animal equivalent to the one you killed. This should be ascertained by two trustworthy *fuqahā'* from among the Muslims. If the animal to be killed was with you on 'Arafah the sacrifice should be made at Minā. Otherwise it should be made in Makkah, the animal concerned having been brought in from outside the Ḥaram territory. You have the choice between doing this or making *kaffārah* by feeding destitute people, in which case you work out the value of the animal killed in terms of food and give that amount away as *ṣadaqah*. Or alternatively you can fast one day for each *mudd*, fasting a whole day for any incomplete *mudd*.

'Umrah is a confirmed *sunnah* to be done at least once in a lifetime. When you leave Makkah after *ḥajj* or *'umrah*, it is recommended to say:

وصفة التمتع أن يحرم بعمرة ثم يحل منها في أشهر الحج، ثم يحج من عامه قبل الرجوع إلى أفقه أو إلى مثل أفقه في البعد، ولهذا أن يحرم من مكة إن كان بها، ولا يحرم منها من أراد أن يعتمر حتى يخرج إلى الحل.

وصفة القران أن يحرم بحجة وعمرة معا، ويبدأ بالعمرة في نيته، وإذا أردف الحج على العمرة قبل أن يطوف ويركع فهو قارن، وليس على أهل مكة هدي في تمتع ولا قران، ومن حل من عمرته أشهر الحج ثم حج من عامه فليس بمتمتع.

ومن أصاب صيدا فعليه جزاء مثل ما قتل من النعم يحكم به ذوا عدل من فقهاء المسلمين، ومحله منى إن وقف به بعرفة، وإلا فمكة، ويدخل به من الحل، وله أن يختار ذلك، أو كفارة طعام مساكين، أو ينظر إلى قيمة الصيد طعاما فيتصدق به، أو عدل ذلك صياما، أن يصوم عن كل مد يوما، ولكسر المد يوما كاملا.

والعمرة سنة مؤكدة مرة في العمر، ويستحب لمن انصرف من مكة من حج أو عمرة أن يقول :

Āyibūna tā'ibūna 'ābidūna lirabbinā ḥāmidūn, ṣadaqa-llāhu wa'dahu wa naṣara 'abdahu wa hazama-l-aḥzāba waḥdah.

"Returning, repentant, worshipping, praising our Lord. Allah has been true to His promise and given victory to His slave and defeated the confederates by Himself."

ءَايِبُونَ تَائِبُونَ عَابِدُونَ لِرَبِّنَا حَامِدُونَ، صَدَقَ اللّٰهُ وَعْدَهُ وَنَصَرَ عَبْدَهُ وَهَزَمَ الْأَحْزَابَ وَحْدَهُ.

29. Sacrifices, slaughter of animals,
animals sacrificed for the birth of a child, hunting, circumcision and forbidden food and drinks

Sacrificing an animal for the *'Īd* is a *sunnah* which is obligatory for all who are able to do so. The least which is acceptable for it in the case of sheep is a *jadha'ah*, which is a one year old ram, although some have said eight months and some ten months old. In the case of goats it should be a *thaniyyah*, which means a male in its second year and likewise only *thaniyyah* animals are acceptable in the case of cattle and camels. A *thaniyyah* in respect of cattle is a male in its fourth year and in respect of camels it is a six-year-old male.

Rams which have not been castrated are better for sacrifice than those which have been, but castrated rams are better than ewes. Ewes are better than either male or female goats. Male goats which have not been castrated are better than camels and cattle for *'Īd* sacrifices. As regards '*hady*s' (animals to be sacrificed as part of the *ḥajj*) camels are best and then cattle and then sheep and then goats.

In none of these circumstances is it acceptable to sacrifice a one-eyed animal, a sick animal, a markedly lame animal, or an emaciated animal. In fact you should avoid using for sacrifice any animal that has something wrong with it. You should also avoid any split-eared animal unless the split is only slight. The same applies to an animal whose ear has been cut off or one with a broken horn. If it is bleeding it is not acceptable for sacrifice. However, if it is not bleeding, it is acceptable.

It is good to sacrifice your animal yourself after the imam has made his sacrifice on the morning of the Day of Sacrifice. If you slaughter

٢٩ - باب في الضحايا والذبائح والعقيقة والصيد والختان وما يحرم من الأطعمة والأشربة

والأضحية سنة واجبة على من استطاعها. وأقل ما يجزئ فيها من الأسنان الجذع من الضأن، وهو ابن ثمانية أشهر، وقيل: ابن عشرة أشهر، والثني من المعز، وهو ما أوفى سنة ودخل في الثانية، ولا يجزئ في الضحايا من المعز والبقر والإبل إلا الثني، والثني من البقر ما دخل في السنة الرابعة، والثني من الإبل ابن ست سنين.

وفحول الضأن في الضحايا أفضل من خصيانها، وخصيانها أفضل من إناثها، وإناثها أفضل من ذكور المعز ومن إناثها، وفحول المعز أفضل من إناثها، وإناث المعز أفضل من الإبل والبقر، في الضحايا، وأما في الهدايا فالإبل أفضل ثم البقر، ثم الضأن، ثم المعز.

ولا يجوز في شيء من ذلك عوراء ولا مريضة ولا العرجاء البين ضلعها، ولا العجفاء التي لا شحم فيها، ويتقى فيها العيب كله، ولا المشقوقة الأذن إلا أن يكون يسيرا، وكذلك القطع، ومكسورة القرن إن كان يدمي فلا يجوز، وإن لم يدم فذلك جائز.

وَلْيَلِ الرجل ذبح أضحيته بيده بعد ذبح الإمام أو نحره يوم النحر

your animal before the imam, you must repeat your sacrifice. If there is no imam with you, you should make sure you do not do it before the time the imam nearest to you would do so. The sacrifice must not be done at night.

There are three 'days of sacrifice' and you can make your sacrifice any time up until *Maghrib* on the last of these days but the best time to make your sacrifice is on the first day. If you do not manage to make your sacrifice before midday on the first day some of the people of knowledge say that it is better to wait until the morning of the second day. No part of an animal sacrificed for the *'Īd* may be sold; neither its skin nor anything else.

The animal you are intending to sacrifice should be made to face the *qiblah* and when you slaughter it you should say:

Bismillāh, Allāhu Akbar

"In the name of Allah. Allah is greater."

If, when sacrificing for the *'Īd* you add:

Rabbanā taqabbal minnā

"Our Lord, accept this from us", there is no harm in that. If you forget to say *Bismillāh* when sacrificing an animal for the *'Īd* or at any other time you are permitted to eat it. However, if the *Bismillāh* is left out deliberately, then the animal cannot be eaten. The same thing applies to sending hunting animals out after game.

It is not permissible to sell the meat, skin, fat, innards, or any other part of an animal that has been sacrificed either for the *'Īd* or for a new-born child or as part of the *ḥajj*, but you are allowed to eat from such an animal and it is recommended to give some away as *ṣadaqah,* although it is not obligatory to do this. You may not, however, eat from an animal you have sacrificed in expiation for breaking one of the conditions of *iḥrām* nor for one sacrificed on account of having

ضحوة. ومن ذبح قبل أن يذبح الإمام أو ينحر أعاد أضحيته. ومن لا إمام لهم فليتحروا صلاة أقرب الأئمة إليهم وذبحه. ومن ضحى بليل أو أهدى لم يجزه.

وأيام النحر ثلاثة يذبح فيها أو ينحر إلى غروب الشمس من آخرها، وأفضل أيام النحر أولها. ومن فاته الذبح في اليوم الأول إلى الزوال فقد قال بعض أهل العلم: يستحب له أن يصبر على ضحى اليوم الثاني. ولا يباع شيء من الأضحية: جلد ولا غيره.

وتوجه الذبيحة عند الذبح إلى القبلة، وليقل الذابح :

بِسْمِ اللهِ اللهُ أَكْبَرُ

وإن زاد في الأضحية:

رَبَّنَا تَقَبَّلْ مِنَّا

فلا باس بذلك، ومن نسي التسمية في ذبح أضحية أو غيرها فإنها تؤكل، وإن تعمد ترك التسمية لم تؤكل، وكذلك عند إرسال الجوارح على الصيد.

ولا يباع من الأضحية والعقيقة والنسك لحم ولا جلد ولا ودك ولا عصب ولا غير ذلك. ويأكل الرجل من أضحيته، ويتصدق منها أفضل له، وليس بواجب عليه، ولا يأكل من فدية الأذى وجزاء الصيد ونذر المساكين وما عطب من هدي التطوع قبل محله، ويأكل مما سوى ذلك إن شاء الله.

killed something while in *iḥrām* nor from one sacrificed as part of a vow you have made to feed the poor nor from *'hadys'* intended as voluntary sacrifices, which for some reason become defective before reaching the place of sacrifice. In any other instances you can eat from your sacrifice if you want inshā'Allāh.

The correct method of slaughtering is to sever the throat and the carotid arteries and nothing short of that is acceptable. If you take your hand away after severing only part of that and then resume and complete the cutting, the animal cannot be eaten. If you cut the head right off you have committed a wrong action, but the animal can be eaten. You may not eat an animal which has been slaughtered from the back of the neck. Cattle should be slaughtered with a knife but if their throats are pierced with a spear they can still be eaten. Camels should be pierced in the throat with a spear and if they are slaughtered with a knife they may not be eaten, although there is a difference of opinion about this. Sheep and goats should be slaughtered with a knife and if their throats are pierced with a spear they should not be eaten, although there is a difference of opinion about this as well. The slaughter of a mother includes what is in the womb provided that the foetus is fully formed and its hair has grown.

An animal which has been strangled by a rope or suchlike, one that has been beaten with a stick or some other object, one that has fallen from a height, one that has been gored, or one that has been attacked by a wild beast may not be slaughtered and eaten if the animal is going to die from the wounds it has received. There is no harm in eating carrion (*maytah*) if you are in dire need – you can eat from it until you are satisfied and take provision from it so long as you throw it away when the need for it no longer exists.

There is no harm in using the skin of a carrion animal if it has been tanned, but you cannot pray on it nor can it be sold. There is no

والذكاة قطع الحلقوم والأوداج، ولا يجزئ أقل من ذلك، وإن رفع يده بعد قطع بعض ذلك ثم أعاد يده فأجهز فلا تؤكل، وإن تمادى حتى قطع الرأس أساء ولتؤكل ، ومن ذبح من القفا، لم توكل، والبقر تذبح، فإن نحرت أكلت، والإبل تنحر فإن ذبحت لم تؤكل، وقد اختلف في أكلها ، والغنم تذبح فإن نحرت لم تؤكل، وقد اختلف أيضا في ذلك . وذكاة ما في البطن ذكاة أمه إذا تم خلقه ونبت شعره.

والمنخنقة بحبل ونحوه ، والموقوذة بعصا وشبهها، والمتردية والنطيحة وأكيلة السبع، إن بلغ ذلك منها في هذه الوجوه مبلغا لا تعيش معه لم تؤكل بذكاة. ولا بأس للمضطر أن يأكل الميتة ويشبع ويتزود، فإن استغنى عنها طرحها.

ولا بأس بالانتفاع بجلدها إذا دبغ، ولا يصلى عليه ولا يباع، ولا

harm in doing the prayer on skins of wild animals or selling them if they have been killed correctly. You can use wool of a carrion animal or its hair or any other thing which could be taken from the animal when alive, but according to us it is better for it to be washed first. You cannot use feathers from birds which are carrion or the horns, hooves and teeth of carrion animals. It is disliked to use elephant tusks although there is a difference of opinion about this.

Any ghee, oil or liquid honey in which a mouse has died should be thrown away and not eaten although there is no harm in using such oil for lighting purposes, provided it is not in a mosque, in which case it should be carefully avoided. If the substance is solid, then the mouse should be thrown away along with what is around it and the rest may be eaten, although Ṣaḥnūn said this was the case only if it had not stayed in it a long time, otherwise all of it should be thrown away.

There is no harm in the food of the people of the Book and their slaughtered animals. However, it is disliked to eat the fat from animals slaughtered by Jews, although it is not actually unlawful. It is not permissible to eat animals slaughtered by Magians, although any of their food that does not involve slaughtering is not *ḥarām*.

Hunting for mere pleasure is disliked but any other kind of hunting is permissible. Any prey killed by your trained dog or falcon can be eaten if you sent the trained animal after it. The same applies if your hunting animal kills any prey out of sight before you are able to slaughter it. If you reach the prey before it has been killed it can only be eaten if you slaughter it.

You may eat anything you kill with a spear or arrow but if you get the chance to slaughter it you should do so. You can still eat an animal even if it runs off, provided you are sure that it is your arrow that has killed it, as long as you reach it before nightfall. Some say that this refers only to prey that has been killed by trained hunting

بأس بالصلاة على جلود السباع إذا ذكيت وبيعها، وينتفع بصوف الميتة وشعرها وما ينزع منها في حال الحياة، وأحب إلينا أن يغسل، ولا ينتفع بريشها ولا بقرنها وأظلافها وأنيابها. وكره الانتفاع بأنياب الفيل، وقد اختلف في ذلك.

وما ماتت فيه فأرة من سمن أو زيت أو عسل ذائب طرح ولم يؤكل، ولا بأس أن يستصبح بالزيت وشبهه في غير المساجد، وليتحفظ منه، وإن كان جامدا طرحت وما حولها وأكل ما بقي. قال سحنون: إلا أن يطول مقامها فيه فإنه يطرح كله.

ولا بأس بطعام أهل الكتاب وذبائحهم، وكره أكل شحوم اليهود منهم من غير تحريم. ولا يؤكل ما ذكاه المجوسي، وما كان مما ليس فيه ذكاة من طعامهم فليس بحرام.

والصيد للهو مكروه، والصيد لغير اللهو مباح، وكل ما قتله كلبك المعلم أو بازك المعلم فجائز أكله إذا أرسلته عليه، وكذلك ما أنفذت الجوارح مقاتله قبل قدرته على ذكاته، وما أدركته قبل إنفاذها لمقاتله لم يؤكل إلا بذكاة.

وكل ما صدته بسهمك أو رمحك فكله، فإن أدركت ذكاته فذكه، وإن فات بنفسه فكله إذا قتله سهمك ما لم يبت عنك، وقيل: إنما ذلك فيما بات عنك مما قتلته الجوارح، وأما السهم يوجد في مقاتله

animals. If your arrow is found piercing a vital organ, then you can eat the animal. You may not eat a domestic animal which has been killed in the way game is killed.

Sacrificing an animal for the birth of a child (*'aqīqah*) is a recommended *sunnah*. It should be done on the seventh day after the birth of the child, using a sheep similar in age and characteristics to what has been previously mentioned concerning sacrifices for the *'Īd*. The day on which the child is born is not counted as one of the seven days. The animal should be sacrificed in the morning. The child should not be smeared with any of the animal's blood. It can be eaten and given away as *ṣadaqah* and its bones can be broken. If the baby's head is shaved and the weight of hair in gold or silver given away as *ṣadaqah* that is a good practice. If, instead of being rubbed with blood as was the custom before Islam, the baby's head is rubbed with a lotion consisting of perfume mixed with rose water, there is no harm in this.

Circumcision is an obligatory *sunnah* for males, and female circumcision (*khifāḍ*) is praiseworthy (*makrumah*).

فلا بأس بأكله، ولا تؤكل الإنسية بما يؤكل به الصيد.

والعقيقة سنة مستحبة، ويعق عن المولود يوم سابعه بشاة مثل ما ذكرناه من سن الأضحية وصفتها، ولا يحسب في السبعة الأيام اليوم الذي ولد فيه. وتذبح ضحوة، ولا يمس الصبي بشيء من دمها، ويؤكل منها ويتصدق، وتكسر عظامها، وإن حلق شعر رأس المولود وتصدق بوزنه من ذهب أو فضة فذلك مستحب حسن، وإن خلق رأسه بخلوق بدلا من الدم الذي كانت تفعله الجاهلية فلا بأس بذلك.

والختان سنة في الذكور واجبة، والخفاض في النساء مكرمة.

30. *Jihād*

Jihād is an obligation which can be taken on by some of the people on behalf of others. And it is preferable, according to us, that the enemy are not fought until they have been invited to the *dīn* of Allah unless they attack first. They can either accept Islam or pay the *jizyah* (tax on non-Muslims); if not they are to be fought. *Jizyah* is only acceptable in places where they are subject to our law. If they are a long way from our jurisdiction *jizyah* can only be accepted from them if they move to our territory. If they do not do this they are to be fought.

Fleeing from the enemy is a major wrong action when their number is twice that of the Muslims or less. If there are more than that there is nothing wrong in doing so. The enemy are to be fought whether the commander of the Muslims is right-acting or not.

There is no harm in killing an enemy prisoner but you may not kill anyone after a pledge of security has been given, nor may you break a treaty, nor may you kill women and children. Killing monks and priests should be avoided unless they are involved in the fighting. Similarly, women who fight can also be killed. A pledge of security given by the least of the Muslims is binding on the rest of then. This also applies when women do this, and also children, provided they are able to understand what is involved. It is also said that this is only acceptable if the man in charge says it is acceptable.

When the Muslims gain booty by having fought and won it, their leader takes one fifth and divides the remaining four-fifths between those doing the fighting. It is better for this dividing up to take place where the battle was fought. Only booty that has been fought for

٣٠ - باب في الجهاد

والجهاد فريضة يحمله بعض الناس عن بعض. وأحب إلينا أن لا يقاتل العدو حتى يدعوا إلى دين الله إلا أن يعاجلونا فإما أن يسلموا أو يؤدوا الجزية وإلا قوتلوا، وإنما تقبل منهم الجزية إذا كانوا حيث تنالهم أحكامنا. فأما إن بعدوا منا فلا تقبل منهم الجزية إلا أن يرتحلوا إلى بلادنا، وإلا قوتلوا.

والفرار من العدو من الكبائر إذا كانوا مثلي عدد المسلمين فأقل، فإن كانوا أكثر من ذلك فلا بأس بذلك، ويقاتل العدو مع كل بر وفاجر من الولاة.

ولا بأس بقتل من أسر من الأعلاج. ولا يقتل أحد بعد أمان، ولا يخفر لهم بعهد، ولا يقتل النساء والصبيان، ويجتنب قتل الرهبان والأحبار، إلا أن يقاتلوا، وكذلك المرأة تقتل إذا قاتلت، ويجوز أمان أدنى المسلمين على بقيتهم، وكذلك المرأة والصبي إذا عقل الأمان، وقيل: إن جاز ذلك الإمام جاز.

وما غنم المسلمون بإيجاف فليأخذ الإمام خمسه ويقسم الأربعة الأخماس بين أهل الجيش، وقسم ذلك ببلد الحرب أولى، وإنما يخمس ويقسم ما أوجف عليه بالخيل والركاب وما غنم بقتال، ولا

using horses and camels or taken after combat is to be divided up in this way. If part of the spoils consist of food or fodder, there is no harm in any who need it taking some before the division takes place.

A share of the booty is only given to those who took part in the fighting or who were prevented from doing so because they were occupied with the *jihād* in some other way. Anyone who falls sick is given a share as is any horse that falls sick. A horse gets two shares and a rider gets one share. Slaves do not get a share nor do women or children, unless the children are actually able to fight, have been given permission by the leader, and do actually participate in the fighting in which case they are given a share. A hired servant is not given a share unless he actually fights.

If anyone from the enemy becomes a Muslim and has in his possession property previously belonging to the Muslims, that property remains in his possession. If anyone buys any of it from him it becomes theirs and the original owner can only get it back by paying the correct price for it. If property of this kind is divided up as part of the booty, the original owner of a particular piece of property has the first right to it provided he pays the correct price for it. If the division has not yet been made, he can reclaim his property without having to pay anything for it.

No one is permitted to receive more than their allotted share unless it is given by the leader at his discretion from the fifth apportioned to him and this cannot be done before the basic division has been made. The arms, clothing and personal effects of enemy soldiers killed in the battle are treated as part of the fifth that can be given away at the leader's discretion.

Guarding a frontier post (*ribāṭ*) is an action of great excellence, which increases in virtue according to the amount of danger experienced by the people manning that post and the amount of caution they

بأس أن يؤكل من الغنيمة قبل أن يقسم الطعام والعلف لمن احتاج إلى ذلك، وإنما يسهم لمن حضر القتال أو تخلف عن القتال في شغل المسلمين من أمر جهادهم، ويسهم للمريض وللفرس الرهيص، ويسهم للفرس سهمان وسهم لراكبه، ولا يسهم لعبد ولا لامرأة ولا لصبي إلا أن يطيق الصبي الذي لم يحتمل القتال، ويجيزه الإمام ويقاتل فيسهم له، ولا يسهم للأجير إلا أن يقاتل.

ومن أسلم من العدو على شيء في يده من أموال المسلمين فهو له حلال، ومن اشترى شيئا منها من مال العدو لم يأخذه ربه إلا بالثمن. وما وقع في المقاسم منها فربه أحق به بالثمن، وما لم يقع في المقاسم فربه أحق به بلا ثمن.

ولا نفل إلا من الخمس على الاجتهاد من الإمام، ولا يكون ذلك قبل القسم. والسلب من النفل.

والرباط فيه فضل كبير، وذلك بقدر كثرة خوف أهل ذلك الثغر وكثرة تحرزهم من عدوهم. ولا يغزي بغير إذن الأبوين إلا أن

have to take. You cannot go on *jihād* without the permission of your parents unless the enemy makes a surprise attack, raiding your town, in which case it is obligatory for you to put up a defence. In such case parents' permission is not required.

يفجأ العدو مدينة قوم ويغيرون عليهم ففرض عليهم دفعهم، ولا يستأذن الأبوان في مثل هذا.

31. Oaths and vows

Anyone who swears an oath should either do so by Allah or keep quiet. Anyone who swears an oath to divorce a wife or free a slave is to be punished for doing so although he still has to hold to his oath. No one should make an oath containing the safety clause "if Allah wills" and there is no *kaffārah* (expiation) except in the case of an oath made using the name Allah or one of His other names or attributes. If someone does use the expression "Allah willing", he does not have to do *kaffārah* as long as he intends that provision and says *'Insha-allāh'* at the same time as he makes his oath. If this is not the case such a provision bears no weight.

There are four kinds of oaths which can be sworn by Allah. You do *kaffārah* for two of these: namely, if you swear by Allah, "If I do such-and-such a thing, I will do such-and-such a thing", or if you swear by Allah, "I will do such-and-such a thing." The two kinds you do not do *kaffārah* for are: firstly when you make an oath about something, thinking at the time it is true and later realising that it is not. In this case you do not do *kaffārah*, nor is there any wrong action involved. The other kind is if you swear an oath about something knowing it to be untrue or having doubt about it. In this case there is a wrong action involved but no *kaffārah*. You must, however, repent to Allah, glory be to Him, on account of it.

Kaffārah for oaths consists of feeding ten needy people, who are Muslim and free, giving one *mudd* to each measuring by the *mudd* of the Prophet ﷺ, but we believe that it is better to increase that by a third or a half. You add a third or a half according to what the prevailing standard of living is and whether the price of staples at

٣١ - باب في الأيمان والنذور

ومن كان حالفا فليحلف بالله أو ليصمت، ويؤدب من حلف بطلاق أو عتاق، ويلزمه، ولا ثنيا ولا كفارة إلا في اليمين بالله عز وجل أو بشيء من أسمائه وصفاته. ومن استثنى فلا كفارة عليه إذا قصد الاستثناء، وقال إن شاء الله، ووصلها بيمينه قبل أن يصمت، وإلا لم ينفعه ذلك.

والأيمان بالله أربعة، فيمينان تكفران وهو أن يحلف بالله إن فعلت، أو يحلف ليفعلن، ويمينان لا تكفران: إحداهما لغو اليمين، وهو أن يحلف على شي يظنه كذلك في يقينه ثم يتبين له خلافه فلا كفارة عليه ولا إثم/ والأخرى الحالف متعمدا للكذب أو شاكا فهو آثم، ولا تكفر ذلك الكفارة، وليتب من ذلك إلى الله سبحانه وتعالى.

والكفارة إطعام عشرة مساكين من المسلمين الأحرار مدا لكل مسكين بمد النبي صلى الله عليه وسلم. وأحب إلينا أن لو زاد على المد مثل ثلث مد أو نصف مد، وذلك بقدر ما يكون من وسط عيشهم

the time is high or low. However if you only give one *mudd* regardless of these considerations, you have fulfilled the obligation. If you give clothing you should give a man a robe and a woman a robe and a head-covering. *Kaffārah* can also be done by freeing a believing slave but if you cannot do this or feed people, then you should fast three consecutive days, although if you do them separately you have still fulfilled the obligation. You can do *kaffārah* either before or after failing to fulfil a vow, although doing it afterwards is preferable according to us.

Anyone who makes a vow involving obedience to Allah must fulfil it whereas anyone who makes a vow involving disobedience to Allah must not fulfil it and no reparation is necessary. Anyone who makes a vow to give *ṣadaqah* with someone else's money or to free a slave belonging to someone else is not under any obligation to fulfil it. Anyone who makes a vow that if he does a particular thing, he will do a specific good action, such as praying or fasting or going on *ḥajj* or *'umrah*, or giving away something specific as *ṣadaqah*, must do what he said he was going to do even if he fails to fulfil his vow straightaway. This is the case even if his vow is not backed up by an oath. If anyone makes a vow without specifying a particular good action to be done if he fails to fulfil it, and then does fail to fulfil it, should atone for it by doing the *kaffārah* for oaths.

Anyone who makes a vow to do a wrong action such as killing someone, drinking wine or something similar, or to do something which is neither a good action nor a wrong action, does not have to make any reparation for failing to fulfil it, but should seek forgiveness from Allah. If anyone swears by Allah to do a wrong action he should do the *kaffārah* for oaths and not do the thing he swore to do. However, if he is so bold as to do the thing he swore to do, he has committed the wrong action but does not have to do the *kaffārah* for breaking his oath.

في غلاء أو رخص، ومن أخرج مدا على كل حال أجزأه، وإن كساهم للرجل قميص وللمرأة قميص وخمار، أو عتق رقبة مؤمنة، فإن لم يجد ذلك ولا إطعاما فليصم ثلاثة أيام يتابعهن، فإن فرقهن أجزأه، وله أن يكفر قبل الحنث أو بعده، وبعد الحنث أحب إلينا.

ومن نذر أن يطيع الله فليطعه، ومن نذر أن يعصي الله فلا يعصه، ولا شيء عليه. ومن نذر صدقة مال غيره أو عتق عبد غيره لم يلزمه شيء. ومن قال: إن فعلت كذا فعلي نذر كذا، وكذا لشيء يذكره من فعل البر من صلاة أو صوم أو حج أو عمرة أو صدقة شيء سماه فذلك يلزمه إن حنث، كما يلزمه لو نذره مجردا من غير يمين، وإن لم يسم لنذره مخرجا من الأعمال فعليه كفارة يمين.

ومن نذر معصية من قتل نفس أو شرب خمر أو شبهه أو ما ليس بطاعة ولا معصية فلا شيء عليه، وليستغفر الله. وإن حلف بالله ليفعلن معصية فليكفر عن يمينه، ولا يفعل ذلك، وإن تجرأ وفعله أثم ولا كفارة عليه ليمينه.

Anyone who says in his oath "By the pact of Allah and His covenant" and then fails to fulfil it has to do a double *kaffārah*. However, anyone who emphasises his oath about one specific thing by repeating it would only have to do a single *kaffārah*. Anyone who says, "I am a *mushrik*," or that he is a Jew or a Christian if he does such-and-such, does not have to make any reparation and nothing is binding on him, except that he must seek Allah's forgiveness. Anyone who makes something unlawful for himself, which Allah has made lawful, does not have to do *kaffarah*, except in the case of his wife, who then does become unlawful for him until after she has been through another marriage.

If you make an oath or vow to give your wealth away as *ṣadaqah* or as a free gift [to the House of Allah], giving away a third is sufficient to fulfil the oath. If you make an oath to sacrifice your son then, if you remember what happened with Ibrāhīm, you should sacrifice an animal which should be slaughtered in Makkah. The minimum sacrifice for this is a sheep. If, however, the example of Ibrāhīm does not enter your thoughts, there is no need for you to make any reparation. If you make an oath to walk to Makkah and fail to do so, it is still binding on you to walk from the place where you made the oath and it is up to you whether you go for *ḥajj* or *'umrah*. If it becomes impossible for you to walk at any point you should ride. But if you later become able to walk you should walk that part of the journey where you rode. If you are certain you will not be able to fulfil the oath you stay where you are and make a sacrifice. What 'Aṭā' said about this is that you should not go over any part of your journey a second time and that you can sacrifice instead.

If you have not yet gone on *ḥajj* (and it was not part of your intention when you made the oath to walk to Makkah to do so) you must do an *'umrah* first and when you have finished your *ṭawāf* and *sa'y* and shortened your hair, you may then go into *iḥrām* from Makkah for

ومن قال: علي عهد الله وميثاقه في يمين فحنث فعليه كفارتان، وليس على من وكد اليمين فكررها في شيء واحد غير كفارة واحدة. ومن قال: أشركت بالله أو هو يهودي أو نصراني إن فعل كذا فلا يلزمه غير الاستغفار. ومن حرم على نفسه شيئا مما أحل الله له فلا شيء عليه إلا في زوجته فإنها تحرم عليه إلا بعد زوج. ومن جعل ماله صدقة أو هديا أجزأه ثلثه.

ومن حلف بنحر ولده فإن ذكر مقام إبراهيم أهدى هديا يذبح بمكة وتجزئه شاة، وإن لم يذكر المقام فلا شيء عليه. ومن حلف بالمشي إلى مكة فحنث فعليه المشي من موضع حلفه، فليمش إن شاء في حج أو عمرة، فإن عجز عن المشي ركب، ثم يرجع ثانية إن قدر فيمشي أماكن ركوبه، فإن علم أنه لا يقدر قعد وأهدى. وقال عطاء: لا يرجع ثانية وإن قدر، ويجزئه الهدي.

وإذا كان ضرورة جعل ذلك في عمرة، فإذا طاف وسعى وقصر أحرم من مكة بفريضة وكان متمتعا. والحلاق في غير هذا أفضل، وإنما يستحب له التقصير في هذا استبقاء للشعث في الحج.

the obligation of *ḥajj* to perform *tamattu'*. In any other case you should shave your head but in this instance it is recommended to merely shorten the hair in order to retain an unkempt appearance during the *ḥajj*.

If you make an oath to walk to Madīnah or to Jerusalem it is all right to ride to them if your original intention was to do the prayer in either of the two mosques. If you meant something else you do not have to fulfil you oath at all. If you make an oath to pray in any mosque other than one of these three, you should not go either walking or riding, but you should do that prayer in the place where you are. If you make an oath to man a post in any place on the frontiers of Islam you have to do it.

ومن نذر مشيا إلى المدينة أو إلى بيت المقدس أتاهما راكبا إن نوى الصلاة بمسجديها وإلا فلا شيء عليه، وأما غير هذه الثلاثة مساجد فلا يأتيها ماشيا ولا راكبا لصلاة نذرها، وليصل بموضعه. زمن نذر رباطا بموضع من الثغور فذلك عليه أن يأتيه

32. Marriage and Divorce,

Remarriage, *Ẓihār*-Repudiation, Vows of Celibacy within Marriage, *Liʿān*-Divorce, *Khulʿ*-Separation, and Suckling

Marriage is not legally valid without a guardian (*walī*), a dowry, and two legally acceptable witnesses. If these two are not present to witness the actual making of the contract, it is not permissible for the couple to consummate their marriage until the witnessing has taken place. The least acceptable amount for a dowry is a quarter of a dinar.

A father may arrange the marriage of his virgin daughter without her permission even if she is beyond the age of puberty. It is up to him whether he consults her or not. However, if anyone other than the father is arranging the marriage of a virgin, such as a guardian appointed in the father's will or anyone else, he cannot give her in marriage unless she is beyond the age of puberty and has given her consent. In this case her silence is taken as consent. A woman who has already been married cannot be given in marriage, by her father or anyone else, unless she herself agrees to it and gives verbal consent.

A woman can only be married if she has the consent of her guardian or someone suitably qualified from among her people, such as one of her male relations, or the governor. There is a difference of opinion regarding lowly women (*daniyyah*) as to whether they can have a guardian that is not related to them or not. A woman's son has more right to be her marriage guardian than her father and her father has more right than her brother. After this the nearer the relationship the greater the right. However, if the more distant relative acts as guardian, the marriage is nevertheless still valid.

٣٢ - باب في النكاح والطلاق والرجعة والظهار والإيلاء واللعان والخلع والرضاع

ولا نكاح إلا بولي وصداق وشاهدي عدل، فإن لم يشهدا في العقد فلا يبني بها حتى يشهدا. وأقل الصداق ربع دينار.

وللأب إنكاح ابنتيه البكر بغير إذنها وإن بلغت، وإن شاء شاورها، وأما غير الأب في البكر وصي أو غيره فلا يزوجها حتى تبلغ وتأذن، وإذنها صماتها. ولا يزوج الثيب أب ولا غيره إلا برضاها، وتأذن بالقول.

ولا تنكح المرأة إلا بإذن وليها أو ذي الرأي من أهلها كالرجل من عشيرتها أو السلطان، وقد اختلف في الدنية أن تولي أجنبيا، والابن أولى من الأب، والأب أولى من الأخ، ومن قرب من العصبة أحق، وإن زوجها البعيد مضى ذلك.

A guardian appointed in a will can arrange the marriage of a male child under his guardianship but he cannot arrange the marriage of a female child unless the father has given him specific instructions to do so. Male relatives on the maternal side are not considered suitable as marriage guardians, who should rather come from the paternal side.

No one should propose marriage to a woman if another proposal has already been accepted, nor should anyone try to outbid his brother, if an agreement has already been reached. A '*shighār*' marriage – which is when there is a direct exchange of daughters without any dowry – is not permitted; neither is marriage without a dowry; nor is temporary marriage – which is marriage for a specified limited period. Marriage during a woman's *'iddah* period is also forbidden as is any marriage involving uncertainty (*gharar*) either in the terms of the contract or the amount of the dowry, or any marriage in which the dowry includes anything whose sale is forbidden.

Any marriage, which is invalid because of some defect in the dowry, should be dissolved before consummation takes place. If, however, the marriage has been consummated, it is considered valid and the man should then pay the dowry appropriate to the circumstances of the woman he has married. If it is the contract that is defective, but the marriage is not dissolved until after it has been consummated, the specified dowry must be paid and any marriage bars (*maḥārim*) that would have applied if the marriage had been valid, still apply. Such a marriage does not make it possible for a man to remarry a woman whom he has previously divorced with a triple divorce. Nor do the two parties involved attain '*muḥṣan*' status.

Allah has made it unlawful to marry seven categories of women through blood relationship and seven through suckling and marriage relationship. He says, may He be exalted:

وللوصي أن يزوج الطفل في ولايته، ولا يزوج الصغيرة إلا أن يأمره الأب بإنكاحها. وليس ذوو الأرحام من الأولياء، والأولياء من العصبة.

ولا يخطب أحد على خطبة أخيه، ولا يسوم على سومه، وذلك إذا ركنا وتقاربا. ولا يجوز نكاح الشغار، وهو البضع بالبضع. ولا نكاح بغير صداق، ولا نكاح المتعة وهو نكاح إلى أجل، ولا النكاح في العدة، ولا ما جر إلى غرر في عقد أو صداق، ولا بما لا يجوز بيعه.

وما فسد من النكاح لصداقه فسخ قبل البناء، فإن دخل بها مضى وكان فيه صداق المثل. وما فسد من النكاح لعقده وفسخ بعد البناء ففيه المسمى، وتقع به الحرمة كما تقع بالنكاح الصحيح، ولكن لا تحل به المطلقة ثلاثا، ولا يحصن به الزوجان.

وحرم الله سبحانه من النساء سبعا بالقرابة وسبعا بالرضاع والصهر: فقال عز وجل:

"Unlawful for you are your mothers and your daughters and your sisters, your paternal aunts and maternal aunts, and your brothers' daughters and your sisters' daughters." (4:23)

These are the ones who are unlawful through blood relationship. Those who are unlawful through suckling or marriage relationship are, as Allah says:

"Your foster mothers who have suckled you and your sisters by suckling, your wives' mothers, your step-daughters who are under your protection: the daughters of your wives with whom you have had sexual relations (though if you have not had sexual relations with them there is nothing blameworthy for you in it) the wives of your sons whom you have fathered, or marrying two sisters at the same time except for what has already taken place." (4:23)

Allah *ta'ālā* also says,

"Do not marry any of women your fathers married." (4:22)

And the Prophet ﷺ made suckling the same as blood regarding the categories of relationship which are unlawful for marriage. And he also made it unlawful for a woman to marry a man who is married to any aunt of hers.

When a man has married a woman, the existence of the contract, even without the marriage having been consummated, makes that bride unlawful for his father and grandfathers and his sons. In the same way, the bride's mother and grandmothers become unlawful for him. However, her daughters are not unlawful unless either he has had sexual intercourse with her or has experienced physical pleasure from contact with her, as a result of having married her or owned her as a slave-girl or the same thing having happened as a result of a doubtful

حُرِّمَتْ عَلَيْكُمْ أُمَّهَٰتُكُمْ وَبَنَاتُكُمْ وَأَخَوَٰتُكُمْ وَعَمَّٰتُكُمْ وَخَٰلَٰتُكُمْ وَبَنَاتُ ٱلْأَخِ وَبَنَاتُ ٱلْأُخْتِ

فهؤلاء من القرابة. واللواتي من الرضاع والصهر. قوله تعالى:

وَأُمَّهَٰتُكُمُ ٱلَّٰتِىٓ أَرْضَعْنَكُمْ وَأَخَوَٰتُكُم مِّنَ ٱلرَّضَٰعَةِ وَأُمَّهَٰتُ نِسَآئِكُمْ وَرَبَٰٓئِبُكُمُ ٱلَّٰتِى فِى حُجُورِكُم مِّن نِّسَآئِكُمُ ٱلَّٰتِى دَخَلْتُم بِهِنَّ فَإِن لَّمْ تَكُونُوا۟ دَخَلْتُم بِهِنَّ فَلَا جُنَاحَ عَلَيْكُمْ وَحَلَٰٓئِلُ أَبْنَآئِكُمُ ٱلَّذِينَ مِنْ أَصْلَٰبِكُمْ وَأَن تَجْمَعُوا۟ بَيْنَ ٱلْأُخْتَيْنِ إِلَّا مَا قَدْ سَلَفَ

وقال تعالى:

وَلَا تَنكِحُوا۟ مَا نَكَحَ ءَابَآؤُكُم مِّنَ ٱلنِّسَآءِ

و حرم النبي صلى الله عليه وسلم بالرضاع ما يحرم من النسب. ونهى أن تنكح المرأة على عمتها أو خالتها.

فمن نكح امرأة حرمت بالعقد- دون أن تمس- على آبائه وأبنائه، وحرمت عليه أمهاتها، ولا تحرم عليه بناتها حتى يدخل بالأم أو يتلذذ بها بنكاح أو ملك يمين أو بشبهة من نكاح أو ملك.

marriage or ownership.

Zinā (fornication or adultery) does not make partners unlawful who would normally be lawful. Allah has made it unlawful to have sexual intercourse with an unbelieving woman not from the People of the Book either through marriage or ownership. It is lawful to have sexual intercourse with women of the People of the Book if you own them as slaves or are married to any of their free women, but it is not lawful for either a free man or a slave to have sexual intercourse with slave-girls from among the People of the Book through marriage to them.

A woman may not marry her slave, nor her son's slave, and a man may not marry his slave-girl, nor his son's slave-girl. He may, however, marry his father's slave-girl and his mother's slave-girl. A man is permitted to marry his stepmother's daughter from a previous marriage. And a woman may marry her stepmother's son from a previous marriage.

Both free men and slaves are permitted to marry four free women, whether Muslims or from the People of the Book. Slaves can marry four Muslim slave-girls, and free men can also do this but only if they are afraid of committing fornication and do not possess the means to marry free women. A man should treat his wives equally. He is responsible for their maintenance and housing to the extent that his means allow. A man's slave-girls and or a slave-girl by whom a man has had a child (*umm walad*) are not allotted nights in the same way as his wives are. A man is not responsible for maintenance until his marriage has been consummated or he has been called on to consummate his marriage, provided that it is with someone with whom sexual intercourse is possible.

Marriage by proxy is acceptable. This is when the husband and the guardian make a contract without mentioning a dowry, in which case the marriage cannot be consummated until the amount of the dowry

ولا يحرم بالزنا حلال. وحرم الله سبحانه وطء الكوافر ممن لسن من أهل الكتاب بملك أو نكاح، ويحل وطء الكتابيات بالملك. ويحل وطء حرائرهن بالنكاح، ولا يحل وطء إمائهن بالنكاح لحر ولا لعبد.

ولا تتزوج المرأة عبدها ولا عبد ولدها، ولا الرجل أمته ولا أمة ولده، وله أن يتزوج أمة والده، وأمة أمه، وله أن يتزوج بنت امرأة أبيه من رجل غيره، وتتزوج المرأة ابن زوجة أبيها من رجل غيره.

ويجوز للحر والعبد نكاح أربع حرائر مسلمات أو كتابيات، وللعبد نكاح أربع إماء مسلمات، وللحر ذلك إن خشي العنت ولم يجد للحرائر طولا. وليعدل بين نسائه. وعليه النفقة والسكنى بقدر وجده. ولا قسم في المبيت لأمته ولا لأم ولده، ولا نفقة للزوجة حتى يدخل بها أو يدعى إلى الدخول وهي ممن يوطأ مثلها.

ونكاح التفويض جائز، وهو أن يعقداه ولا يذكران صداقا ثم لا يدخل بها حتى يفرض لها. فإن فرض لها صداق المثل لزمها، وإن

has been fixed. If the stipulated dowry is appropriate to the status of the woman in question she must accept it. However, if it is less than her due the choice is hers. If she does not want to accept it, the couple are separated. If she is satisfied with it, or if the husband makes the amount to what is appropriate, then the marriage is binding on her.

If either one of a married couple leaves Islam, their marriage is annulled and they automatically become divorced, although another opinion is that the marriage is annulled but no actual divorce takes place. If a non-Muslim couple both become Muslim their marriage remains valid. If only one of the couple becomes a Muslim, the marriage is automatically invalidated, but no actual divorce takes place. If the woman becomes a Muslim, her previous husband has the first claim on her if he becomes a Muslim during her *'iddah* period. If the man becomes a Muslim and the woman is one of the People of the Book, their marriage remains valid. If the woman is a fire-worshipper (Magian) and becomes a Muslim immediately after her husband, they remain married. If there is a delay in her accepting Islam, separation takes place. If an idol-worshipper, who has more than four wives, becomes a Muslim he must select four of them and separate from the rest.

If someone divorces his wife by a curse (*li'ān*) he can never marry her again. The same applies to a man who marries a woman during her *'iddah* period and consummates the marriage during it. It is not permitted for a slave or a slavegirl to marry unless their master gives permission. It is not permitted for a woman, or a slave, or a non-Muslim to draw up a woman's marriage contract. It is not permitted for a man to marry a woman in order to make it *ḥalāl* for her to remarry a man who has previously divorced her by a triple divorce, and if such a marriage did take place it would not make a remarriage of this kind valid. A man in a state of *iḥrām* may neither get married

كان أقل فهي مخيرة، فإن كرهته فرق بينهما إلا أن يرضيها، أو يفرض لها صداق مثلها فليلزمها.

وإذا ارتد أحد الزوجين انفسخ النكاح بطلاق، وقد قيل بغير طلاق. وإذا أسلم الكافران ثبتا على نكاحهما، وإن أسلم أحدهما فذلك فسخ بغير طلاق، فإن أسلمت هي كان أحق بها إن أسلم في العدة، وإن أسلم هو وكانت كتابية ثبت عليها، فإن كانت مجوسية فأسلمت بعده مكانها كانا زوجين، وإن تأخر ذلك فقد بانت منه، وإذا أسلم مشرك وعنده أكثر من أربع فليختر أربعا ويفارق باقيهن.

ومن لاعن زوجته لم تحل له أبدا، وكذلك الذي يتزوج المرأة في عدتها، ولا نكاح لعبد ولا لأمة إلا أن يأذن السيد، ولا تعقد امرأة ولا عبد ولا من على غير دين الإسلام نكاح امرأة، ولا يجوز أن يتزوج الرجل امرأة ليحلها لمن طلقها ثلاثا، ولا يحلها ذلك، ولا يجوز نكاح المحرم لنفسه ولا يعقد نكاحا لغيره. ولا يجوز نكاح المريض ويفسخ، وإن بنى فلها الصداق في الثلث مبدأ، ولا ميراث لها. ولو طلق المريض امرأته لزمه ذلك. وكان لها الميراث منه إن

himself nor draw up a marriage contract for someone else. It is not permitted for a man with a very serious illness to get married and it is annulled, but if he does get married and consummates the marriage, then his bride's dowry is the first thing to be paid from the third of his wealth he is permitted to leave as he wills. She does not receive the fixed share of his estate that would normally go to a wife. If a man with a very serious illness divorces a wife, that divorce is binding on him, but, if he dies from his illness, his wife still inherits from him.

If anyone divorces his wife by a triple divorce she is no longer lawful for him either by right of ownership or marriage until she has married another husband. It is an innovation (*bid'ah*) to divorce a wife by a triple divorce said on one occasion but if it happens it is nevertheless binding. A *sunnah* divorce is acceptable, which is when a man divorces his wife by one pronouncement made while she is pure, having not had sexual intercourse with her since she became pure, and then does not make a second pronouncement until her *'iddah* period is over.

He can go back to her provided that she has not begun her third menstrual period from the time of the pronouncement of divorce (assuming she has menstrual periods and is a free woman). If the wife is a slave-girl who has menstrual periods, he can go back to her provided she has not yet begun her second period. If the wife has not yet begun to have menstrual periods or has ceased to have them, he can divorce her at any time he wants and the same applies to a woman who is pregnant. A man can go back to his pregnant wife up until the time she gives birth, in the same way that he can go back to a wife who is having periods before the end of her *'iddah*.

It is forbidden for a man to divorce his wife while she is menstruating, but if he does do so the divorce is valid; however, he is compelled to take her back if her *'iddah* period has not finished. If a man has not yet consummated his marriage he can divorce his wife at any time.

مات في مرضه ذلك.

ومن طلق امرأته ثلاثا لم تحل له بملك ولا نكاح حتى تنكح زوجا غيره. وطلاق الثلاث في كلمة واحدة بدعة، ويلزم إن وقع. وطلاق السنة مباح، وهو أن يطلقها في طهر لم يقربها فيه طلقة، ثم لا يتبعها طلاقا حتى تنقضي العدة.

وله الرجعة في التي تحيض ما لم تدخل في الحيضة الثالثة في الحرة أو الثانية في الأمة، فإن كانت ممن لم تحض أو ممن قد يئست من المحيض طلقها متى شاء، وكذلك الحامل. وترتجع الحامل ما لم تضع. والمعتدة بالشهور ما لم تنقض العدة، والأقراء هي الأطهار.

وينهى أن يطلق في الحيض، فإن طلق لزمه، ويجبر على الرجعة ما لم تنقض العدة، والتي لم يدخل بها يطلقها متى شاء، والواحدة تبينها، والثلاث تحرمها إلا بعد زوج. ومن قال لزوجته: أنت طالق فهي

One pronouncement of divorce ends the marriage and three makes her unlawful for him until she has been married to someone else. If a man says, "You are divorced," to his wife that is considered one pronouncement unless he intended more than that.

Khul' is a type of divorce which precludes any possibility of remarriage, even though it is not technically called a divorce, and it takes place when the husband accepts something from his wife in return for her release.

If someone says to his wife, "You are divorced once and for all," it is as if he had pronounced the triple divorce, regardless of whether the marriage has been consummated or not. Similarly, if someone says, "You are no longer my responsibility," or "You are on your own," or "You are unlawful for me," or "Your rein is on your hump" (i.e. you can go wherever you like), that is also considered as a triple divorce if the marriage has been consummated. If the marriage has not been consummated the husband is asked to specify what he intended.

When a woman who has been previously married is divorced before the marriage has been consummated, she receives half her dowry unless she chooses of her own free will to forgo it. If she is a virgin the decision is left to her father and in the case of a slave-girl it is left to her master. When a man divorces his wife it is recommended for him to give her something by way of consolation although this is not obligatory. If the marriage has not been consummated but the dowry has been paid, nothing need be given by way of consolation. The same thing applies when a woman asks for a *khul'* divorce.

If a man dies without having either paid over the dowry or consummated his marriage, his wife receives her share of his estate but does not receive any dowry. If the marriage has been consummated she should receive a dowry appropriate for someone of her status if no particular amount has been agreed beforehand.

واحدة حتى ينوي أكثر من ذلك.

والخلع طلقة لا رجعة فيها وإن لم يسم طلاقا إذا أعطته شيئا نخلعها به من نفسه.

ومن قال لزوجته: أنت طالق البتة فهي ثلاث، دخل بها أو لم يدخل، وإن قال: برية أو خلية أو حرام أو حبلك على غاربك فهي ثلاث في التي دخل بها، وينوي في التي لم يدخل بها.

والمطلقة قبل البناء لها نصف الصداق إلا أن تعفو عنه هي إن كانت ثيبا، وإن كانت بكرا فذلك إلى أبيها، وكذلك السيد في أمته. ومن طلق فينبغي له أن يمتع ولا يجبر، والتي لم يدخل بها وقد فرض لها فلا متعة لها ولا للمختلعة.

وإن مات عن التي لم يفرض لها ولم يبن بها فلها الميراث، ولا صداق لها، ولو دخل بها كان لها صداق المثل إن لم تكن رضيت بشيء معلوم.

The marriage contract can be annulled if a bride is found to be mad or suffering from leprosy or a disease of the vagina. If the man consummates his marriage to such a woman in ignorance, he must pay her dowry and then claim it back from her father. The same applies if it was the bride's brother who acted as her marriage guardian. If the marriage guardian is not one of her close relatives, the man does not have to pay any previously agreed dowry, but instead the bride receives only a quarter of a dinar (i.e. the minimum possible dowry).

An impotent man is allowed one year and, if he is still not capable of having sexual intercourse, the marriage can be dissolved if the wife so wishes. If a man disappears his wife should wait four years from the day she brings the matter to the notice of the appropriate authority. When this period of time has elapsed she should observe the same *'iddah* period as a woman whose husband has died. Then she may remarry if she wishes to. The wealth of such a man is not distributed as inheritance until such a time has passed that he could no longer be reasonably supposed to be alive.

A woman may not be asked for in marriage during her *'iddah* period although there is no harm in an indirect suggestion being made provided it is done in an acceptable way. A man who marries a virgin can spend seven consecutive nights with her, overriding the rights of any other wives for that period. If the woman has previously been married the period is three nights.

If a man has two slave-girls who are sisters he may not have sexual intercourse with both of them. If, having had sexual intercourse with one of them, he desires to have sexual intercourse with the other, he must separate himself from the first, making her unlawful for himself, by either selling her, or making an arrangement with her for her to buy her freedom (*kitābah*), or by setting her free, or by any other means by which she would become unlawful for him. If a man has had sexual

وترد المرأة من الجنون والجذام والبرص وداء الفرج، فإن دخل بها ولم يعلم أدى صداقها ورجع به على أبيها، وكذلك إن زوجها أخوها، وإن زوجها ولي ليس بقريب القرابة فلا شيء عليه، ولا يكون لها إلا ربع دينار.

ويؤخر المعترض سنة، فإن وطيء وإلا فرق بينهما إن شاءت. والمفقود يضرب له أجل أربع سنين من يوم ترفع ذاك، وينتهي الكشف عنه ثم تعتد كعدة الميت، ثم تتزوج إن شاءت، ولا يورث ماله حتى يأتي عليه من الزمان ما لا يعيش إلى مثله.

ولا تخطب المرأة في عدتها، ولا بأس بالتعريض بالقول المعروف. ومن نكح بكرا فله أن يقيم عندها سبعا دون سائر نسائه، وفي الثيب ثلاثة أيام.

ولا يجمع بين الأختين في ملك اليمين في الوطء، فإن شاء وطء الأخرى فليحرم عليه فرج الأولى ببيع أو كتابة أو عتق وشبهه مما تحرم به. ومن وطئ أمة بملك لم تحل له أمها ولا ابنتها وتحرم على آبائه وأبنائه كتحريم النكاح.

intercourse with one of his slave-girls, her mother and daughters become unlawful for him and she also becomes unlawful for his father and sons as is the case in marriage.

A slave can divorce without getting his master's permission. A child, however, cannot divorce. A woman whose husband has given her the authority to divorce, or the option to do so, can do so as long as the two are in the same meeting, where the permission was given. The husband may deny the right of other than a single divorce. If she has the option, it can only be a triple divorce and he does not have the night to deny it.

A man who swears not to have intercourse for more than four months is considered to have pronounced an *īlā'*. The divorce is only implemented after the end of the *īlā'*, which is four months if the man is free, and two months if he is a slave. Then the ruler gives him an ultimatum. If he resumes marital relations, then the *īlā'* is cancelled.

If someone pronounces a *ẓihār* (a statement that sex with his wife is tantamount to incest) then he may not have intercourse with her until he expiates that by freeing a believing slave who is free of faults, who is not partially owned by others or in the process of obtaining freedom. If he cannot do that, then he must fast two consecutive months. If he is unable to do that, he should feed sixty poor people two *mudd*s each. He may not have intercourse with her night or day until the end of the expiation. If he does so, he must repent to Allah Almighty. If he has intercourse after doing part of the expiation by feeding or fasting, he must start it over again. There is no harm in freeing a one-eyed slave or a bastard for the *ẓihār*. A child is sufficient, but we think it better to free someone who fasts and prays.

The *li'ān* (divorce) between a couple is when the man denies paternity, provided that he claims that he has been apart from his wife since her last menstrual period, or by actually witnessing adultery, like a kohl

والطلاق بيد العبد دون السيد. ولا طلاق لصبي. والمملكة والمخيرة لهما أن يقضيا ما داماتا في المجلس، وله أن يناكر المملكة خاصة فيما فوق الواحدة، وليس لها في التخيير أن تقضي إلا بالثلاث ثم لا نكرة له فيها.

وكل حالف على ترك الوطء أكثر من أربعة أشهر فهو مول، ولا يقع عليه الطلاق إلا بعد أجل الإيلاء، وهو أربعة أشهر للحر، وشهران للعبد حتى يوقفه السلطان.

ومن ظاهر من امرأته فلا يطؤها حتى يكفر بعتق رقبة مؤمنة سليمة من العيوب، ليس فيها شرك ولا طرف من حرية، فإن لم يجد صام شهرين متتابعين، فإن لم يستطع أطعم ستين مسكينا مدين لكل مسكين، ولا يطؤها في ليل أو نهار حتى تنقضي الكفارة، فإن فعل ذلك فليتب إلى الله عز وجل، فإن كان وطؤه بعد أن فعل بعض الكفارة بإطعام أو صوم فليبتدئها، ولا بأس بعتق الأعور في الظهار وولد الزنا، ويجزئ الصغير، ومن صلى وصام أحب إلينا.

واللعان بين كل زوجين في نفي حمل يدعى قبله الاستبراء أو رؤية الزنا كالمرود في المكحلة، واختلف في اللعان في القذف، وإذا افترقا

stick in its case. There is disagreement about whether *li'ān* in the case of slander is allowed. If a couple divorce by *li'ān*, they can never remarry. The husband begins the *li'ān* by testifying four times by Allah and then the fifth time he curses himself. Then she does the same four times and the fifth invokes Allah's anger, as Allah Almighty has mentioned (in the Qur'an 24:6-9). If the wife refuses to testify, she is stoned if she is free and *muḥṣanah* by virtue of intercourse with her husband or another husband. Otherwise, she receives a hundred lashes. If the husband refuses to testify, he is flogged eighty lashes for slander and the child is considered to be his.

A woman may ransom herself from her husband by her dower, or a sum more or less, unless the *khul'* is due to some injury to her. If there was an injury to her, she may reclaim what she gave him and the *khul'* is still binding. The *khul'* is a divorce which cannot be retracted except by a new marriage contracted of her own accord.

A woman freed from slavery, who is married to a slave, can choose between remaining married to him or separating from him. If someone buys his wife, then his marriage is void. A slave is allowed only two divorces and the *'iddah* of a slave-girl consists of two menstrual periods. The expiations of the slave are the same as the free man except for the differences in the *ḥadd* punishments and divorce.

Any milk that reaches the stomach of a nursing child in the first two years, even one suck, makes marriage unlawful. Nursing after the age of two years does not cause these prohibitions, unless it is close to it, like a month or so, or some say two months. If the child is weaned before the age of two so that it eats food without milk, any nursing which happens after that does not create these prohibitions. Nursing by pouring milk into the mouth or nose creates the same prohibitions. If a woman nurses a boy, her daughters and her husband's daughters, whether born before or after the boy, are his sisters. However the boy's brother may marry them.

باللعان لم يتناكحا أبدا، ويبدأ الزوج فيلتعن أربع شهادات بالله ثم يخمس باللعنة، ثم تلتعن هي أربعا أيضا، وتخمس بالغضب كما ذكر الله سبحانه وتعالى، وإن نكلت هي رجمت إن كانت حرة محصنة بوطء تقدم من هذا الزوج أو زوج غيره، وإلا جلدت مائة جلدة، وإن نكل الزوج جلد حد القذف ثمانين، ولحق به الولد.

وللمرأة أن تفتدي من زوجها بصداقها أو أقل أو أكثر إذا لم يكن عن ضرر بها، ورجعت بما أعطته ولزمه الخلع. والخلع طلقة لا رجعة فيها إلا بنكاح جديد برضاها.

والمعتقة تحت العبد لها الخيار أن تقيم معه أو تفارقه. ومن اشترى زوجته انفسخ نكاحه. وطلاق العبد طلقتان. وعدة الأمة حيضتان. وكفارات العبد كالحر بخلاف معاني الحدود والطلاق.

وكل ما وصل إلى جوف الرضيع في الحولين من اللبن فإنه يحرم، وإن مصة واحدة، ولا يحرم ما أرضع بعد الحولين إلا ما قرب منهما كالشهر ونحوه، وقيل: والشهرين، ولو فصل قبل الحولين فصالا استغنى فيه بالطعام لم يحرم ما أرضع بعد ذلك. ويحرم بالوجور والسعوط. ومن أرضعت صبيا فبنات تلك المرأة وبنات فحلها ما تقدم أو تأخر، إخوة له، ولأخيه نكاح بناتها.

33. *'IDDAH, ISTIBRĀ'* AND MAINTENANCE

The *'iddah* for a free woman is three periods (*qurū'*), whether she is Muslim or one of the People of the Book. For a slave or partial slave, it is two periods. It does not matter whether the husband is free or a slave. A 'period (*qur'*)' means the period of purity between two menstruations. If the woman is not menstruating or has ceased menstruation, then it is three months for a woman, free or slave. The *'iddah* for a divorced woman with constant bleeding is one year, slave or free. The *'iddah* for a pregnant woman who is widowed or divorced is when she gives birth, whether free or slave or one of the People of the Book. A divorced woman whose marriage has not been consummated has no *'iddah*.

The *'iddah* for a free woman who is widowed is four months and ten nights, whether a child or adult, whether the marriage has been consummated or not, whether Muslim or one of the People of the Book. For a slave-girl, who is partially free, it is two months and five days, except in the case of an older woman whose period is delayed. Then she waits until the doubt is removed. As for the one who does not menstruate because of youth or old age, and her marriage was consummated, she may not marry until three months after the death of the husband.

Mourning for a woman who is in *'iddah* because of being widowed takes the form of her not using any adornment in the form of jewellery, kohl or other things, and avoiding all dyed colours except black and also all perfume. She should not use henna or perfumed oil nor comb perfumed substances into her hair. Mourning should be observed by the slave and free woman, child and adult. There is disagreement

٣٣ - باب في العدة والنفقة والاستبراء

وعدة الحرة المطلقة ثلاثة قروء، كانت مسلمة أو كتابية، والأمة ومن فيها بقية رق قرآن، كان الزوج في جميعهن حرا أو عبدا. والأقراء هي الأطهار التي بين الدمين، فإن كانت ممن لم تحض أو ممن قد يئست من المحيض فثلاثة أشهر في الحرة و الأمة، وعدة الحرة المستحاضة أو الأمة في الطلاق سنة. وعدة الحامل في وفاة أو طلاق وضع حملها، كانت حرة أو أمة أو كتابية. والمطلقة التي لم يدخل بها لا عدة عليها.

وعدة الحرة من الوفاة أربعة أشهر وعشر، كانت صغيرة أو كبيرة، دخل بها أو لم يدخل، مسلمة كانت أو كتابية، وفي الأمة ومن فيها بقية رق شهران وخمس ليال، ما لم ترتب الكبيرة ذات الحيض بتأخيره عن وقته فتقعد حتى تذهب الريبة، وأما التي لا تحيض لصغر أو كبر وقد بنى بها فلا تنكح في الوفاة إلا بعد ثلاثة أشهر.

والإحداد أن لا تقرب المعتدة من الوفاة شيئا من الزينة بحلي أو كحل أو غيره، وتجتنب الصباغ كله إلا الأسود، وتجتنب الطيب كله ولا تختضب بحناء، ولاتقرب دهنا مطيبا، ولا تمتشط بما يختمر في رأسها، وعلى الأمة والحرة الصغيرة والكبيرة الإحداد. واختلف

about one of the People of the Book. A divorced woman does not have to observe mourning. A free woman of the People of the Book should be compelled to observe the *'iddah* for a Muslim husband who has died or divorced her. The *'iddah* of an *umm walad* after the death of her master is one menstrual period. It is the same when he frees her. If she does not menstruate, it is three months.

Istibrā' is observed in the case of a slave-girl who changes ownership. It is one menstruation. This is whether ownership changes by selling, giving away, capture, or any other way. If the woman menstruates after being in the possession of the new master before he has bought her, then she does not have to observe an *istibrā'* if she has not gone out. The *istibrā'* for a child when she is sold is three months as it is for a woman who no longer menstruates. There is no *istibrā'* for a woman who has never had sexual intercourse. If someone buys a pregnant woman from another person or gains possession of her without a sale, he should not go near her or enjoy her in any manner until she gives birth.

A divorced woman whose marriage has been consummated has the right to lodging but not maintenance unless she was divorced by less than three divorces or is pregnant. If pregnant, she has a right to maintenance whether it is one or three divorces. A woman with a *khul'* divorce has no right to maintenance unless she is pregnant. The woman divorced by *li'ān* has no maintenance, even if she is pregnant. In the *'iddah* period on account of being widowed, a woman has no right to maintenance but she does have a right to lodging if the house belonged to the deceased or he rented it. When she is divorced or widowed, a woman should not leave her house until her *'iddah* is over unless the owner of the house evicts her and will not accept a normal rent. Then she leaves and stays in the place to which she moves until the end of the *'iddah*.

في الكتابية، وليس على المطلقة إحداد، وتجبر الحرة الكتابية على العدة من المسلم في الوفاة و الطلاق، وعدة أم الولد من وفاة سيدها حيضة كذلك إذا أعتقها، فإن قعدت عن الحيض فثلاثة أشهر.

الاستبراء: معناه، وأسبابه وأحكامه:

واستبراء الأمة في انتقال الملك حيضة، انتقل الملك ببيع أو هبة أو سبي أو غير ذلك، ومن هي في حيازته قد حاضت عنده ثم إنه اشتراها فلا استبراء عليها إن لم تكن تخرج. واستبراء الصغيرة في البيع، إن كانت توطأ، ثلاثة أشهر، واستبراء اليائسة من المحيض ثلاثة أشهر، والتي لا توطأ فلا استبراء فيها، ومن ابتاع حاملا من غيره أو ملكها بغير البيع فلا يقربها ولا يتلذذ منها بشيء حتى تضع.

حكم السكنى والنفقة للمطلقة والحامل:

والسكنى لكل مطلقة مدخول بها، ولا نفقة إلا للتي طلقت دون الثلاث، وللحامل، كانت مطلقة واحدة أو ثلاثا، ولا نفقة للمختلعة إلا في الحمل، ولا نفقة للملاعنة وإن كانت حاملا، ولا نفقة لكل معتدة من وفاة، ولها السكنى إن كانت الدار للميت أو قد نقد كراءها، ولا تخرج من بيتها في طلاق أو وفاة حتى تتم العدة إلا أن يخرجها رب الدار، ولم يقبل من الكراء ما يشبه كراء المثل فلتخرج وتقيم بالموضع الذي تنتقل إليه حتى تنقضي العدة.

حكم إرضاع المرأة لولدها:

A woman should nurse her child in the marriage unless someone of her status should not do so. A divorced woman can nurse the child for the father and she can take a fee for nursing if she wishes. After a divorce, the woman has custody of a boy until he reaches puberty and a girl until she marries and the marriage is consummated. After the mother, if she dies or remarries, custody goes to the grandmother and then the maternal aunt. If there are no female relatives of the mother, then it goes to one of the sisters and paternal uncles. If there are none, then to the agnate relatives.

A man is only responsible for the maintenance of his wife, whether she is rich or poor, and his poor parents and his young children who have no wealth. He is responsible for sons until they reach puberty, if they have no crippling disability, and for girls until they marry and their marriages are consummated. These are the only relatives whose maintenance he is responsible for. If he is wealthy enough, he should provide his wife with servants. He must also maintain his slaves and shroud them if they die. There is disagreement about shrouding the wife: Ibn al-Qāsim said that it is done using her own money, and 'Abd al-Malik says that it should come from the husband's money. Ṣaḥnūn said that if she is wealthy her money is used, and if she is poor, it is done from her husband's money.

والمرأة ترضع ولدها في العصمة إلا أن يكون مثلها لا يرضع، وللمطلقة رضاع ولدها على أبيه، ولها أن تأخذ أجرة رضاعها إن شاءت.

الحضانة وأحكامها:

والحضانة للأم بعد الطلاق إلى احتلام الذكر ونكاح الأنثى ودخول بها، وذلك، بعد الأم إن ماتت أو نكحت، للجدة، ثم للخالة، فإن لم يكن من ذوي رحم الأم أحد فالأخوات والعمات، فإن لم يكونوا فالعصبة.

حكم النفقة على الزوجة:

ولا يلزم الرجل النفقة إلا على زوجته، كانت غنية أو فقيرة، وعلى أبويه الفقيرين، وعلى صغار ولده الذين لا مال لهم، على الذكور حتى يحتلموا ولا زمانة بهم، وعلى الإناث حتى ينكحن ويدخل بهن أزواجهن. ولا نفقة لمن سوى هؤلاء من الأقارب، وإن اتسع فعليه إخدام زوجته. وعليه أن ينفق على عبيده، ويكفنهم إذا ماتوا، واختلف في كفن الزوجة، فقال ابن القاسم: في مالها. وقال عبد الملك: في مال الزوج. وقال سحنون: إن كانت ملية ففي مالها، وإن كانت فقيرة ففي مال الزوج

34. Sales and other business transactions

"Allah has permitted trade and forbidden usury." (2:275)

The usury practised in the *Jāhiliyyah* with respect to debts was that when they were due, they were either paid or delayed in exchange for a payment of usurious interest. Besides usury in exchange for delay, usury also consists of selling silver for silver, hand to hand in unequal amounts. The same applies in the case of gold for gold. Silver for silver and gold for gold are not permitted except like for like, hand to hand. Gold for silver is usury except hand to hand.

The same applies to food grains, beans and similar foods or condiments which can be stored. It is not permitted to exchange one category of them for the same category except hand to hand, like for like. It is not permitted for there to be a delay in this. It is not permitted to exchange food for food with a delay, whether in the same category or different categories, and whether that can be stored or not. There is nothing wrong with exchanging fruits and vegetables that cannot be stored, in unequal amounts, even if they are of the same kind, provided it is hand to hand. It is not permitted to have a disparity in the same category of dried fruits and other condiments, food or drink which can be stored, except for water. There is nothing wrong in exchanging different categories of other grains and fruit and foods in equal amounts from hand to hand. It is not permitted to have a disparity in the same category except in the case of fresh fruits and vegetables.

Wheat, barley and sult-barley comprise one category in respect of

٣٤ - باب في البيوع وما شاكل البيوع

وَأَحَلَّ ٱللَّهُ ٱلْبَيْعَ وَحَرَّمَ ٱلرِّبَوٰاْ

وكان ربا الجاهلية في الديون: إما أن يقضيه دينه وإما أن يربي له فيه. ومن الربا في غير النسيئة بيع الفضة بالفضة يدا بيد متفاضلا، وكذلك الذهب بالذهب، ولا يجوز فضة بفضة ولا ذهب بذهب إلا مثلا بمثل يدا بيد. والفضة بالذهب ربا إلا يدا بيد.

والطعام من الحبوب والقطنية وشبهها مما يدخر من قوت أو إدام لا يجوز الجنس منه بجنسه إلا مثلا بمثل يدا بيد، ولايجوز فيه تأخير، ولا يجوز طعام بطعام إلى أجل، كان من جنسه أو من خلافه، كان مما يدخر أو لا يدخر. ولا بأس بالفواكه والبقول وما لا يدخر متفاضلا وإن كان من جنس واحد يدا بيد. ولا يجوز التفاضل في الجنس الواحد فيما يدخر من الفواكه اليابسة وسائر الإدام والطعام والشراب إلا الماء وحده، وما اختلفت أجناسه من ذلك ومن سائر الحبوب والثمار والطعام فلا بأس بالتفاضل فيه يدا بيد، ولا يجوز التفاضل في الجنس الواحد منه إلا في الخضر والفواكه.

والقمح والشعير والسلت كجنس واحد فيما يحل منه ويحرم،

lawfulness and unlawfulness. All sorts of raisins comprise one category. All sorts of dates comprise one category. Beans have different categories in regard to sales. The position of Mālik varies regarding this, but his position about them being one category for *zakāt* purposes does not vary. The meat of quadrupeds and wild animals is considered to be one category; the meat of all types of fowl is one category; and the flesh of all water creatures is one category. Fat falls into the category of the flesh from which it is extracted. Yoghurt, cheese and butter are classified according to the category of the animals from which they are taken.

Someone who buys food is not permitted to sell it before he takes possession of it, as long as the purchase was by weight, volume or number rather than unmeasured. That is the case for every food, condiment or drink except water. Medicines and crops that are not pressed for oil are not among the foods which it is forbidden to sell before taking possession of them or which cannot be exchanged for unequal amounts of the same category. There is nothing wrong with selling borrowed food before taking possession of it. There is nothing wrong with partnership in buying, in cost resale, or in revocation of a sale before taking possession, in the case of food which is measured.

Every sales contract, hire or lease which contains danger or risk in respect of the price, the item purchased, or the term at which payment is due is not permitted. It is not permitted to sell something uncertain or to sell something unknown or to sell to an unknown term. In selling, it is not permitted to conceal faults or to adulterate things or to overrate or mislead or to conceal defects. It is not permitted to mix the bad with the good or to conceal something about the goods which, if known, would make the buyer dislike them or which would reduce the price if it were known.

والزبيب كله صنف، والتمر كله صنف، والقطنية أصناف في البيوع، واختلف فيهما قول مالك، ولم يختلف قوله في الزكاة أنها صنف واحد. ولحوم ذوات الأربع من الأنعام والوحش صنف، ولحوم الطير كله صنف، ولحوم دواب الماء كلها صنف، وما تولد من لحوم الجنس الواحد من شحم فهو كلحمه، وألبان ذلك الصنف وجبنه وسمنه صنف.

ومن ابتاع طعاما فلا يجوز بيعه قبل أن يستوفيه إذا كان شراؤه ذلك على وزن أو كيل أو عدد، بخلاف الجزاف، وكذلك كل طعام أو إدام أو شراب إلا الماء وحده، وما يكون من الأدوية و الزراريع التي لا يعتصر منها زيت فلا يدخل ذلك فيما يحرم من بيع الطعام قبل قبضه أو التفاضل في الجنس الواحد منه. ولا باس ببيع الطعام القرض قبل أن يستوفيه. ولا بأس بالشركة والتولية والإقالة في الطعام المكيل قبل قبضه.

وكل عقد بيع أو إجارة أو كراء بخطر أو غرر في ثمن أو مثمون أو أجل فلا يجوز. ولا يجوز بيع الغرر ولا بيع شيء مجهول، ولا إلى أجل مجهول، ولا يجوز في البيوع التدليس ولا الغش ولا الخلابة ولا الخديعة ولا كتمان العيوب ولا خلط دنيء بجيد، ولا أن يكتم من أمر سلعته ما إذا ذكره كرهه المبتاع، أو كان ذكره أبخس له في الثمن.

If someone buys a slave and finds a defect in him, he can keep him without any compensation, or return him and get his money back, unless the slave has acquired a new corrupting defect while in his possession. If this is the case, the new owner may claim back the amount of the original defect from the price he paid, or he can return the slave and pay the depreciation caused by the new defect. If he returns a slave because of a defect and has put him to work to earn revenue while he was with him, he keeps the revenue.

A sale with an option to cancel is permitted when the two parties stipulate a short period in which the buyer can test the goods or in which to seek advice. Immediate payment is not permitted in such a sale. Nor is immediate payment permitted in the case of a slave with a three day guarantee. Nor is there immediate payment in the case of a slave-girl placed in seclusion to ascertain whether she is pregnant. The responsibility and maintenance during that period are that of the seller. A slave-girl is usually only secluded to see whether she is pregnant when she is purchased to take to bed or when the seller states that he has had intercourse with her, even if she is ugly. The buyer cannot absolve the seller from the responsibility for the pregnancy unless it is clear and obvious. Absolving the seller of responsibility in things about the slave about which the seller has no knowledge is allowed. A mother and her child are not separated in a sale until the child has grown his second set of teeth.

In an invalid sale the seller remains responsible for the goods. But if the buyer has taken possession of them, he is responsible for them from the time he has them in his possession. So if the market price changes or the commodity is altered, then the buyer must pay its price on the day he bought it and does not return it. If, however, it is something sold by measure or weight, he must return its equivalent. Real estate is unaffected by market changes.

ومن ابتاع عبدا فوجد به عيبا فله أن يحبسه ولا شيء له، أو يرده ويأخذ ثمنه، إلا أن يدخله عنده عيب مفسد فله أن يرجع بقيمة العيب القديم من الثمن، أو يرده ويرد ما نقصه العيب عنده، وإن رد عبدا بعيب وقد استغله فله غلته.

والبيع على الخيار جائز إذا ضربا لذلك أجلا قريبا إلى ما تختبر فيه تلك السلعة أو ما تكون فيه المشورة، ولا يجوز النقد في الخيار، ولا في عهدة الثلاث، ولا في المواضعة بشرط، والنفقة في ذلك والضمان على البائع، وإنما يتواضع للاستبراء الجارية التي للفراش في الأغلب، أو التي أقر البائع بوطئها وإن كانت وخشا.ولا تجوز البراءة من الحمل إلا حملا ظاهرا. والبراءة في الرقيق جائزة مما لم يعلم البائع، ولا يفرق بين الأم وولدها في البيع حتى يثغر.

وكل بيع فاسد فضمانه من البائع، فإن قبضه المبتاع فضمانه من المبتاع من يوم قبضه، فإن حال سوقه أو تغير في بدنه فعليه قيمته يوم قبضه ولا يرده، وإن كان مما يوزن أو يكال فليرد مثله. ولا يفيت الرباع حوالة الأسواق.

It is not permitted to make a loan in exchange for some benefit [for the lender]. It is not permitted to combine a sale and a loan in a single transaction. The same applies if the loan is combined with hire or rental. A loan is permitted in everything except slave-girls or silver ore. A reduction in the debt is not permitted in order to hasten its collection nor can it be delayed in exchange for an increase in the amount due. Goods may not be collected sooner in exchange for increase in them when there is a sale involved. There is no harm in returning a loan early with an increase which is only in the quality.

There is disagreement about when someone repays a trade loan (*qarḍ*) with an additional amount at the time of repayment when there was no stipulation, promise or custom to do so. Ashhab allowed that but Ibn al-Qasim disliked it and did not allow it. If someone owes dinars or dirhams as the result of a sale or a loan which has a set term, he can pay them before they are due. He can also hand over goods or food early from a loan but not when it is a question of a sale.

It is not permitted to sell fruits or grain whose ripeness has not appeared, but it is permitted to sell them when the ripeness of some of them has appeared, even if that is on one palm tree among many. It is not permitted to sell fish which are still in rivers or pools, nor can one sell a foetus still in its mother's womb, nor the foetus of what is in the wombs of animals. It is not permitted to sell the offspring of unborn camels nor to sell the sperm of male camels nor to sell a runaway slave or stray camel. Selling dogs is forbidden. There is disagreement about whether one can sell those dogs which are permitted to be kept. If someone kills such a dog, he is liable for its price. It is not permitted to sell meat for a live animal of the same species.

It is not permitted to have two sales in the same contract. That is when someone buys goods for either five in cash or ten on credit, the sale

ولا يجوز سلف يجر منفعة، ولا يجوز بيع وسلف، وكذلك ما قارن السلف من إجازة أو كراء. والسلف جائز في كل شيء إلا في الجواري، وكذلك تراب الفضة. ولا تجوز الوضيعة من الدين على تعجيله، ولا التأخير به على الزيادة فيه، ولا تعجيل عرض على الزيادة فيه إذا كان من بيع، ولا بأس بتعجيله ذلك من قرض إذا كانت الزيادة في الصفة.

ومن رد في القرض أكثر عددا في مجلس القضاء، فقد اختلف في ذلك إذا لم يكن فيه شرط ولا وأي ولا عادة. فأجازه أشهب، وكرهه ابن القاسم ولم يجزه. ومن عليه دنانير أو دراهم من بيع أو قرض مؤجل فله أن يعجله قبل أجله ، وكذلك له أن يعجل العروض والطعام من قرض، لا من بيع.

ولا يجوز بيع تمر أو حب لم يبد صلاحه، ويجوز بيعه إذا بدا صلاح بعضه وإن نخلة من نخيل كثيرة. ولا يجوز بيع ما في الأنهار والبرك من الحيتان، ولا بيع الجنين في بطن أمه، ولا بيع ما في بطون سائر الحيوانات، ولا بيع نتاج ما تنتج الناقة، ولا بيع ما في ظهور الإبل، ولا بيع الآبق والبعير الشارد. ونهي عن بيع الكلاب. واختلف في بيع ما أذن في اتخاذه منها، وأما من قتله فعليه قيمته. ولا يجوز بيع اللحم بالحيوان من جنسه

ولا بيعتان في بيعة، وذلك أن يشتري سلعة إما بخمسة نقدا أو عشرة

already being binding on one of the two prices. It is not permitted to sell dried dates for fresh ones, nor raisins for grapes, whether for disparate amounts or equal amounts, nor any type of fresh fruit for the dried fruit of the same type. This is *muzābanah* which is forbidden. One may not sell an undetermined amount for a measured amount of the same commodity, nor an undetermined amount for an undetermined amount of the same category unless the difference between the two is clear and it is something in which disparity in the same category is permitted.

There is nothing wrong with selling an absent article based on its description. Prepayment is not to be stipulated unless its location is close or it is something safe from change, like a house, land or a tree. Prepayment can be made for these. An indemnification is permitted in selling a slave when that is stipulated or it is the local custom. In the three day indemnification the seller is completely responsible for all defects in that slave, and in a year's indemnification, he is only responsible for insanity or either type of leprosy.

There is nothing wrong in advance payment (*salam*) for goods, slaves, animals, food and condiments, provided the goods have a known description and there is a set date of delivery. The price is to be paid immediately, or with a short delay of something like two or three days, if that is stipulated in the contract. We prefer the delivery of the goods paid for in advance to be fifteen days, or for it to be collected from another town, even if that is two or three days distant. According to more than one scholar, it is permitted to pay three days in advance and collect it in the same town in which the advance was paid. Others dislike that. It is not permitted for the payment to consist of the same type of goods as that for which the advance payment is made. No advance is made of the same type or similar type of goods unless he lends him something to be repaid with something of the same quality and quantity, and the borrower enjoys the benefit.

إلى أجل قد لزمته بأحد الثمنين، ولا يجوز بيع التمر بالرطب، ولا الزبيب بالعنب، لا متفاضلا ولا مثلا بمثل، ولا رطب بيابس من جنسه من سائر الثمار والفواكه، وهو مما نهي عنه من المزابنة. ولا يباع جزاف بمكيل من صنفه، ولا جزاف بجزاف من صنفه إلا أن يتبين الفضل بينهما إن كان مما يجوز التفاضل في الجنس الواحد منه.

ولا بأس ببيع الشيء الغائب على الصفة، ولا ينقد فيه بشرط، إلا أن يقرب مكانه، أو يكون مما يؤمن تغيره من دار أو أرض أو شجر، فيجوز النقد فيه. والعهدة جائزة في الرقيق إن اشترطت أو كانت جارية بالبلد، فعهدة الثلاث الضمان فيها من البائع من كل شيء، وعهدة السنة من الجنون والجذام والبرص.

ولا بأس بالسلم في العروض والرقيق والحيوان والطعام والإدام بصفة معلومة وأجل معلوم، ويعجل رأس المال أو يؤخره إلى مثل يومين أو ثلاثة، وإن كان بشرط، وأجل السلم أحب إلينا أن يكون خمسة عشر يوما، أو على أن يقبض ببلد آخر، وإن كانت مسافته يومين أو ثلاثة. ومن أسلم إلى ثلاثة أيام يقبضه ببلد أسلم فيه. فقد أجازه غير واحد من العلماء، وكرهه آخرون، ولا يجوز أن يكون رأس المال من جنس ما أسلم فيه، ولا يسلم شيء في جنسه أو فيما يقرب منه إلا أن يقرضه شيئا في مثله صفة ومقدارا والنفع للمتسلف.

It is not permitted to sell a debt for a debt. One form of that is to stipulate delay of payment for the *salam* sale until the goods are delivered, or to delay payment more than three days after the contract. Nor is it permitted to cancel one debt by another debt. That is when someone owes you something and you cancel it by allowing him to pay you something else at a later date. It is not permitted to sell something which you do not have if it is stipulated that you must deliver it immediately.

When you sell some goods to be paid for later, you may not buy them back by paying in cash less than you sold them for or by taking a shorter term to pay for them than the term given to the original buyer, nor can you pay more for them or take a longer time to pay for them than the original time stipulated. It is permitted to buy them at the original date, and that is fair exchange (*muqāṣṣah*).

There is nothing wrong in buying undetermined amounts of things which can be measured or weighed, except for dinars and dirhams that are minted. It is, however, permitted in the case of pieces of gold and silver. It is not permitted to buy slaves and garments in undetermined amounts, nor other things which can be counted without difficulty.

If someone sells date palms after they have been pollinated, the fruit belongs to the seller unless the buyer stipulates that as part of the sale. It is the same with other types of fruit. Pollinating (*ibār*) is using the male blossoms to pollinate the female, but in respect of crops, it means when they sprout from the soil. If someone sells a slave who owns some property, that property belongs to the seller, unless the buyer stipulates otherwise. There is nothing wrong in buying what is in bags with a known description on rosters. It is not permitted, however, to buy cloth which is not unfolded nor described nor to buy if it is a dark night when the buyer and seller cannot see it or know what is in it. The same holds for buying an animal on a dark night.

ولا يجوز دين بدين، وتأخير رأس المال بشرط إلى محل السلم أو ما بعد من العقدة من ذلك. ولا يجوز فسخ دين في دين ، وهو أن يكون لك شيء في ذمته فتفسخه في شيء آخر لا تتعجله. ولا يجوز بيع ما ليس عندك على أن يكون عليك حالا.

وإذا بعت سلعة بثمن مؤجل فلا تشترها بأقل منه نقدا أو إلى أجل دون الأجل الأول ولا بأكثر منه إلى أبعد من أجله. وأما إلى الأجل نفسه فذلك كله جائز، وتكون مقاصة.

ولا بأس بشراء الجزاء فيما يكال أو يوزن سوى الدنانير والدراهم ما كان مسكوكا، وأما نقار الذهب والفضة فذلك فيهما جائز. ولا يجوز شراء الرقيق والثياب جزافا، ولا ما يمكن عدده بلا مشقة جزافا.

ومن باع نخلا قد أبرت فثمرها للبائع إلا أن يشترطه المبتاع، وكذلك غيرها من الثمار، والإبار التذكير، وإبار الزرع خروجه من الأرض. ومن باع عبدا وله مال فماله للبائع إلا أن يشترطه المبتاع. ولا بأس بشراء ما في العدل على البرنامج بصفة معلومة، ولا يجوز شراء ثوب لا ينشر ولا يوصف. أو في ليل مظلم لا يتأملانه ولا يعرفان ما فيه، وكذلك الدابة في ليل مظلم.

No one should bid against his brother's bid when the two parties are satisfied and near to closing a deal, but he can do so at the beginning of the bidding. A sale is finalised verbally, even if the two parties have not physically separated.

Hiring services (*ijārah*) is permitted when the two parties set the length of time and the payment. No term is fixed in a contract to recover a runaway slave or a lost camel, or to dig a well, to sell a garment or similar things. The contractor receives nothing until the work is complete. If someone is hired to sell something by the end of a term and he still has not sold it at the end of the time, he is entitled to his full wage. If he sells it after half the term, he only receives half the wage.

Renting is like selling as far as what is lawful or unlawful is concerned. If someone rents a particular riding animal to go to a certain place and the animal dies, the rest of the hire is cancelled. It is the same when an employee dies, or when a house is rented but collapses before the end of the term. There is nothing wrong in a teacher teaching the Qur'an being paid when the student has mastered it and for a doctor to be employed provided he cures the patient. The rental of an animal or house does not end with the death of the renter nor does the hire of a shepherd end with the death of the sheep. The sheep should be replaced with a similar flock.

If someone rents out an animal with a guarantee and then the animal dies, he should provide another. If the rider dies, the rental is not cancelled and his heirs must hire another rider. If someone rents a household implement or something else, he is not liable for it if it is destroyed or lost while in his possession. His word is believed about that until it can be proven that he is lying. Artisans are responsible for things they lose, whether they are working for a wage or not. The owner of a public bathhouse is not liable [for belongings lost by

ولا يسوم أحد على سوم أخيه، وذلك إذا ركنا وتقاربا، لا في أول التساوم. والبيع ينعقد بالكلام وإن لم يفترق المتبايعان.

والإجارة جائزة إذا ضربا لها أجلا وسميا الثمن، ولا يضرب في الجعل أجل في رد آبق أو بعير شارد أو حفر بئر أو بيع ثوب ونحوه، ولا شيء له إلا بتمام العمل: والأجير على البيع إذا تم الأجل ولم يبع وجب له جميع الأجر، وإن باع في نصف الأجل فله نصف الإجارة.

والكراء كالبيع فيما يحل ويحرم. ومن اكترى دابة بعينها إلى بلد فماتت انفسخ الكراء فيما بقي، وكذلك الأجير يموت، والدار تنهدم قبل تمام مدة الكراء. ولا بأس بتعليم المعلم القرآن على الحذاق، ومشارطة الطبيب على البرء، ولا ينتقض الكراء بموت الراكب، أو الساكن، ولا بموت غنم الرعاية، وليأت بمثلها.

ومن اكترى كراء مضمونا فماتت الدابة فليأت بغيرها، وإن مات الراكب لم ينفسخ الكراء وليكتروا مكانه غيره. ومن اكترى ماعونا أو غيره فلا ضمان عليه في هلاكه بيده، وهو مصدق إلا أن يتبين كذبه. والصناع ضامنون لما غابوا عليه، عملوه بأجر أو بغير أجر. ولا ضمان على صاحب الحمام، ولا ضمان على صاحب السفينة، ولا

clients]. The owner of a ship is not liable [for lost cargo or damage]. A ship-owner is not paid his hire until he delivers his cargo.

There is nothing wrong in having a partnership in physical labour when the two partners work in the same place doing the same work, or do work that is similar. A partnership in pooled capital is permitted provided the profit is shared between the two partners according to the size of the investment of each of them. The work of each is also in proportion to the percentage of the profit stipulated for him. It is not permitted to share the profit equally if their investments differ.

An investment loan in trade (*qirāḍ*) is permitted with dirhams and dinars, and it is also allowed with unminted gold and silver. A *qirāḍ* made in goods is not permitted. In such a case, the borrower is like an employee who sells them. If he then trades with the price, this then becomes an investment loan. The agent has a right to clothing and food if he travels with a considerable amount of capital. He is only entitled to clothing for a long trip. The profit is not divided until the capital is in cash.

Leasing an orchard or plantation of trees is permitted, provided that the two parties agree on the shares. All the work is done by the lessee. No other work can be stipulated for him other than that entailed by the *musāqāh* (irrigation) and nor is he required to start any work in the orchard unless it is of no consequence, like mending a fence and repairing a reservoir, without that involving actually initiating the work. Pollination of the trees is done by the lessee as well as cleaning the places where the water settles among the trees, mending the place where the water falls from the bucket, cleaning the water source and similar tasks. The *musāqāh* does not permit the expulsion of animals in the orchard. If some of them die, then the owner must replace them. The lessee must maintain the animals and the employees.

The lessee should cultivate an unplanted area if it is slight. There is

كراء له إلا على البلاغ.

ولا بأس بالشركة بالأبدان إذا عملا في موضع واحد عملا واحدا أو متقاربا. وتجوز الشركة بالأموال على أن يكون الربح بينهما بقدر ما أخرج كل واحد منهما، والعمل عليهما بقدر ما شرطا من الربح لكل واحد، ولا يجوز أن يختلف رأس المال ويستويا في الربح.

والقراض جائز بالدنانير والدراهم، وقد أرخص فيه بنقار الذهب والفضة، ولا يجوز بالعروض، ويكون إن نزل أجيرا في بيعها وعلى قراض مثله في الثمن، وللعامل كسوته وطعامه إذا سافر في المال الذي له بال، وإنما يكتسى في السفر البعيد، ولا يقتسمان الربح حتى ينض رأس المال.

والمساقاة جائزة في الأصول على ما تراضيا عليه من الأجزاء، والعمل كله على المساقى، ولا يشترط عليه عملا غير عمل المساقاة، ولا عمل شيء ينشئه في الحائط إلا مما له بال من شد الحظيرة وإصلاح الضفيرة، وهي مجتمع الماء من غير أن ينشيء بناءها. والتذكير على العامل وتنقية مناقع الشجر، وإصلاح مسقط الماء من الغرب. وتنقية العين، وشبه ذلك جائز أن يشترط على العامل. ولا تجوز المساقاة على إخراج ما في الحائط من الدواب. وما مات منها فعلى ربه خلفه. ونفقة الدواب والأجراء على العامل.

وعليه زريعة البياض اليسير. ولا بأس أن يلغى ذلك للعامل وهو

no harm in leaving that up to the lessee, and this is the most lawful course. If there is a lot of unplanted land, however, it is not permitted to include it in the *musāqāh* contract of the orchard. It can only be included if it is a third or less of the orchard.

It is permitted to have a crop-sharing partnership if both parties share in the cultivation and the profit is shared between them, whether one owns the land and the other does the work, or the work and rent are shared between them, or they both own the land. If one provides the seeds and the other owns the land, with the profit to be shared between them, that is not permitted, whether one or both do the work. If they both rent the land and the seed comes from one and the work from the other, it is permitted if the values of the two undertakings are close. No payment is made on renting land whose irrigation is uncertain until it is watered.

If someone buys fruit still on the trees, and then a third or more of it is destroyed by cold, locusts, frost or something else, the cost of that is deducted from the price the buyer pays. If it is less than a third, then the buyer bears the loss. There is no crop damage in a crop or what is bought after the fruit has been dried. There is a reduction in the case of crop damage to vegetables, even if it is little. It is also said that there is only a reduction if a third is damaged.

If someone gives a man an *'āriyah* (a gift) of the fruit of palm trees from his garden, there is no harm in him buying them when they are ripe in exchange for dry dates, based on estimation of their measure. He is given that when they are cut, if it is five *wasq*s or less. It is not permitted to buy more than five *wasq*s except with money or merchandise.

أحله، وإن كان البياض كثيرا لم يجز أن يدخل في مساقاة النخل إلا أن يكون قدر الثلث من الجميع فأقل.

والشركة في الزرع جائزة إذا كانت الزريعة منهما جميعا والربح بينهما، كانت الأرض لأحدهما والعمل على الآخر أو العمل بينهما واكتريا الأرض، أو كانت بينهما، أما إن كان البذر من عند أحدهما ومن عند الآخر الأرض والعمل عليه أو عليهما والربح بينهما لم يجز. ولو كانا اكتريا الأرض والبذر من عند واحد وعلى الآخر العمل جاز إذا تقاربت قيمة ذلك، ولا ينقد في كراء أرض غير مأمونة قبل أن تروى.

ومن ابتاع ثمرة في رؤوس الشجر فأجيح ببرد أو جراد أو جليد أو غيره، فإن أجيح قدر الثلث فأكثر وضع عن المشتري قدر ذلك من الثمن، وما نقص عن الثلث فمن المبتاع. ولا جائحة في الزرع ولا فيما اشتري بعد أن يبس من الثمار. وتوضع جائحة البقول وإن قلت، وقيل : لا يوضع إلا قدر الثلث.

ومن أعرى ثمر نخلات لرجل من جنانه فلا بأس أن يشتريها إذا أزهت بخرصها تمرا يعطيه ذلك عند الجذاذ إن كان فيها خمسة أوسق إلا بالعين والعرض.

35. Bequests and freeing slaves (the *mudabbar*, *mukātab*, emancipation, the *umm walad* and *walā'*)

It is imperative for someone who has property to make a will. Bequests can be made from the disposable third. Anything which exceeds that is rejected unless the heirs allow it. In respect of the disposable third, one should begin by freeing a slave who has been specified. Next in priority is freeing a *mudabbar* so long as the *tadbīr* declaration was made when the master was healthy. This precedes emancipation or any other bequests made when he was ill, including unpaid *zakāt*. A bequest to pay *zakāt* is taken from the third before other bequests, but a *tadbīr* made when the master was healthy takes precedence over it. If the third is not enough for them, the people of shares who have no precedence receive proportional shares of the rest. A man may revoke his bequest of emancipation or other things.

A *tadbīr* is contracted when a man says to his slave, "You are *mudabbar*" or "You are free afterwards," (i.e. after my death). Then he is not permitted to sell such slave but is still entitled to his work and, as long as the master is not ill, he can confiscate the slave's possessions. If it is a slave-girl, he can have intercourse with her. He is not permitted to have sexual intercourse with a slave-girl who is going be set free at a certain date nor can he sell her. He can demand her work and can confiscate her possessions as long as the term for her emancipation is not near. When the master dies, the emancipation payment of the *mudabbar* comes out of the disposable third, while that of a slave promised freedom at a certain date comes from the total estate.

A slave with a *kitābah* agreement (*mukātab*) remains a slave as long

٣٥ - باب في الوصايا والمدبر والمكاتب والمعتق وأم الولد والولاء

ويحق على من له ما يوصي فيه أن يعد وصيته. "ولا وصية لوارث". والوصايا خارجة من الثلث، ويرد ما زاد عليه إلا أن يجيزه الورثة. والعتق بعينه مبدأ عليها. والمدبر في الصحة مبدأ على ما في المرض من عتق وغيره، وعلى ما فرط فيه من الزكاة فأوصى به. فإن ذلك في ثلثه مبدأ على الوصايا، ومدبر الصحة مبدأ عليه، وإذا ضاق الثلث تحاص أهل الوصايا التي لا تبدئة فيها. وللرجل الرجوع عن وصيته من عتق وغيره.

والتدبير أن يقول الرجل لعبده: أنت مدبر أو أنت حر عن دبر مني، ثم لا يجوز له بيعه، وله خدمته، وله انتزاع ماله ما لم يمرض، وله وطؤها إن كانت أمة، ولا يطأ المعتقة إلى أجل، ولا يبيعها، وله أن يستخدمها، وله أن ينتزع مالها ما لم يقرب الأجل . وإذا مات فالمدبر من ثلثه، والمعتق إلى أجل من رأس ماله.

والمكاتب عبد ما بقي عليه شيء. والكتابة جائزة على ما رضيه العبد

as he still owes anything. The *kitābah* agreement is permitted when made with the agreement of the slave and master for an amount to be paid in instalments, however many or few they are. If he is unable to pay, he reverts to being a full slave and the master can keep what he has already received. A slave can only be deemed insolvent by the ruler after failing to pay if he refuses to acknowledge his insolvency. If a woman has a *kitābah* or *tadbīr* agreement, or a date is set for her emancipation, or she is pledged as security, any child she bears shares her status. The children of an *umm walad* fathered by someone other than her master have the same status as her.

A slave's property belongs to him unless the master confiscates it. If the master frees him or grants him a *kitābah*, and does not exclude the slave's property, then he cannot confiscate it. A master may not have intercourse with a slave-girl who has a *kitābah* contract. Any children born to a man or woman slave with a *kitābah* contract after they have concluded a *kitābah* have the same status and they are free when the parents are free. A slave with a *kitābah* cannot free his own slaves or waste his property until he is free. He cannot marry nor undertake a long journey without his master's permission.

If a slave with a *kitābah* dies leaving a child, he takes his place and pays from his estate whatever is still unpaid, which becomes immediately due. His children inherit any remaining property. If there is not enough to settle the amount, the children should trade with what there is and pay it off in instalments if they are adults. If they are children, and the estate is not enough to cover the instalments until they come of age and can trade, they revert to being full slaves. If he does not have any children with him in his *kitābah*, his master inherits from him.

If a man has a child by a slave-girl, he can enjoy her while he is alive and then she is set free from the main estate when he dies. He

والسيد من المال منجما، قلت النجوم أو كثرت، فإن عجز رجع رقيقا وحل له ما أخذ منه، ولا يعجزه إلا السلطان بعد التلوم إذا امتنع عن التعجيز. وكل ذات رحم فولدها بمنزلتها من مكاتبة أو مدبرة أو معتقة إلى أجل أوم رهونة، وولد أم الولد من غير السيد بمنزلتها.

ومال العبد له إلا أن ينتزعه السيد، فإن أعتقه أو كاتبه ولم يستثن ماله فليس له أن ينتزعه، وليس له وطء مكاتبته، وما حدث للكاتب والمكاتبة من ولد دخل معهما في الكتابة وعتق بعتقهما. وتجوز كتابة الجماعة ولا يعتقون إلا بأداء الجميع. وليس للمكاتب عتق ولا إتلاف ماله حتى يعتق ، ولا يتزوج ولا يسافر السفر البعيد بغير إذن سيده.

وإذا مات وله ولد قام مقامه وأدى من ماله ما بقي عليه حالا، وورث من معه من ولده ما بقي، وإن لم يكن في المال وفاء فإن ولده يسعون فيه ويؤدون نجوما إن كانوا كبارا، وإن كانوا صغارا وليس في المال قدر النجوم إلى بلوغهم السعي رقوا ، وإن لم يكن له ولد معه في كتابته ورثه سيده.

ومن أولد أمة فله أن يستمتع منها في حياته، وتعتق من رأس ماله بعد مماته، ولا يجوز بيعها، ولا له عليها خدمة ولا غلة، وله ذلك

is not permitted to sell her or demand her work or demand revenue from her, although he may, however, demand that from her child by another man. Such a child has the same status as his mother regarding emancipation and is free when she is free. Any miscarriage of a slavegirl, known to be a child, makes her an *umm walad.* He cannot claim *coitus interruptus* in order to deny paternity of the child if he admits to having had intercourse with her. If he claims that he has observed *istibrā'* and not had intercourse with her afterwards, the paternity of her child born after that is not attributed to him.

It is not permitted for someone whose property is encumbered by debts to set a slave free. If someone frees part of his slave, he is made to free all of him. If someone else has a share in the slave, the share of his partner is estimated on the day the emancipation is settled, and the slave is set free. If he does not have the money to pay the partner, the portion of the partner in the slave remains. If someone mutilates his slave in an overt way, such as cutting off a limb and the like, the slave is set free. If someone obtains ownership of his parents, his children or grandchildren, grandfather or grandmother, or uterine, paternal or full brother, that slave is freed automatically. If someone frees a pregnant woman, her unborn child is free with her.

In freeing a slave to discharge an obligation, one may not free a slave who is already in the process of being freed, such as one with a *tadbīr* or a *kitābah* or something similar, nor one who is blind, or has had a hand or the like amputated, or a non-Muslim, a child, or someone who is subject to enforced guardianship.

The *walā'* belongs to the one who sets a slave free. It is not permitted to sell it or give it away. If someone frees a slave on behalf of another man, that man still has the *walā'*. If someone becomes Muslim at someone's hand, the *walā'* does not go to him, but to the Muslims as a whole. When a woman sets a slave free, she has the *walā'* of that

في ولدها من غيره، وهو بمنزلة أمة في العتق، يعتق بعتقها، وكل ما أسقطته مما يعلم أنه ولد فهي به أم ولد، ولا ينفعه العزل إذا أنكر ولدها وأقر بالوطء، فإن ادعى استبراء لم يطأ بعده لم يلحق به ما جاء من ولد.

ولا يجوز عتق من أحاط الدين بماله، ومن أعتق بعض عبده استتم عليه، وإن كان لغيره معه فيه شركة قوم عليه نصيب شريكه بقيمته يوم يقام عليه وعتق، فإن لم يوجد له مال بقي سهم الشريك رقيقا. ومن مثل بعبده مثلة بينة من قطع جارحة ونحوه عتق عليه. ومن ملك أبويه أو أحدا من ولده أو ولد ولده أو ولد بناته، أو جده أوجدته أو أخاه لأم أو لأب أو لهما جميعا عتق عليه. ومن أعتق حاملا كان جنينها حرا معها.

ولا يعتق في الرقاب الواجبة من فيه معنى من عتق بتدبير أو كتابة أو غيرهما، ولا أعمى ولا أقطع اليد وشبهه، ولا من على غير الإسلام، ولا يجوز عتق الصبي ولا المولى عليه.

والولاء لمن أعتق ولا يجوز بيعه ولا هبته. ومن أعتق عبدا عن رجل فالولاء للرجل، ولا يكون الولاء لمن أسلم على يديه، وهو للمسلمين. وولاء ما أعتقت المرأة لها، وولاء من يجر من ولد أو عبد

person as well as the *walā'* of the person's children and any slaves that person frees. In the case of someone she has not set free, she does not inherit the *walā'* from her father, son, husband or anyone else.

The estate left by a slave without a *walī* (*sā'ibah*) goes to the Muslim community. The *walā'* is inherited by the closest agnatic heir of the dead person. If he has two sons, they share the *walā'* between them. If one of them dies, leaving sons, the *walā'* goes to his brother rather than his sons. If one of them dies leaving one son, and the other dies leaving two sons, the *walā'* is shared between all three.

أعتقته، ولا ترث ما أعتق غيرها من أب أو ابن أو زوج أو غيره. وميراث السائبة لجماعة المسلمين، والولاء للأقعد من عصبة الميت الأول، فإن ترك ابنين فورثا ولاء مولى لأبيهما ثم مات أحدهما وترك ابنين رجع الولاء إلى أخيه دون بنيه، وإن مات واحد وترك ولدا ومات أخوه وترك ولدين فالولاء بين الثلاثة أثلاثا.

36. Property rights

Pre-emption (*shufʿah*), gifts, *ṣadaqah*, *waqf*s, pledges, the *ʿāriyah*, deposits, lost items, and misappropriation

Pre-emption is allowed in respect of something which is jointly owned. There is no pre-emption in respect of what has been divided, nor is there pre-emption in respect of a neighbour, a road, the courtyard of a house whose rooms have been divided, a male palm tree or a well when the palm trees or the land have been divided. There is only pre-emption in respect of land and the buildings and trees on it. There is no pre-emption for someone present after a year has passed. The person who is absent still has his right, even if it has been a long time. A buyer must guarantee the one with the right of pre-emption. A possible pre-emptor may be forced to exercise his right or forgo it. Pre-emption may not be given away or sold. The right is divided between partners according to their shares.

A gift, *ṣadaqah* or *waqf* is only complete by taking actual possession of it. If the giver dies before a gift is collected, then it becomes part of his inheritance, unless that gift was made during his final illness. Then it is paid out of the disposable third as long as it is for someone other than an heir. A gift to a close relative or poor person is like *ṣadaqah* and cannot be taken back. When someone gives *ṣadaqah* to his son, he cannot take it back. He may, however, take back something he gave to a minor child or adult as long as he has not used it to get married or given it as a loan and nothing has happened to the gift.

A mother may take back a gift as long as the father is alive. When the father is dead, she cannot take it back. One may not take back a gift to an orphan. An orphan is someone who has lost his father. A

٣٦ - باب في الشفعة وواهبة والصدقة والحبس والرهن والعارية والوديعة واللقطة والغصب

وإنما الشفعة في المشاع، ولا شفعة فيما قد قسم ، ولا لجار ولا في طريق ولا عرصة دار قد قسمت بيوتها، ولا في فحل نخل أو بئر إذا قسمت النخل أو الأرض. ولا شفعة إلا في الأرض وما يتصل بها من البناء والشجر، ولا شفعة للحاضر بعد السنة، والغائب على شفعته وإن طالت غيبته، وعهدة الشفيع على المشتري ، ويوقف الشفيع فإما أخذ أو ترك. ولا توهب الشفعة ولا تباع، وتقسم بين الشركاء بقدر الأنصباء.

ولا تتم هبة ولا صدقة ولا حبس إلا بالحيازة، فإن مات قبل أن تحاز عنه فهي ميراث إلا أن يكون ذلك في المرض فذلك نافذ من الثلث إن كان لغير وارث. والهبة لصلة الرحم أو لفقير كالصدقة لا رجوع فيها. ومن تصدق على ولده فلا رجوع له، وله أن يعتصر ما وهب لولده الصغير أو الكبير، ما لم ينكح لذلك أو يداين أو يحدث في الهبة حدثا. والأم تعتصر ما دام الأب حيا، فإذا مات لم تعتصر، ولا يعتصر من يتيم. واليتم من قبل الأب. وما وهبه لابنه الصغير فحيازته له جائزة إذا لم يسكن ذلك أو يلبسه إن كان ثوبا، وإنما يجوز

father is permitted to retain possession of a gift he gives to his minor son so long as he does not live in it or wear it if it is a garment. He can only do that if the gift is a specific article. He cannot do that if the son is an adult.

A man should not take back his *ṣadaqah* nor can he recover it except by inheritance. There is no harm in drinking the milk of an animal he gave as *ṣadaqah*. He may not buy back anything he gave away as *ṣadaqah*. If someone is given a gift for which the giver expects recompense, he should either repay it with something of equal value or return the gift. If he no longer has it, then he must give back its value when he sees that the giver wanted recompense for what he gave him. It is disliked for someone to give all his property to one of his children. Giving part of his property is allowed. There is nothing wrong in someone giving all his property to the poor for the sake of Allah.

If someone who is given something does not take possession of it until the donor is ill or bankrupt, he cannot then take it. If the recipient dies, his heirs can take it if the giver is still in good health.

When someone makes a house a *ḥubus*, it is used for the purpose to which he put it if it is taken before he dies. If it is a *ḥubus* in favour of his minor son, he may hold it for him until he comes of age. He should rent it out for him and not live it in himself. If he continues to live in it until he dies, then the *ḥubus* is nullified. If the beneficiaries of the *ḥubus* die out, the nearest of people to the founder on the day it reverts becomes the beneficiary. If someone gives someone the use of a house for his lifetime as an *'umrā*, it reverts to the owner when they die. It is the same if he gave the use to the children of that person and they die out. This is not the case with the *ḥubus*.

If the one who granted the use dies on the same day, the property

له ما يعرف بعينه، وأما الكبير فلا تجوز حيازته له.

ولا يرجع الرجل في صدقته، ولا ترجع إليه إلا بالميراث. ولا بأس أن يشرب من لبن ما تصدق به، ولا يشتري ما تصدق به. والموهوب للعوض إما أثاب القيمة أو رد الهبة، فإن فاتت فعليه قيمتها، وذلك إذا كان يرى أنه أراد الثواب من الموهوب له. ويكره أن يهب لبعض ولده ماله كله. وأما الشيء منه فذلك سائغ . ولا بأس أن يتصدق على الفقراء بماله كله لله.

.ومن وهب هبة فلم يحزها الموهوب له حتى مرض الواهب أو أفلس فليس له حينئذ قبضها، ولو مات الموهوب له كان لورثته القيام فيها على الواهب الصحيح.

ومن حبس دارا فهي على ما جعلها عليه إن حيزت قبل موته، ولو كانت حبسا على ولده الصغير جازته له إلى أن يبلغ، وليكرها له ولا يسكنها، فإن لم يدع سكناها حتى مات بطلت، وإن انقرض من حبست عليه رجعت حبسا على أقرب الناس بالمحبس يوم المرجع. ومن أعمر رجلا حياته دارا رجعت بعد موت الساكن ملكا لربها، وكذلك إن أعمر عقبه فانقرضوا، بخلاف الحبس.

فإن مات المعمر يومئذ كانت لورثته يوم موته ملكا. ومن مات من

goes to his heirs on the day he dies. If one of the people of the *ḥubus* dies, his share goes to the rest. People in need of lodging and revenue are preferred for the *ḥubus*. If someone is living in it, he should not be evicted in favour of someone else unless that is a precondition in the *ḥubus* which is carried out.

The *ḥubus* may never be sold, even if it falls into ruins. If a horse which is a *ḥubus* becomes rabid, it is sold and the price used for another one like it or to help in paying for one. There is disagreement about replacing a ruined building with a building in good condition.

The use of a pledge is permitted and it is only accomplished by possession of the article pledged. Testimony about possession is only valid if the witness actually saw possession take place. Responsibility for the pledge is held by the one who takes it, if it is something that can be hidden. If it is something that cannot be hidden, he is not liable. The responsibility for the fruit of palm trees in pledge is that of the pledger. The same is true for the revenue of houses. If a slave-girl bears a child while she is acting as a pledge, her child is also a pledge. The possessions of a slave do not go into pledge with him unless that is stipulated. If the pledge is destroyed in the possession of a trustee, it is the responsibility of the pledger.

An *'āriyah* (loan for temporary use) is assigned for a time. The borrower is responsible for what can be hidden, but not for what cannot be hidden, such as a slave or a riding animal, unless he misuses it. If someone given a deposit (*wadī'ah*) says, "I have returned the deposit to you," he is believed unless he received it in the presence of witnesses. If he says, "It has disappeared," he is believed in any case. In the case of an *'āriyah*, however, he is not believed about its destruction if it is something which can be concealed. If someone abuses a deposit, he is liable for it. If it was dinars, which he returns to their original bag and

أهل الحبس فنصيبه على من بقي ، ويؤثر في الحبس أهل الحاجة بالسكنى والغلة. ومن سكن فلا يخرج لغيره إلا أن يكون في أصل الحبس شرط فيمضي.

ولا يباع الحبس وإن خرب ، ويباع الفرس الحبس يكلب، ويجعل ثمنه في مثله، أو يعان به فيه. و اختلف في المعاوضة بالربع الخرب بربع غير خرب.

والرهن جائز، ولا يتم إلا بالحيازة. ولا تنفع الشهادة في حيازته إلا بمعاينة البينة، وضمان الرهن من المرتهن فيما يغاب عليه، ولا يضمن ما لا يغاب عليه. وثمرة النخل الرهن للراهن، وكذلك غلة الدور، والولد رهن مع الأمة الرهن تلده بعد الرهن، ولا يكون مال العبد رهنا إلا بشرط، وما هلك بيد أمين فهو من الراهن.

والعارية مؤداة. يضمن ما يغاب عليه، ولا يضمن ما لا يغاب عليه من عبد أو دابة إلا أن يتعدى. والمودع إن قال رددت الوديعة إليك صدق إلا أن يكون قبضها بإشهاد، وإن قال : ذهبت فهو مصدق بكل حال، والعارية لا يصدق في هلاكها فيما يغاب عليه. ومن تعدى على وديعة ضمنها، وإن كانت دنانير فردها في صرتها ثم هلكت فقد اختلف في تضمينه. ومن اتجر بوديعة فذلك مكروه،

then they are lost, there is disagreement about whether he is liable for them. It is disliked for someone to trade with something deposited with him. If he does so with money, the profit is his. If the deposit was goods and he sells them, the owner can choose between taking the price or the value on the day he infringed.

If someone finds something, he must announce it for a year in a place where it is hoped that it will be recognised. If, after a year, no one comes forward, he can make it a *ḥubus* or give it away as *ṣadaqah*. If he does that, he is responsible for it if its owner should then come forward. If the finder makes use of it, he is responsible for it. If it is destroyed before or after the year is up without action on his part, he is not responsible. If the claimant recognises the purse and the strap, he may take it. A man may not claim a stray camel in the desert, but he can take a sheep and eat it if it is found in uninhabited wasteland. If someone consumes merchandise, then he owes its value. If the goods are weighed or measured, he owes the equivalent.

A misappropriater is liable for what he misappropriated. If he returns it in its original state, he owes nothing. If it has changed while in his possession then the owner can choose between taking it with the defect or making him liable for its price. If the loss was due to his misuse, the owner has a choice between taking it and taking it with compensation for the damage. There is a difference of opinion about that. A misappropriater has no right to any revenue he has received and must return what he consumed of the revenue or pay for any use he had from what he took. If he has intercourse with a slave-girl he takes, then he is subject to the *ḥadd* punishment and his child is a slave of her owner. Someone who has usurped property has no right to its profit up until the time he returns it to the owner. Some of the people of Mālik prefer that he give it away as *ṣadaqah*. There is something about this in the chapter on judgments.

والربح له إن كانت عينا. وإن باع الوديعة وهي عرض فربها مخير في الثمن أو القيمة يوم التعدي.

ومن وجد لقطة فليعرفها سنة بموضع يرجو التعريف بها، فإن تمت سنة ولم يأت لها أحد، فإن شاء حبسها وإن شاء تصدق بها، وضمنها لربها إن جاء، وإن انتفع بها ضمنها، وإن هلكت قبل السنة أو بعدها بغير تحريك لم يضمنها، وإذا عرف طالبها العفاص والوكاء أخذها. ولا يأخذ الرجل ضالة الإبل من الصحراء، وله أخذ الشاة وأكلها إن كانت بفيفاء لا عمارة فيها. ومن استهلك عرضا فعليه قيمته، وكل ما يوزن أو يكال فعليه مثله.

والغاصب ضامن لما غصب، فإن رد ذلك بحاله فلا شيء عليه، وإن تغير في يده فربه مخير بين أخذه بنقصه أو تضمينه القيمة، ولو كان النقص بتعديه خير أيضا في أخذه وأخذ ما نقصه، وقد اختلف في ذلك، ولا غلة للغاصب، ويرد ما أكل من غلة أو انتفع، وعليه الحد إن وطيء، وولده رقيق لرب الأمة، ولا يطيب لغاصب المال ربحه حتى يرد رأس المال على ربه، ولو تصدق بالربح كان أحب إلى بعض أصحاب مالك . وفي باب الأقضية شيء من هذا المعنى.

37. JUDGMENTS ON HOMICIDE AND *ḤADD*-PUNISHMENTS

No one may be killed for homicide except on the basis of just evidence, confession, or by the *qasāmah* when that is necessary. The form that the *qasāmah* takes is that [fifty] relatives [of the victim] swear fifty oaths and then they are entitled to take the life of the accused. If it was premeditated murder, then the minimum required is that two men swear the oaths. It is not permitted to put more than one man to death as a result of the *qasāmah*. *Qasāmah* is obliged by the statement of the dying man, "So-and-so killed me" or there is a witness to the killing, or two witnesses to the wounding if he then survives long enough afterwards to eat and drink.

If those who claim blood refuse to swear, then the accused must swear fifty oaths. If he cannot find those among his relatives who will swear with him, then the accused himself swears fifty oaths. If a group are accused of murder, then each of them must swear fifty oaths. When the relatives seek blood, fifty men swear fifty oaths. If they are less than that, the oaths are divided between them. A woman does not swear in a case of premeditated murder.

In the case of an accidental homicide, the heirs, male or female, swear according to the amount of blood money they inherit. If the division of the oaths is uneven, then the one with the largest share swears the remaining oath. If some of the heirs who are present swear oaths in order to gain blood money on account of accidental killing, they must swear all the oaths. Then those after them later swear according to their shares of the inheritance. They should swear

٣٧ - باب في أحكام الدماء والحدود

ولا تقتل نفس بنفس إلا ببينة عادلة، أو باعتراف أو بالقسامة إذا وجبت، يقسم الولاة خمسين يمينا ويستحقون الدم، ولا يحلف في العمد أقل من رجلين، ولا يقتل بالقسامة أكثر من رجل واحد. وإنما تجب القسامة بقول الميت: دمي عند فلان، أو بشاهد على القتل، أو بشاهدين على الجرح ثم يعيش بعد ذلك ويأكل ويشرب.

وإذا نكل مدعو الدم حلف المدعى عليهم خمسين يمينا، فإن لم يجد من يحلف من ولاته معه غير المدعى عليه وحده حلف الخمسين. ولو ادعي القتل على جماعة حلف كل واحد خمسين يمينا. ويحلف من الولاة في طلب الدم خمسون رجلا خمسين يمينا، وإن كانوا أقل قسمت عليهم الأيمان. ولا تحلف امرأة في العمد.

وتحلف الورثة في الخطإ بقدر ما يرثون من الدية من رجل أو امرأة، وإن انكسرت يمين عليهم حلفها أكثرهم نصيبا منها، وإذا حضر بعض ورثة الخطإ لم يكن له بد أن يحلف جميع الأيمان، ثم يحلف من يأتي بعده بقدر نصيبه من الميراث، ويحلفون في القسامة قياما، ويجلب إلى مكة والمدينة وبيت المقدس أهل أعمالها للقسامة، ولا

the oaths while standing. People living in the provinces of Makkah, Madīnah or Jerusalem should be brought to those places to perform the *qasāmah*. People of other provinces are not summoned to their provincial centre unless they are a short distance from it. There is no *qasāmah* in the case of wounds, nor for slaves, nor for one of the People of the Book, nor if the body is found between the battle lines or found in the residential quarter of people.

There is no pardon in the case of murder done for financial gain. A man may pardon his murderer if he was not killed for financial gain. He may pardon for accidental killing from the disposable third of his state. If one of the sons of the victim grant pardon, then the killer is not killed, but the other heirs still receive their shares of the blood money. Daughters cannot grant pardon when there are sons. Someone who is pardoned for wilful killing receives a hundred lashes and is imprisoned for a year.

The blood money for people with camels is one hundred camels. For those who use gold, it is one thousand dinars, and for those who use silver it is 12,000 dirhams. The blood money for murder, if accepted, in camels is twenty-five four year old she-camels (*ḥiqqah*), twenty-five five year old she-camels (*jadha'ah*), twenty-five three year old she camels (*bint labūn*) and twenty-five two year old she-camels (*bint makhāḍ*). The blood money for accidental homicide is twenty of each type and twenty male three year old camels (*ibn labūn*).

The blood money is made more exacting in the case of a father who kills his son by throwing a piece of iron at him and killing him. He is not put to death for his death, but he must pay thirty five year old she-camels, thirty four year old she-camels and forty *khalifah*s, which are pregnant camels. It is said that the *'āqilah* [the tribe] pay that and it is also said that it comes from his own property. The blood money of a woman is half that of a man. The same applies to the blood money

يجلب في غيرها إلا من الأميال اليسيرة، ولا قسامة في جرح ولا في عبد ولا بين أهل الكتاب، ولا في قتيل بين الصفين، أو وجد في محلة قوم.

وقتل الغيلة لا عفو فيه. وللرجل العفو عن دمه العمد إن لم يكن قتل غيلة، وعفوه عن الخطإ في ثلثه. وإن عفا أحد البنين فلا قتل، ولمن بقي نصيبهم من الدية، ولا عفو للبنات مع البنين، ومن عفي عنه في العمد ضرب مائة وحبس عاما.

والدية على أهل الإبل مائة من الإبل، وعلى أهل الذهب ألف دينار، وعلى أهل الورق اثنا عشر ألف درهم. ودية العمد - إذا قبلت - خمس وعشرون حقة، وخمس وعشرون جذعة، وخمس وعشرون بنت لبون، وخمس وعشرون بنت مخاض. ودية الخطإ مخمسة، عشرون من كل ما ذكرنا، وعشرون بنو لبون ذكورا.

وإنما تغلظ الدية في الأب يرمي ابنه بحديدة فيقتله فلا يقتل به، ويكون عليه ثلاثون جذعة وثلاثون حقة وأربعون خلفة في بطونها أولادها، وقيل: ذلك على عاقلته، وقيل : ذلك في ماله. ودية المرأة على النصف من دية الرجل، وكذلك دية الكتابيين، ونساؤهم على النصف من ذلك، والمجوسي ديته ثمانمائة درهم، ونساؤهم على

of *Kitābīs*, and their women is half of that of their men. A Magian's blood money is 800 dirhams and that of their women half of that. The same principle applies to penalties for wounds.

Full blood money must be paid for loss of both hands or feet or eyes, and half is owed for the loss of one of them. Full blood money is also due for cutting the cartilage of the nose, causing loss of hearing, causing loss of mental understanding, breaking the back, crushing the testicles, cutting off the penis, and cutting off the tongue or damaging it so that the victim cannot speak. Full blood money is due for destroying the breasts of a woman or for causing the loss of the eye of someone with only one eye.

For a *mūḍiḥah* wound, which is a head wound that exposes the skull, the penalty is five camels. The same amount must be paid for loss of a tooth. Ten camels are due for the loss of each finger or toe, three and a third for the tips of fingers and toes, and five for the tips of the thumb or big toe. Fifteen per cent is owed for a *munaqqilah* wound. A *mūḍiḥah* is a head wound which exposes the bone and a *munaqqilah* wound is one that affects the skull, but does not reach the brain. If it reaches the brain it is a *ma'mūmah*, and a third of the blood money is owed for it. The same holds for a *jā'ifah* (abdominal) wound. *Ijtihād* (discretion) must be exercised in the case of a wound less than a *mūḍiḥah* and in the case of other wounds. The blood money for a wound is only paid after it has healed. If a wound less than a *mūḍiḥah* heals without leaving a scar, there is no compensation for it. There is retaliation for deliberate wounds, unless such a wound may prove fatal, such as a *ma'mūmah*, *jā'ifah*, and *munaqqilah*, or breaking a thigh, crushing the testicles, breaking the back, and such injuries. Blood money is paid for such injuries.

The *'āqilah* (tribe) do not have to pay in the case of deliberate murder nor for homicide based on confession. They should pay in

النصف من ذلك، ودية جراحهم كذلك.

وفي اليدين الدية، وكذلك في الرجلين أو العينين، وفي كل واحدة منهما نصفها، وفي الأنف يقطع مارنه الدية، وفي السمع الدية، وفي العقل الدية، وفي الصلب ينكسر الدية، وفي الأنثيين الدية، وفي الحشفة الدية، وفي اللسان الدية، وفيما منع منه الكلام الدية، وفي ثديي المرأة الدية، وفي عين الأعور الدية.

وفي الموضحة خمس من الإبل، وفي السن خمس، وفي كل أصبع عشر، وفي الأنملة ثلاث وثلث، وفي كل أنملة من الإبهامين خمس من الإبل، وفي المنقلة عشر ونصف عشر. والموضحة ما أوضح ما أوضح العظم ، والمنقلة ما طار فراشها من العظم ولم تصل إلى الدماغ، وما وصل إليه فهي المأمونة، ففيها ثلث الدية، وكذلك الجائفة، وليس فيما دون الموضحة إلا الاجتهاد، وكذلك في جراح الجسد. ولا يعقل جرح إلا بعد البرء، وما بريء على غير شين مما دون الموضحة فلا شيء فيه. وفي الجراح القصاص في العمد، إلا في المتآلف مثل المأمومة والجائفة والمنقلة والفخذ والأنثيين والصلب ونحوه ففي كل ذلك الدية.

ولا تحمل العاقلة قتل عمد ولا اعترافا به، وتحمل من جراح الخطإ ما

the case of accidental injuries if the amount is a third or more of the full blood money. Amounts less than a third should be paid by the perpetrator from his own property. As for a deliberate *ma'mūmah* or *jā'ifah* wound, Mālik said that the blood money should be paid by the tribe (*'āqilah*). He also said that it is said that it should be paid from the inflictor's property unless he is without money. Then the *'āqilah* pay it, because there is no retaliation in the case of such wounds when they are deliberate. It is the same with penalties which reach a third of the blood money when there is no retaliation because that might prove fatal. The *'āqilah* do not pay anything in the case of someone who kills himself either deliberately or accidentally.

A woman is paid the same compensation as a man up to a third of the blood money of a man. If compensation reaches a third, it reverts to her portion of the blood money (which is half). When a group murder a man, they are all killed for his murder. If a drunk kills, he is killed. If a madman kills, his tribe pay the blood money. A deliberate injury inflicted by a minor is the same as an accidental one. It is paid by the *'āqilah* if it is a third of the blood money or more. Otherwise it comes from his own property.

A woman is killed for killing a man and a man for killing a woman. Retaliation is exacted from each for wounds. A free man is not killed for killing a slave, but a slave is killed for killing a free man. A Muslim is not killed for killing an unbeliever, but an unbeliever is killed for killing a Muslim. There is no retaliation between a free man and slave in the cause of wounds, nor between a Muslim and an unbeliever.

Someone who is driving, leading or riding an animal is liable for anything that that animal tramples on. If the animal tramples on something and that was not the result of what the person did, or while it is stationary without anything having been done to it, there is no legal liability in that case. If someone dies in a well or a mine without

كان قدر الثلث فأكثر، وما كان دون الثلث ففي مال الجاني. وأما المأمومة والجائفة عمدا فقال مالك: ذلك على العاقلة، وقال أيضا: عن ذلك في ماله، إلا أن يكون عديما فتحمله العاقلة لأنهما لا يقاد من عمدهما. وكذلك ما بلغ ثلث الدية مما لا يقاد منه، لأنه متلف، ولا تعقل العاقلة من قتل نفسه عمدا أو خطأ.

وتعاقل المرأة الرجل إلى ثلث دية الرجل ، فإذا بلغتها رجعت إلى عقلها. والنفر يقتلون رجلا فإنهم يقتلون به. والسكران إن قتل قتل. وإن قتل مجنون رجلا فالدية على عاقلته. وعمد الصبي كالخطإ، وذلك على عاقلته إن كان ثلث الدية فأكثر، وإلا ففي ماله.

وتقتل المرأة بالرجل، والرجل بها. ويقتص لبعضهم من بعض في الجراح، ولا يقتل حر بعبد ويقتل به العبد، ولا يقتل مسلم بكافر ويقتل به الكافر، ولا قصاص بين حر وعبد في جرح، ولا بين مسلم وكافر.

والسائق والقائد والراكب ضامنون لما وطئت الدابة ، وما كان منها من غير فعلهم أو وهي واقفة لغير شيء فعل بها، فذلك هدر. وما مات في بئر أو معدن من غير فعل أحد فهو هدر.

anyone doing something to cause that, there is no liability.

The tribe (*'āqilah*) pay the blood money in instalments over three years. If a third of the blood rate is owed, it should be paid in a year. If it is a half, it should be paid over two years. Blood money is inherited on the basis of the shares of inheritance.

A *ghurrah* is owed for causing the loss of the foetus of a free woman. A *ghurrah* is a slave or slave-girl worth fifty dinars or six hundred dirhams. A *ghurrah* is inherited by the heirs according to the Book of Allah.

Someone who deliberately kills a person may not inherit either his property or his blood money. Someone who kills a relative by accident inherits his property but not the blood money. The same amount is owed for causing the loss of a foetus of a slave-girl pregnant by her master as there is for causing a free woman to miscarry. If she was pregnant by someone else, the fine is a tenth of the value of the mother. If someone kills a slave, he owes his value.

If a group of people kill someone in aggravated robbery (*ḥirābah*) or for financial gain, they should all be killed, even if only one of them did the actual killing.

Atonement (*kaffārah*) for accidental killing is mandatory. It consists of freeing a Muslim slave, or, if that is not possible, then fasting for two consecutive months. He is ordered to do that if he is pardoned for deliberate killing, for this is best for him.

A *zindīq* is killed and his repentance is not accepted. He is the one who conceals disbelief while making an outward display of Islam. The same is true for a sorcerer. His repentance is not accepted. An apostate is killed unless he repents. He is given three days to repent. The same ruling applies to a woman. If someone has not apostatised but affirms the prayer and yet says, "I will not pray," he is given a respite until the time of the next prayer. If he does not pray, he is

وتنجم الدية على العاقلة في ثلاث سنين، وثلثها في سنة، ونصفها في سنتين. والدية موروثة على الفرائض.

وفي جنين الحرة غرة عبد أو وليدة تقوم بخمسين دينارا أو ستمائة درهم، وتورث على كتاب الله.

ولا يرث قاتل العمد من مال ولا دية، وقاتل الخطإ يرث من المال دون الدية. وفي جنين الأمة من سيدها ما في جنين الحرة، وإن كان من غيره ففيه عشر قيمتها. ومن قتل عبدا فعليه قيمته.

وتقتل الجماعة بالواحد في الحرابة والغيلة، وإن ولي القتل بعضهم.

وكفارة القتل في الخطإ واجبة: عتق رقبة مؤمنة، فإن لم يجد فصيام شهرين متتابعين، ويؤمر بذلك إن عفي عنه في العمد فهو خير له.

ويقتل الزنديق ولا تقبل توبته، وهو الذي يسر الكفر ويظهر الإسلام، وكذلك الساحر، ولا تقبل توبته، ويقتل من ارتد إلا أن يتوب، ويؤخر للتوبة ثلاثا، وكذلك المرأة، ومن لم يرتد وأقر الصلاة وقال: لا أصلي، أخر حتى يمضي وقت صلاة واحدة، فإن لم يصلها قتل. ومن امتنع من الزكاة أخذت منه كرها. ومن ترك الحج فالله

killed. If someone refuses to pay *zakāt*, it is taken from him by force. If someone does not go on *ḥajj*, he is left to Allah. Someone who abandons the prayer out of denial of its obligatory nature is like an apostate. He is asked to repent for three days. If he does not repent, he is killed.

If someone curses the Messenger of Allah ﷺ, he is killed and his repentance is not accepted. If one of the people of *dhimmah* abuses him outside of that which constitutes his disbelief or curses Allah Almighty other than what constitutes his disbelief, he is killed unless he becomes Muslim.

The estate of the apostate goes to the Muslim community.

A bandit may not be pardoned when he is caught. If he has killed anyone, he must be killed. If he has not killed anyone, the ruler should exercise his discretion according to the seriousness of his crime and the length of time he has been a robber. He may execute him, or crucify him and then execute him, or cut off his opposite foot and hand, or exile him to another town to be imprisoned there until he repents. If he is not caught until he comes in repentance, none of these rights, which are Allah's rights, are exacted. The rights of people are taken in the form of blood or property.

Each member of a gang of thieves is liable for all the property they take. The entire group is killed for the murder of one person in banditry or for financial gain, even if only one of them did the actual killing. A Muslim is put to death for killing a *dhimmī* in aggravated robbery or for financial gain.

If someone has illicit sex and is a free *muḥṣan*, he is stoned to death. One acquires the status of being *muḥṣan* by marrying a woman in a valid marriage and having valid intercourse with her. If he is not *muḥṣan*, he receives a hundred lashes and is exiled to another town by the ruler and kept there for a year. A slave who commits fornication

حسبه، ومن ترك الصلاة جحدا لها فهو كالمرتد يستتاب ثلاثا، فإن لم يتب قتل.

ومن سب رسول الله صلى الله عليه وسلم قتل، ولا تقبل توبته. ومن سبه من أهل الذمة بغير ما به كفر، أو سب الله عز وجل بغير ما به كفر قتل، إلا أن يسلم.

وميراث المرتد لجماعة المسلمين.

والمحارب لا عفو فيه إذا ظفر به، فإن قتل أحدا فلا بد من قتله، وإن لم يقتل فيسع الإمام فيه اجتهاده بقدر جرمه، وكثرة مقامه في فساده، فإما قتله، أو صلبه ثم قتله، أو يقطعه من خلاف، أو ينفيه إلى بلد يسجن بها حتى يتوب، فإن لم يقدر عليه حتى جاء تائبا وضع عنه كل حق هو لله من ذلك. وأخذ بحقوق الناس من مال أو دم.

وكل واحد من اللصوص ضامن لجميع ما سلبوه من الأموال. وتقتل الجماعة بالواحد في الحرابة والغيلة وإن ولي القتل واحد منهم، ويقتل المسلم بقتل الذمي قتل غيلة أو حرابة.

ومن زنى من حر محصن رجم حتى يموت. والإحصان أن يتزوج امرأة نكاحا صحيحا ويطأها وطأ صحيحا، فإن لم يحصن جلد مائة جلدة، وغربه الإمام إلى بلد آخر، وحبس فيه عاما. وعلى العبد في

receives fifty lashes, as does a slave-girl, even if they are married. They are not exiled nor is a woman exiled.

The *ḥadd* punishment for illicit sex is only carried out when proven by confession, clear pregnancy, or the testimony of four free men who are adult and of good character and who see the actual act, like a kohl stick entering a bottle. They must testify at the same time, and if one of them does not give the full description, the other three who gave it in full are given the *ḥadd* punishment (for slander). A *ḥadd* punishment is not inflicted on someone who has not reached puberty.

The *ḥadd* punishment is carried out on someone who has illicit sex with his father's slave-girl but not on someone who has sex with his son's slave-girl. He must, however, pay him her value, even if she does not become pregnant. A partner in a jointly owned slave-girl is punished if he has sex with her and is liable for her price if he has money. If she does not conceive, the other partner can choose between keeping her or being reimbursed for her value.

If a pregnant woman says that she was forced, she is not believed and receives the *ḥadd* punishment unless there is a witness that she was carried off in such a way that the abductor disappeared with her, or she comes seeking help at the time of the event, or comes bleeding. If a Christian rapes a Muslim woman he is killed. If someone retracts a confession to illicit sex, he is released and let go.

A master imposes the *ḥadd* punishment for illicit sex on his slave or slave-girl if she becomes pregnant or if there is other evidence in the form of four witnesses, or confession. But if the slave-girl has a free husband or her husband is the slave of someone else, the *ḥadd* punishment is only carried out on her by the ruler.

When a man commits the action of the people of Lūṭ with another consenting adult male, they are both stoned, *muḥṣan* or not.

الزنا خمسون جلدة، وكذلك الأمة، وإن كانا متزوجين، ولا تغريب عليهما. ولا على امرأة.

ولا يحد الزاني إلا باعتراف، أو بحمل يظهر، أو بشهادة أربعة رجال أحرار بالغين عدول يرونه كالمرود في المكحلة، ويشهدون في وقت واحد، وإن لم يتم أحدهم الصفة حد الثلاثة الذين أتموها، ولا حد على من لم يحتلم.

ويحد واطئ أمة والده. ولا يحد واطئ أمة ولده، وتقوم عليه وإن لم تحمل، ويؤدب الشريك في الأمة يطؤها، ويضمن قيمتها إن كان له مال، فإن لم تحمل فالشريك بالخيار بين أن يتماسك أو تقوم عليه.

وإن قالت امرأة بها حمل : استكرهت، لم تصدق وحدت إلا أن تعرف بينة أنها احتملت حتى غاب عليها، أو جاءت مستغيثة عند النازلة، أو جاءت تدمى. والنصراني إذا غصب المسلمة في الزنا قتل، وإن رجع المقر بالزنا أقيل وترك.

ويقيم الرجل على عبده وأمته حد الزنا إذا ظهر حمل أو قامت بينة غيره: أربعة شهداء، أو كان إقرار، ولكن إن كان للأمة زوج حر أو عبد لغيره فلا يقيم الحد عليها إلا السلطان.

ومن عمل عمل قوم لوط بذكر بالغ أطاعه رجما، أحصنا أو لم يحصنا.

A free person who slanders is given eighty lashes, while a slave is given forty lashes for slander and fifty for fornication. An unbeliever who slanders also receives eighty lashes. There is no *ḥadd* punishment inflicted on someone who slanders a slave or an unbeliever. There is a *ḥadd* on account of accusing a girl of fornication if she is of an age in which she can have intercourse but there is no *ḥadd* punishment on account of slandering a boy, nor is the punishment carried out on a minor for slander or intercourse. A *ḥadd* punishment for slander is imposed on someone who denies a man's parentage or implies its denial. If someone calls a man a sodomite, he also receives the *ḥadd* punishment. If someone slanders a group, then one of the group may oblige the *ḥadd* punishment once, and then the rest of the group have nothing from him.

If someone drinks wine or fornicates more than once, there is one *ḥadd* punishment for all of that. It is the same with slandering a group of people. As for someone who is liable to both *ḥudūd* punishments and killing, killing him is sufficient in that case – except in the case of slander. He receives the *ḥadd* punishment for that before he is killed.

If someone drinks wine or intoxicating *nabīdh*, he receives a *ḥadd* of eighty lashes, whether he is intoxicated or not, but he is not imprisoned for it.

The one who receives a *ḥadd* punishment is stripped, but a woman is only divested of what would protect her from the blows. They receive the flogging sitting down. A pregnant woman is not flogged until she gives birth, nor is a very sick person until he recovers.

Someone guilty of bestiality is not killed, but is punished.

If someone steals a quarter of a dinar of gold or the equivalent of goods worth three dirhams or the weight of three dirhams in silver on the day of the theft, his hand is cut off if he stole that from a protected place. His hand is not cut off if he snatches them. In such a case of

وعلى القاذف الحر الحد ثمانون، وعلى العبد أربعون في القذف وخمسون في الزنا والكافر يحد في القذف ثمانين، ولا حد على قاذف عبد أو كافر، ويحد قاذف الصبية بالزنا إن كان مثلها يوطأ، ولا يحد قاذف الصبي، ولا حد على من لم يبلغ في قذف ولا وطء. ومن نفى رجلا من نسبه فعليه الحد، وفي التعريض الحد. ومن قال لرجل : يا لوطي حد. ومن قذف جماعة فحد واحد يلزمه لمن قام به منهم، ثم لا شيء عليه.

ومن كرر شرب الخمر أو الزنا فحد واحد في ذلك كله، وكذلك من قذف جماعة، ومن لزمته حدود وقتل فالقتل يجزي عن ذلك إلا في القذف فليحد قبل أن يقتل.

ومن شرب خمرا أو نبيذا مسكرا حد ثمانين، سكر أو لم يسكر، ولا سجن عليه.

ويجرد المحدود، ولا تجرد المرأة إلا مما يقيها الضرب، ويجلدان قاعدين. ولا تحد حامل حتى تضع، ولا مريض مثقل حتى يبرأ.

ولا يقتل واطيء البهيمة، وليعاقب.

ومن سرق ربع دينار ذهبا أو ما قيمته يوم السرقة ثلاثة دراهم من العروض، أو وزن ثلاثة دراهم فضة قطع إذا سرق من حرز، ولا قطع في الخلسة، ويقطع في ذلك يد الرجل والمرأة والعبد، ثم إن

theft, the right hand of a man, woman or slave is cut off. If the person steals a second time, his left foot is cut off. If he steals a third time, his left hand is cut off. If he steals a fourth time, his right foot is cut off. If he then steals again, he is flogged and imprisoned. If someone confesses to theft, his hand is cut off. If he retracts, he is let go. A thief must return what he stole if he has it. Otherwise, he is indebted for that amount.

If someone takes something from a place where it is in safekeeping, his hand is not cut off until he actually removes the stolen object from that place. The same applies to stealing a shroud from a grave. If someone steals from a house that he has permission to enter, his hand is not cut off. The hand of someone who snatches is not cut off.

If a slave confesses to something which obliges a *ḥadd* punishment or amputation on his body, his confession is binding. In that which concerns his person, he cannot confess.

There is no amputation for taking fruit hanging on a tree, a palm pith, or for taking grazing sheep or goats, unless he stole them from their pens, nor for taking fruit unless it is from a store. There is no intercession once a case of theft or illicit sex has reached the ruler. There is disagreement about that in the case of slander. If someone steals from someone's sleeve, his hand is cut off. If someone steals from the granary or treasury or booty, his hand is cut off. It is said that if what he took is three dirhams more than his share of the booty then his hand is cut off.

When a thief has his hand cut off, he is prosecuted for restitution of the value of missing stolen goods if he is solvent. If he has no property, he is not prosecuted. He is, however, prosecuted for an amount which does not reach the level at which the hand is cut off.

سرق قطعت رجله من خلاف، ثم إن سرق فيده، ثم إن سرق فرجله، ثم إن سرق جلد وسجن. ومن أقر بسرقة قطع، وإن رجع أقيل وغرم السرقة إن كانت معه، وإلا اتبع بها.

ومن أخذ في الحرز لم يقطع حتى يخرج السرقة من الحرز، وكذلك الكفن من القبر. ومن سرق من بيت أذن له في دخوله لم يقطع، ولا يقطع المختلس.

وإقرار العبد فيما يلزمه في بدنه من حد أو قطع يلزمه، وما كان في رقبته فلا إقرار له.

ولا قطع في ثمر معلق، ولا في الجمار في النخل، ولا في الغنم الراعية حتى تسرق من مراحها، وكذلك التمر من الأندر. ولا يشفع لمن بلغ الإمام في السرقة والزنا، واختلف في ذلك في القذف. ومن سرق من الكم قطع . ومن سرق من الهري وبيت المال والمغنم فليقطع، وقيل: إن سرق فوق حقه من المغنم بثلاثة دراهم قطع.

ويتبع السارق إذا قطع بقيمة ما فات من السرقة في ملائه، ولا يتبع في عدمه، ويتبع في عدمه بما لا يقطع فيه من السرقة.

38. Judgments and testimony

The plaintiff must produce testimony and the one who denies it must take an oath. No oath is taken unless it is established that they have had dealings or that is suspected. That was the practice of the judges of the people of Madīnah. ʻUmar ibn ʻAbd al-ʻAzīz said, "People have new cases according to the extent that they have new iniquities." If the defendant refuses to take an oath, judgment is not given to the claimant until he swears an oath to what he claims to the best of his knowledge. The oath is:

"By Allah Whom there is no god but Him."

Bi-llāhi-lladhī lā ilāha illā huwa

He should take the oath standing by the minbar of the Messenger of Allah ﷺ if it concerns something worth a quarter of a dinar or more. Outside Madīnah, he takes the oath in the central mosque at the most esteemed place in it. The unbeliever must swear "By Allah" in a place he respects.

When a claimant finds evidence he did not previously know about after the defendant has taken an oath, judgment can be given in his favour by it. If he knew of it before, it is not accepted. There is also another opinion that it is accepted. Judgment can be given on the basis of a single witness and an oath in the case of property, but one witness and an oath is not accepted in the case of marriage, divorce, and *ḥudūd* punishments, nor is one witness and an oath accepted in deliberate wounding or homicide. Homicide alone is decided by the *qasāmah* process. There is another view that wounds can be decided on that basis as well.

The testimony of women is only permitted in respect of property.

٣٨ - باب في الأقضية والشهادات

والبينة على المدعى واليمين على من أنكر ولا يمين حتى تثبت الخلطة أو الظنة، كذلك قضى حكام أهل المدينة. وقد قال عمر بن عبد العزيز: تحدث للناس أقضية بقدر ما أحدثوا من الفجور. وإذا نكل المدعى عليه لم يقض للطالب حتى يحلف فيما يدعي فيه معرفة.

واليمين:

بِاللهِ الذِي لاَ إِلَهَ إِلاَّ هُوَ

ويحلف قائما، وعند منبر الرسول صلى الله عليه وسلم في ربع دينار فأكثر. وفي غير المدينة يحلف في ذلك في الجامع وموضع يعظم منه، ويحلف الكافر بالله حيث يعظم.

وإذا وجد الطالب بينة بعد يمين المطلوب لم يكن علم بها، قضي له بها، وإن كان علم بها فلا تقبل منه، وقد قيل: تقبل منه. ويقضى بشاهد ويمين في الأموال. ولا يقضى بذلك في نكاح أو طلاق أو حد، ولا في دم عمد أو نفس إلا مع القسامة في النفس، وقد قيل: يقضى بذلك في الجراح.

ولا تجوز شهادة النساء إلا في الأموال، ومائة أمرأة كامرأتين،

A hundred women count as two women. Two women count as one man. Judgment is given on the basis of that with one man or an oath in cases where one witness and an oath are permitted. The testimony of two women alone is accepted in matters which men do not observe, such as childbirth, the crying of a new-born child and the like.

The testimony of an adversary or someone who is suspect is not allowed. Only the testimony of reputable witnesses is acceptable. Those who have been punished for a *ḥadd* punishment are not acceptable as witnesses, nor the testimony of a slave, child, or unbeliever. If someone who has received the *ḥadd* for illicit sex repents, then his testimony may be accepted except in cases involving illicit sex. It is not permitted for a son to testify in favour of his parents or vice versa, nor a husband to testify in favour of his wife or vice versa. It is, however, permitted for a man of good character to testify in favour of his brother. The testimony of a habitual liar, of someone who openly commits a major wrong action, of someone seeking his own self-interest or seeking to avert harm from himself, or of a guardian in favour of his orphan ward is not allowed. A guardian may, however, testify against his ward.

It is not permitted for women to testify to the good or bad character of a witness. Declaring someone to have good character (*tazkiyah*) is only accepted when someone says, "He is reputable and pleasing (*'adlun riḍā*)." A single witness to the character or bad character of a witness is not accepted. The testimony of minors in respect of wounds may be accepted as long as it is given before they have left the scene and no adult has been with them.

When two parties to a contract disagree, the seller is asked to swear an oath and then the buyer either accepts that or swears an oath and is free of the contract. When two claimants disagree about something in their possession, they must swear an oath and then the disputed

وذلك كرجل واحد يقضى بذلك مع رجل أو مع اليمين فيما يجوز فيه شاهد ويمين، وشهادة امرأتين فقط فيما لا يطلع عليه الرجال من الولادة والاستهلال وشبهه جائزة.

ولا تجوز شهادة خصم ولا ظنين، ولا يقبل إلا العدول، ولا يجوز شهادة المحدود، ولا شهادة عبد ولا صبي ولا كافر، وإذا تاب المحدود في الزنا قبلت شهادته إلا في الزنا، ولا تجوز شهادة الابن للأبوين ولا هما له، ولا الزوج للزوجة، ولا هي له، وتجوز شهادة الأخ العدل لأخيه، ولا تجوز شهادة مجرب في كذب، أو مظهر لكبيرة، ولا جار لنفسه، ولا دافع عنها، ولا وصي ليتيمه، وتجوز شهادته عليه.

ولا يجوز تعديل النساء ولا تجريحهن، ولا يقبل في التزكية إلا من يقول : عدل رضا، ولا يقبل في ذلك ولا في التجريح واحد. وتقبل شهادة الصبيان في الجراح قبل أن يفترقوا، أو يدخل بينهم كبير.

وإذا اختلف المتبايعان استحلف البائع ثم يأخذ المبتاع، أو يحلف ويبرأ. وإذا اختلف المتداعيان في شيء بأيديهما حلف وقسم بينهما. وإن أقاما بينتين قضي بأعدلهما، فإن استويا حلفا وكان بينهما.

property is divided between them. If the two produce witnesses, judgment is given in favour of the one with better character. If the two witnesses are equal, then the two parties swear an oath and the property is divided between them.

When a witness retracts his testimony after judgment, he is liable for any losses which resulted if he admits to perjury. The people of Mālik said that. When someone says, "I have returned to you what you entrusted to me to pay" or "to sell" or "I paid you its price" or "I have returned your deposit or your loan," then his statement is accepted. If someone says, "I gave it to so-and-so as you commanded," and that person denies it, then the one who delivered it must produce proof. Otherwise he is liable. The same is true in the case of the guardian of orphans. He needs proof about what he spent on them or gave to them. If, however, they are in his direct custody, then he is believed about their maintenance when it seems probable.

An amicable settlement is permitted unless it leads to the unlawful. It is permitted in both affirmation or denial.

If a deceitful slave-girl marries a man on the basis that she is free, her master can reclaim her and claim the value of any child on the day of the judgment. When someone establishes his claim to a slave-girl who has borne (her new master) a child, he is entitled to her value and the value of her child on the day of the judgment. It is also said that he takes her and the price of the child. And it is also said that he only takes her price, or the price she was subsequently sold for. If he chooses to take her price, he takes it from the abductor who sold her. If she is still in the possession of the abductor, then he receives the *ḥadd* punishment and the child and its mother are slaves of her true owner.

If someone establishes his claim to land after it has been built on, he should pay the price of the buildings which are standing. If he

وإذا رجع الشاهد بعد الحكم أغرم ما أتلف بشهادته إن اعترف أنه شهد بزور، قاله أصحاب مالك. ومن قال: رددت إليك ما وكلتني عليه أو على بيعه أو دفعت إليك ثمنه أو وديعتك أو قراضك فالقول قوله. ومن قال: دفعت إلى فلان كما أمرتني فأنكر فلان فعلى الدافع البينة وإلا ضمن، وكذلك على ولي الأيتام البينة أنه أنفق عليهم، أو دفع إليهم، وإن كانوا في حضانته صدق في النفقة فيما يشبه.

والصلح جائز إلا ما جر إلى حرام، ويجوز على الإقرار والإنكار.

والأمة الفارة تتزوج على أنها حرة فلسيدها أخذها وأخذ قيمة الولد يوم الحكم له. ومن استحق أمة قد ولدت فله قيمتها وقيمة الولد يوم الحكم، وقيل يأخذها وقيمة الولد، وقيل: له قيمتها فقط إلا أن يختار الثمن فيأخذه من الغاصب الذي باعها، ولو كانت بيد غاصب فعليه الحد، وولده رقيق معها لربها.

ومستحق الأرض بعد أن عمرت يدفع قيمة العمارة قائماً، فإن أبى دفع إليه المشتري قيمة البقعة براحا، فإن أبى كانا شريكين بقيمة

refuses to do that, the buyer of the land should pay him the price of the undeveloped land. If the buyer refuses to do that, they become partners in the property according to the value which each of them owns. A usurper, however, is ordered to remove his buildings, crops and trees. If he wishes, their owner can be paid the price of the debris and trees, after deducting the cost of hiring someone to remove them. He owes nothing for what has no value after it is uprooted or demolished.

Someone who unlawfully acquired it must return any revenue, but only someone who has acquired it unlawfully is obliged to return it. In the case of the offspring of animals and slave-girls, if they have children by other than the (new) master, they are taken by the one entitled to the mothers from the person who purchased them or has gained possession of them for some other reason. If someone unlawfully abducts a slave-girl and has sexual intercourse with her, the child is a slave and [the abductor] receives the *ḥadd* punishment.

The owner of the ground floor is responsible for maintenance of the ground floor if it becomes weak and dilapidated and also for the wood of the ceiling and the support for the rooms above it until it is sound. He is compelled to make the repairs or to sell it to someone who will repair it. "No harm should be done to others nor any exceeding of harm done to you." No one should do anything which will harm his neighbour: like putting in a window facing him through which he can see him, or opening a door directly in front of his door, or digging in a way that will harm his neighbour, even in his own property. Judgment regarding the ownership of a wall is given in favour of the one whose house has wooden or masonry joints in the wall. A man ought not to prevent his neighbour from

Excess water may not be denied in an effort to prevent people from grazing animals. People with wells for their livestock have the first

ما لكل واحد. والغاصب يؤمر بقلع بنائه وزرعه وشجره، وإن شاء أعطاه ربها قيمة ذلك النقض والشجر ملقى بعد قيمة أجر من يقلع ذلك، ولا شيء عليه فيما لا قيمة له بعد القلع والهدم.

ويرد الغاصب الغلة، ولا يردها غير الغاصب. والولد في الحيوان وفي الأمة إذا كان الولد من غير السيد يأخذه المستحق للأمهات من يد مبتاع أو غيره. ومن غصب أمة ثم وطئها فولده رقيق، وعليه الحد.

وإصلاح السفل على صاحب السفل، والخشب للسقف عليه، وتعليق الغرف عليه إذا وهى السفل وهدم يصلح، ويجبر على أن يصلح أو يبيع ممن يصلح. ولا ضرر ولا ضرار، فلا يفعل ما يضر بجاره من فتح كوة قريبة يكشف جاره منها، أو فتح باب قبالة بابه، أو حفر ما يضر بجاره في حفره وإن كان في ملكه. ويقضى بالحائط لمن إليه القمط والعقود.

ولا يمنع فضل الماء ليمنع به الكلأ. وأهل آبار الماشية أحق بها حتى يسقوا، ثم الناس فيها سواء. ومن كان في أرضه عين أو بئر فله

claim on water for their animals and then the rights of other people are the same. If someone has a spring or well on his land, he may prevent others from using it unless his neighbour's well has caved in and he has plants he fears he will lose. Then he cannot deny him his excess water. There is disagreement about whether he can take payment for that or not.

Someone should not refuse to allow his neighbour to insert beams into his wall but he cannot be compelled to accept it.

If livestock ruin crops and gardens during the night, the owners of the animals are liable for that. They do not owe anything for damage done during the day.

If someone finds his goods in the possession of someone who has become bankrupt, he can either take his share [with the other creditors] or recover his actual property if he can identify the individual items. If, however, the debtor has died, he must take his share with the rest of the creditors.

The one who gives a guarantee is liable, and the one who guarantees the appearance of the debtor is liable if he does not bring the person, unless he stipulated that he would not be liable. If someone agrees to have a debt transferred to a third party, he cannot go back to the first debtor, even if the third party becomes bankrupt, unless the first one deceived him. The transfer is based on an original debt. Otherwise it is a guarantee. A guarantor is not liable except in the bankruptcy or the absence of the debtor. The death of the subject or his bankruptcy makes every debt he owes immediately due, but not debts which other people owe to him.

A slave permitted to trade is not sold in order to discharge his debts nor is his master prosecuted for them. A debtor may be imprisoned until his debt is cleared. He is not imprisoned if he is known to be insolvent.

منعها إلا أن تنهدم بئر جاره وله زرع يخاف عليه فلا يمنعه فضله، واختلف هل عليه في ذلك ثمن أم لا؟.

وينبغي ألا يمنع الرجل جاره أن يغرز خشبة في جداره، ولا يقضى عليه.

ما أفسدت الماشية من الزرع والحوائط بالليل فذلك على أرباب الماشية، ولا شيء عليهم في فساد النهار.

ومن وجد سلعته في التفليس، فإما حاصص، وإلا أخذ سلعته إن كانت تعرف بعينها، وهو في الموت أسوة الغرماء.

والضمان غارم، وحميل الوجه إن لم يأت به غرم حتى يشترط أن لا يغرم. ومن أحيل بدين فرضي فلا رجوع له على الأول وإن أفلس هذا إلا أن يغره منه، وإنما الحوالة على أصل دين، وإلا فهي حمالة، ولا يغرم الحميل إلا في عدم الغريم أو غيبته. ويحل بموت المطلوب أو تفليسه كل دين عليه، ولا يحل ما كان له على غيره.

ولا تباع رقبة المأذون فيما عليه، ولا يتبع به سيده. ويحبس المديان ليستبرأ. ولا حبس على معدم.

Buildings and property which can be divided without harm are divided (in case of dispute). In the case of something that cannot be divided without harm, if one party wishes to sell it, the other partner can be compelled to sell it. Division by lots is only done with the same category of thing. None of the partners can be given a price [while others take the goods]. If they decide to equalise the shares, the division is only permitted by mutual consent.

A guardian appointed by the original guardian is like the original guardian. A guardian can trade with the property of orphans and arrange the marriage of their slave-girls. If an untrustworthy guardian is appointed, he may be removed.

In the distribution of the estate of someone deceased one begins with the cost of the shroud, then paying debts, then fulfilling bequests and then the shares of inheritance.

If someone lives in a house belonging to someone else for ten years, it then becomes his if the owner was present and then did not claim anything from him. Living in the house of a relative or in-law, however, for this period of time does not establish this for him.

It is not permitted for a sick person to admit to a debt owed to an heir or to state that the heir has paid him a debt he owes him.

If someone leaves an instruction in his will that the *ḥajj* should be performed (on his behalf), his instruction is carried out, but we prefer a bequest of *ṣadaqah*. If the person hired to make *ḥajj* dies before completing it, he receives the fee for the amount he travelled and the rest must be returned. What he spent is his liability, unless he took it on the basis that he would be paid on completing it. Then the liability is that of those who hired him. If anything is left it is returned.

وما انقسم بلا ضرر قسم من ربع وعقار، وما لم ينقسم بغير ضرر، فمن دعا إلى البيع أجبر عليه من أباه. وقسم القرعة لا يكون إلا في صنف واحد، ولا يؤدي أحد الشركاء ثمنا، وإن كان في ذلك تراجع لم يجز القسم إلا بتراض.

ووصي الوصي كالوصي. وللوصي أن يتجر بأموال اليتامى، ويزوج إماءهم. ومن أوصى إلى غير مأمون فإنه يعزل.

ويبدأ بالكفن ثم الدين ثم الوصية ثم الميراث.

ومن حاز دارا عن حاضر عشر سنين تنسب إليه وصاحبها حاضر عالم لا يدعى شيئا فلا قيام له. ولا حيازة بين الأقارب والأصهار في مثل هذه المدة.

ولا يجوز إقرار المريض لوارثه بدين أو بقبضه.

ومن أوصى بحج أنفذ، والوصية بالصدقة أحب إلينا. وإذا مات أجير الحج قبل أن يصل فله بحساب ما سار ويرد ما بقي، وما هلك بيده فهو منه إلا أن يأخذ المال على أن ينفق على البلاغ، فالضمان من الذين واجروه، ويرد ما فضل إن فضل شيء.

39. Shares of Inheritance

There are only ten male heirs: the son, the son's son – to the furthest generation, the father, the paternal grandfather – to the furthest generation, the brother and the son of the brother – to the furthest generation, the paternal uncle and the son of the paternal uncle – to the furthest generation, the husband and the male client. There are only seven female heirs: daughter, daughter of the son, mother, grandmother, sister, wife and female client.

If a wife has no children or grandchildren, the husband inherits half her estate. If she has children or grandchildren by him or by another husband, he gets a quarter. If a husband has no children or grandchildren, the wife inherits a quarter. If he has children or grandchildren by her or by another wife, she gets an eighth. A mother inherits a third from her son if he leaves neither child nor grandchild or two or more brothers, except in two cases: first, when someone leaves a wife and both parents and then the wife gets a quarter and the mother a third of what remains, and the rest goes to the father; second, when a woman leaves a husband and both parents and then the husband gets a half and the mother a third of what remains and the rest is taken by the father. In other cases, the mother receives a third unless her share is decreased by *'awl* (adjustment) except if the deceased leaves a child or grandchild through a son, or two or more brothers, of whatever sort, then the mother receives a sixth.

If the father is the only heir, he inherits the entire estate of his child. If the deceased has a son or grandson by the son, the father takes a

٣٩ - باب في الفرائض

ولا يرث من الرجال إلا عشرة: الابن، وابن الابن وإن سفل، والأب، والجد للأب وإن علا، والأخ، وابن الأخ وإن بعد، والعم، وابن العم وإن بعد، والزوج، ومولى النعمة. ولا يرث من النساء غير سبع: البنت، وبنت الابن ، والأم، والجدة، والأخت، والزوجة، ومولاة النعمة.

فميراث الزوج من الزوجة إن لم تترك ولدا ولا ولد ابن النصف، فإن تركت ولدا أو ولد ابن منه أو من غيره فله الربع. وترث هي منه الربع إن لم يكن له ولد ولا ولد ابن، فإن كان له ولد أو ولد ابن منها أو من غيرها فلها الثمن. وميراث الأم من ابنها الثلث إن لم يترك ولدا أو ولد ابن أواثنين من الإخوة ما كانوا فصاعدا، إلا في فريضتين: في زوجة وأبوين، فللزوجة الربع وللأم ثلث ما بقي، وما بقي للأب، وفي زوج وأبوين ، فللزوج النصف، وللأم ثلث ما بقي وما بقي للأب، ولها في غير ذلك الثلث إلا ما نقصها العول، إلا أن يكون للميت ولد أو ولد ابن أو اثنان من الإخوة ما كانا فلها السدس حينئذ.

وميراث الأب من ولده إذا انفرد ورث المال كله، ويفرض له مع الولد الذكر أو ولد الابن السدس، فإن لم يكن له ولد ولا ولد ابن

sixth. If the deceased has neither child nor grandson by the son, the father gets a sixth and all the others entitled to shares are given their shares and then he takes the rest. An only son inherits the entire estate, or he takes what is left after the shares of those entitled to a share, such as a wife, parents, or grandfather or grandmother. A son's son is in the position of the son if the son has died.

If there are a son and a daughter, the male receives twice the share of the female. It is the same whether there are several or few sons and daughters. They inherit at this ratio either the entire estate or what is left after people take their shares. The son of a son is like the son in his absence in respect of inheritance and exclusion of other heirs. An only daughter inherits half the estate. Two daughters inherit two-thirds of it. If there are more, they do not receive more than two-thirds. The daughter of a son is like a daughter when there is no daughter. Similarly, the son's daughters are like daughters when the deceased himself has no daughters.

If there is a daughter and the daughter of a son, the daughter gets one half and the daughter of the son gets a sixth to complete the two-thirds. If the son has several daughters, they do not get more than the sixth if they have no brother with them. The remainder goes to the agnates. If there are two daughters, then the daughters of the son get nothing unless they have a brother. In that case the remainder of the estate is divided between them, the male getting twice the share of the females. When there is a male in the generation below them, the estate is also shared between him and them.

It is the same if the daughters of the son inherit a sixth with the daughter, and in the generation below them there are daughters of a son or in the generation below them a male: the residual estate is shared between him and his sisters or paternal aunts in the same way.

فرض للأب السدس وأعطي من شركة من أهل السهام سهامهم، ثم كان له ما بقي. وميراث الولد الذكر جميع المال إن كان وحده، أو يأخذ ما بقي بعد سهام من معه من زوجة وأبوين أو جد أو جدة. وابن الابن بمنزلة الابن إذا لم يكن ابن.

فإن كان ابن وابنة فللذكر مثل حظ الأنثيين، وكذلك في كثرة البنين والبنات وقلتهم، يرثون كذلك جميع المال أو ما فضل منه بعد من شركهم من أهل السهام. وابن الابن كالابن في عدمه فيما يرث ويحجب. وميراث البنت الواحدة النصف، والاثنتين الثلثان، فإن كثرن لم يزدن على الثلثين شيئا. وابنة الابن كالبنت إذا لم تكن بنت، وكذلك بناته كالبنات في عدم البنات.

فإن كانت ابنة وابنة ابن فللابنة النصف ولابنة الابن السدس تمام الثلثين، وإن كثرت بنات الابن لم يزدن على ذلك السدس شيئا، إن لم يكن معهن ذكر، وما بقي للعصبة. وإن كانت البنات اثنتين لم يكن لبنات الابن شيء إلا أن يكون معهن أخ، فيكون ما بقي بينهن وبينه للذكر مثل حظ الأنثيين، وكذلك إذا كان ذلك الذكر تحتهن كان ذلك بينه وبينهن كذلك.

وكذلك لو ورث بنات الابن مع الابنة السدس وتحتهن بنات ابن معهن أو تحتهن ذكر كان ذلك بينه وبين أخواته أو من فوقه من عماته، ولا يدخل في ذلك من دخل في الثلثين من بنات الابن.

The daughters of the son who take a share in the two-thirds have no share in the residual estate.

A full sister inherits half. Two or more sisters share in two-thirds. If there are several full or consanguine brothers and sisters, then the entire property is divided between them, with the male receiving the share of two females, whether they are many or few. If there are daughters, then the sisters become like the *'aṣabah* (agnates) inheriting what is left over, but they are not enriched at the daughters' expense. Brothers and sisters receive no inheritance when there is a father or a son or a grandson. In the absence of full siblings, consanguine siblings are like full siblings, both male and female.

If there is a full sister and one or more consanguine sisters, the full sister gets half and the remaining sisters share in the sixth. If there are two full sisters, the half-sisters receive nothing unless there is a brother with them. Then they take whatever remains, with the male receiving the share of two females. The inheritance of a uterine sister and brother is the same: a sixth, the same for either. If there are several of them, then the third is shared between them, each receiving the same amount. They are excluded from the inheritance by a child and his or her children, a father, or a paternal grandfather.

A brother inherits the entire estate if he is the sole heir, if he is a full brother or has the same father (consanguine). A full brother excludes a consanguine brother. If there are one or more brothers and sisters, full or consanguine, then the estate is shared between them, with the male having twice the share of a female. If there are those entitled to specific shares as well as the brother, one begins with those with specific shares and he takes what is left. Similarly what remains goes to the brothers and sisters, with a male receiving twice the share of a female. If nothing is left, they receive nothing unless there are uterine

وميراث الأخت الشقيقة النصف، والاثنتين فصاعدا الثلثان، فإن كانوا إخوة وأخوات شقائق أو لأب فالمال بينهم للذكر مثل حظ الأنثيين، قلوا أو كثروا. والأخوات مع البنات كالعصبة لهن، يرثن ما فضل عنهن، ولا يربى لهن معهن. ولا ميراث للإخوة والأخوات مع الأب ولا مع الولد الذكر، أو مع ولد الولد. والإخوة للأب في عدم الشقائق كالشقائق ذكورهم وإناثهم.

فإن كانت أخت شقيقة وأخت أو أخوات لأب فالنصف للشقيقة، ولمن بقي من الأخوات للأب السدس، ولو كانتا شقيقتين لم يكن للأخوات للأب شيء إلا أن يكون معهن ذكر فيأخذون ما بقي للذكر مثل حظ الأنثيين. وميراث الأخت للأم والأخ للأم سواء السدس لكل واحد، وإن كثروا فالثلث بينهم، الذكر والأنثى فيه سواء، ويحجبهم عن الميراث الولد وبنوه والأب والجد للأب.

والأخ يرث المال إذا انفرد، كان شقيقا أو لأب، والشقيق يحجب الأخ للأب، وإن كان أخ وأخت فأكثر شقائق أو لأب فالمال بينهم للذكر مثل حظ الأنثيين ، وإن كان مع الأخ ذو سهم بديء بأهل السهام وكان له ما بقي، وكذلك يكون ما بقي للإخوة والأخوات للذكر مثل حظ الأنثيين، فإن لم يبق شيء فلا شيء لهم إلا أن يكون في أهل السهام إخوة لأم قد ورثوا الثلث، وقد بقي

brothers among the people of shares who inherited a third. Then any full siblings, male and female, share equally with the uterine brothers in their third. This share is called "shared" (*mushtarikah*). Consanguine brothers do not share with uterine brothers because they do not have the same mother. If there remain any full or consanguine brothers or sisters, accommodation is made for them.

If there is only one uterine brother or sister, the case is not *mushtarikah*. The residual estate goes to the siblings whether they are males, or males and females. If there are only full or consanguine sisters, there is adjustment made for them. A consanguine brother is like a full brother in the absence of a full brother, except in the case of *mushtarikah*. The son of a brother is like the brother in the absence of the brother, whether he is a full or consanguine brother. The son of a uterine brother does not inherit. A full brother excludes a consanguine brother, but a consanguine brother takes precedence over the son of a full brother. The son of a full brother takes precedence over the son of a consanguine brother.

A son of a consanguine brother excludes a full paternal uncle. A full paternal uncle excludes a consanguine paternal uncle. A consanguine paternal uncle excludes the son of a full paternal uncle. The son of a full paternal uncle excludes the son of a consanguine paternal uncle. So the nearer relative always has the greater entitlement.

Those who do not inherit include the children of sisters of whatever sort, the sons of daughters, the daughters of a brother of whatever sort, the daughters of a paternal uncle, the maternal grandfather, and a uterine paternal uncle. A slave does not inherit, nor does a slave who is in the process of being freed. A Muslim does not inherit from

أخ شقيق أو إخوة ذكور أو ذكور وإناث شقائق معهم فيشاركون كلهم الإخوة للأم في ثلثهم فيكون بينهم بالسواء، وهي الفريضة التي تسمى المشتركة، ولو كان من بقي إخوة لأب لم يشاركوا الإخوة للأم لخروجهم عن ولادة الأم، وإن كان من بقي أختا أو أخوات لأبوين أو لأب أعيل لهن.

وإن كان من قبل الأم أخ واحد أو أخت لم تكن مشتركة، وكان ما بقي للإخوة إن كانوا ذكورا أو ذكورا وإناثا، وإن كن إناثا لأبوين أو لأب أعيل لهن. والأخ للأب كالشقيق في عدم الشقيق إلا في المشتركة. وابن الأخ كالأخ في عدم الأخ، كان شقيقا أو لأب، ولا يرث ابن الأخ للأم. والأخ للأبوين يحجب الأخ للأب، والأخ للأب أولى من ابن أخ شقيق.

وابن أخ شقيق أولى من ابن أخ لأب، وابن أخ لأب يحجب عما لأبوين. وعم لأبوين يحجب عما لأب، وعم لأب يحجب ابن عم لأبوين، وابن عم لأبوين يحجب ابن عم لأب، وهكذا يكون الأقرب أولى.

ولا يرث بنو الأخوات ما كن، ولا بنو البنات، ولا بنات الأخ ما كان، ولا بنات العم، ولا جد لأم، ولا أخو أبيك لأمه، ولا يرث عبد، ولا من فيه بقية رق، ولا يرث المسلم الكافر، ولا الكافر

an unbeliever nor an unbeliever from a Muslim. Others who do not inherit are the son of a uterine brother, the maternal grandfather and the mother of the maternal grandfather. Nor does the paternal grandmother inherit along with her son, the father of the deceased. Uterine brothers do not inherit if there is a paternal grandfather, nor if there are sons or daughters or grandchildren through a son. Siblings of any sort do not inherit if there is a father. A paternal uncle does not inherit if there is a paternal grandfather nor the son of a brother if there is a paternal grandfather.

A murderer does not inherit either the estate or blood money. Someone guilty of accidental homicide does not inherit any of the blood money, but does inherit from the estate. Anyone who does not inherit for some reason cannot then exclude another heir. A woman who has been trebly divorced in the final illness of her husband inherits from her husband, but if she dies first, he does not inherit from her. The same ruling applies if the divorce was a single one and he dies of that illness after her *'iddah* has finished. If someone in good health pronounces a single divorce against his wife, they still inherit from one another as long as she is still in her *'iddah*. If the *'iddah* has finished, they do not inherit from one another. If a man marries in his illness, the couple do not inherit from one another.

A maternal grandmother inherits a sixth as does a paternal grandmother. If there are both of them, then the sixth is shared between them, unless the maternal grandmother is a degree closer, in which case she is more entitled to it because there is a text about her. If it is the paternal grandmother who is closer, then the sixth is shared between them. According to Mālik, only two grandmothers inherit: the father's mother and the mother's mother or their respective mothers. Zayd ibn Thābit is reported to have allowed three grandmothers to inherit: one on the mother's side and two on

المسلم، ولا ابن أخ لأم، ولا جد لأم، ولا أم أبي الأم. ولا ترث أم الأب مع ولدها أبي الميت، ولا ترث إخوة لأم مع الجد للأب، ولا مع الولد، وولد الولد ذكرا كان الولد أو أنثى، ولا ميراث للإخوة مع الأب ما كانوا، ولا يرث عم مع الجد، ولا ابن أخ مع الجد.

ولا يرث قاتل العمد من مال ولا دية، ولا يرث قاتل الخطإ من الدية ويرث من المال، وكل من لا يرث بحال فلا يحجب وارثا. والمطلقة ثلاثا في المرض ترث زوجها إن مات من مرضه ذلك، ولا يرثها، وكذلك إن كان الطلاق واحدة وقد مات من مرضه ذلك بعد العدة. وإن طلق الصحيح امرأته طلقة واحدة فإنهما يتوارثان ما كانت في العدة، فإن انقضت فلا ميراث بينهما بعدها. ومن تزوج امرأة في مرضه لم ترثه ولا يرثها.

وترث الجدة للأم السدس، وكذلك التي للأب، فإن اجتمعتا فالسدس بينهما إلا أن تكون التي للأم أقرب بدرجة فتكون أولى به لأنها التي فيها النص، وإن كانت التي للأب أقربهما فالسدس بينهما نصفين. ولا يرث عند مالك أكثر من جدتين: أم الأب وأم الأم وأمهاتهما. ويذكر عن زيد بن ثابت أنه ورث ثلاث جدات. واحدة من قبل الأم، واثنتين من قبل الأب، وأم أبي الأب، ولم يحفظ

the father's side: the father's mother and the mother of the father's father. None of the Caliphs is reported to have allowed more than two grandmothers to inherit.

If there is only the paternal grandfather, he takes the entire estate. If there is also a son or a son's son, the paternal grandfather takes a sixth. If there are people with specific shares other than brothers and sisters, he is given a sixth. If there is anything left over, it is his. If there are also brothers along with the people of shares, the grandfather has three choices and he can select whichever he prefers, i.e. whichever is best for him. He can share with the brothers, take a sixth of the total estate, or take a third of the residue. If there are only brothers inheriting with him, he shares with them if it is one or two brothers, or what is their equivalent: four sisters. If there are more than two brothers, he takes a third. So when inheriting with brothers, he takes a third, or he divides the estate with them, whichever seems better for him.

Consanguine brothers inherit with the grandfather in the same manner as full brothers if there are no full brothers. If there are both full brothers and consanguine brothers, the full brothers may count the consanguine brothers with them to reduce the share of the grandfather. Then they are more entitled than them to that. An exception is when there is, in addition to the grandfather, a full sister who has a consanguine brother or sister or both. She takes her half of the estate and surrenders what is left to them. Sisters are not enriched at the expense of the grandfather, except in the case of *al-gharrā'* which will be explained later.

When the *mawlā* (emancipator) is the only heir, he or she inherits all of the estate, whether the emancipator is a man or a woman. If there are people with shares as well, then the emancipator takes what is left after they have taken their shares. An emancipator inherits nothing when there are agnates (*'aṣabah*), but he is more entitled than

عن الخلفاء توريث أكثر من جدتين.

وميراث الجد إذا انفرد فله المال، وله مع الولد الذكر أو مع ولد الذكر السدس، فإن شركه أحد من أهل السهام غير الإخوة والأخوات فليقض له بالسدس، فإن بقي شيء من المال كان له، فإن كان مع أهل السهام إخوة فالجد مخير في ثلاثة أوجه، يأخذ أي ذلك أفضل له. إما مقاسمة الإخوة أو السدس من رأس المال، أو ثلث ما بقي، فإن لم يكن معه غير الإخوة فهو يقاسم أخا أو أخوين أو عدلهما أربع أخوات، فإن زادوا فله الثلث، فهو يرث الثلث مع الإخوة إلا أن تكون المقاسمة أفضل له.

والإخوة للأب معه في عدم الشقائق كالشقائق، فإن اجتمعوا عاده الشقائق بالذين للأب فمنعوه بهم كثرة الميراث، ثم كانوا أحق منهم بذلك، إلا أن يكون مع الجد أخت شقيقة ولها أخ لأب أو أخت لأب أو أخ وأخت لأب فتأخذ نصفها مما حصل، وتسلم ما بقي إليهم، ولا يربى للأخوات مع الجد إلا في الغراء وحدها، وسنذكرها بعد هذا.

ويرث المولى الأعلى إذا انفرد جميع المال، رجلا أو امرأة. فإن كان معه أهل سهم كان للمولى ما بقي بعد أهل السهام، ولا يرث المولى مع العصبة، وهو أحق من ذوي الأرحام الذين لا سهم لهم في

uterine relatives, who have no share in the Book of Allah Almighty. Only uterine relatives who have a share in the Book of Allah inherit. A woman only inherits by *walā'* from those she herself set free, or through subsequent freeing or childbirth (by the slave she set free).

When the combined shares known in the Book of Allah are more than the estate, then all of them are reduced proportionately.

There is no adjustment (*'awl*) for a sister when there is a grandfather, except in the *gharrā'* case, which is when a woman dies leaving a husband, mother, full or consanguine sister and a paternal grandfather. The husband gets half, the mother a third, and the grandfather a sixth. Since the estate is exhausted, there must be adjustment for the sister's share of a half, which is three. Then the share of the grandfather is added to her share, and the total of that is divided between them in thirds. She has a third and he has two-thirds, and so there are twenty-seven shares.

كتاب الله عز وجل. ولا يرث من ذوي الأرحام إلا من له سهم في كتاب الله، ولا يرث النساء من الولاء إلا ما أعتقن أو جره من أعتقن إليهن بولادة أو عتق.

وإذا اجتمع من له سهم معلوم في كتاب الله وكان ذلك أكثر من المال أدخل عليهم كلهم الضر، وقسمت الفريضة على مبلغ سهامهم. ولا يعال للأخت مع الجد إلا في الغراء وحدها، وهي امرأة تركت زوجها وأمها وأختها لأبوين أو لأب، وجدها، فللزوج النصف، وللأم الثلث، وللجد السدس، فلما فرغ المال أعيل للأخت بالنصف ثلاثة، ثم جمع إليها سهم الجد فيقسم جميع ذلك بينهما على الثلث لها والثلثين له، فتبلغ سبعة وعشرين سهما.

40. A GENERAL CHAPTER ON THE LEGAL STATUS OF VARIOUS PRACTICES

Wuḍū' for the prayer is obligatory. It is derived from *waḍā'ah* (cleanliness). However, the rinsing of the mouth, inhaling water through the nose and wiping of the ears in it are *sunnah*. *Siwāk* is recommended and desired. Wiping over leather socks is an allowance (*rukhṣah*) and dispensation.

Ghusl on account of *janābah*, menstruation and lochia is obligatory. The *ghusl* on *Jumu'ah* is *sunnah*. A *ghusl* for the two *'Īd*s is recommended. It is obligatory for someone who becomes Muslim to perform *ghusl*, because he is in *janābah*. *Ghusl* for the dead is a *sunnah*.

The five prayers are obligatory, as is saying the *takbīr al-iḥrām*. The rest of the *takbīr*s are *sunnah*. Beginning the prayer with the intention of performing the obligation is obligatory. Raising the hands is *sunnah*. Recitation of the *Fātiḥah* in the prayer is obligatory and reciting more of the Qur'an is a mandatory *sunnah*. Standing, bowing and prostration are obligatory. The first sitting is *sunnah* and the second is obligatory. Saying the *salām* is obligatory and turning the head to right a little while saying it is *sunnah*. Not speaking in the prayer is obligatory and the *tashahhud* is *sunnah*. The *qunūt* in the *Ṣubḥ* prayer is good, but not *sunnah*. Facing *qiblah* is obligatory.

The *Jumu'ah* prayer and going to it are obligatory. The *witr* prayer is a mandatory *sunnah*, as are the two *'Īd* prayers, the eclipse prayer, the rain prayer, and the fear prayer. The fear prayer is a mandatory *sunnah* since Allah Almighty commanded it. It is an act by which those doing

٤٠ - باب جمل من الفرائض والسنن الواجبة والرغائب

الوضوء للصلاة فريضة، وهو مشتق من الوضاءة، إلا المضمضة والاستنشاق ومسح الأذنين منه فإن ذلك سنة. والسواك مستحب مرغب فيه. والمسح على الخفين رخصة وتخفيف.

والغسل من الجنابة ودم الحيض والنفاس فريضة. وغسل الجمعة سنة، وغسل العيدين مستحب، والغسل على من أسلم فريضة لأنه جنب، وغسل الميت سنة.

والصلوات الخمس فريضة. وتكبيرة الإحرام فريضة، وباقي التكبير سنة، والدخول في الصلاة بنية الفرض فريضة، ورفع اليدين سنة، والقراءة بأم القرآن في الصلاة فريضة، وما زاد عليها سنة واجبة، والقيام والركوع والسجود فريضة، والجلسة الأولى سنة، والثانية فريضة، والسلام فريضة، والتيامن به قليلا سنة، وترك الكلام في الصلاة فريضة، والتشهدان سنة، والقنوت في الصبح حسن وليس بسنة، واستقبال القبلة فريضة.

وصلاة الجمعة والسعي إليها فريضة، والوتر سنة واجبة، وكذلك صلاة العيدين والخسوف والاستسقاء. وصلاة الخوف واجبة أمر الله سبحانه وتعالى بها، وهو فعل يستدركون به فضل الجماعة. والغسل

it obtain the excellence of the group prayer. It is recommended to have a *ghusl* before entering Makkah.

Joining prayers on a rainy night is a dispensation. The Rightly-guided Caliphs did it. Joining the prayers at 'Arafah and Muzdalifah is a mandatory *sunnah*. A traveller joining prayers during a strenuous journey is an allowance. A sick person joining prayers when he fears he will lose consciousness is a concession. The same applies to joining them because it is easier for one. Not fasting while travelling is an allowance and shortening the prayer while travelling is mandatory.

The two *rak'ats* of *Fajr* are desirable, and it is said that they are *sunnah*. The *Ḍuḥā* prayer is supererogatory. Praying at night in Ramadan is supererogatory and there is great virtue in it. If someone does it with faith and in anticipation of a reward, he will be forgiven his past wrong actions. Praying at night in Ramadan and other times is desirable and supererogatory. The prayer over dead Muslims is obligatory but the duty is satisfied by those who perform it. The same applies to taking them to burial. Washing them is a mandatory *sunnah*. The same is true of seeking knowledge. It is a general obligation which is satisfied by those who perform it except for that knowledge which is obliged individually for a person.

The obligation of *jihād* is general and is satisfied by those who perform it, unless the enemy attack the settlement of a people in which case it become obligatory for them to fight them provided the enemy are not twice their number or more. *Ribāṭ* at the frontiers of the Muslims and defending them and fortifying them is mandatory but the duty is satisfied by those who undertake this.

Fasting the month of Ramadan is an obligation. *I'tikāf* is supererogatory. Voluntary fasting is desirable. It is desirable to fast the day of 'Āshūrā', the month of Rajab, the month of Sha'bān, the

لدخول مكة مستحب.

والجمع ليلة المطر تخفيف، وقد فعله الخلفاء الراشدون. والجمع بعرفة والمزدلفة سنة واجبة، وجمع المسافر في جد السير رخصة، وجمع المريض يخاف أن يغلب على عقله تخفيف، وكذلك جمعه لعلة به فيكون ذلك أرفق به، والفطر في السفر رخصة، والإقصار فيه واجب.

وركعتا الفجر من الرغائب، وقيل من السنن، وصلاة الضحى نافلة، وكذلك قيام رمضان نافلة، وفيه فضل كبير، ومن قامه إيمانا واحتسابا غفر له ما تقدم من ذنبه، والقيام من الليل في رمضان وغيره من النوافل المرغب فيها. والصلاة على موتى المسلمين فريضة يحملها من قام بها، وكذلك مواراتهم بالدفن، وغسلهم سنة واجبة، وكذلك طلب العلم فريضة عامة يحملها من قام بها إلا ما يلزم الرجل في خاصة نفسه.

وفريضة الجهاد عامة يحملها من قام بها إلا أن يغشى العدو محلة قوم فيجب فرضا عليهم قتالهم إذا كانوا مثلي عددهم، والرباط في ثغور المسلمين وسدها وحياطتها واجب يحمله من قام به.

وصوم شهر رمضان فريضة، والاعتكاف نافلة، والتنفل بالصوم مرغب فيه، وكذلك صوم يوم عاشوراء، ورجب وشعبان ويوم

day of 'Arafah and the Day of Tarwiyah. Fasting the Day of 'Arafah is better for someone not performing *ḥajj* than for the one on *ḥajj*.

Zakāt on money, crops and livestock is obligatory. The *zakāt al-fiṭr* is a *sunnah* made obligatory by the Messenger of Allah ﷺ.

Making *ḥajj* to the House is obligatory and *'umrah* is a mandatory *sunnah*. The *talbiyah* is a mandatory *sunnah*. The intention to perform the *ḥajj* is obligatory. *Ṭawāf al-Ifāḍah* is obligatory and the *sā'y* between Ṣafā and Marwah is obligatory. The *ṭawāf* connected to it is mandatory but the *Ṭawāf al-Ifāḍah* is more stressed than it. The *Ṭawāf* of Farewell is *sunnah*. Spending the night at Minā on the Night before 'Arafah is *sunnah*. Joining prayers at 'Arafah is mandatory and standing at 'Arafah is obligatory. Spending the night at Muzdalifah is a mandatory *sunnah*. Stopping at the Mash'ar al-Ḥarām is commanded. Stoning the *jamrah*s is a mandatory *sunnah*. That is also true of shaving the head. Kissing the Black Stone is a mandatory *sunnah*. A *ghusl* for assuming *iḥrām* is *sunnah* and two *rak'at*s at that time is *sunnah*. A *ghusl* at 'Arafah is *sunnah* and a *ghusl* for entering Makkah is recommended.

Doing the prayer in a group is twenty-seven times better than praying alone. Only praying in the Masjid al-Ḥarām and the Mosque of the Messenger ﷺ are better than praying in other mosques. There is disagreement about the difference in the amount of excellence between the Masjid al-Ḥarām and the Mosque of the Messenger ﷺ. There is no disagreement that praying in the Mosque of the Messenger ﷺ is better than a thousand prayers in any mosque other than the Masjid al-Ḥarām. The people of Madīnah say that the prayer in the Prophet's Mosque is better than the prayer in the Masjid al-Ḥarām, but less than a thousand times better. This is all about obligatory prayers. As for voluntary prayers, they are better done at home. We

عرفة والتروية، وصوم يوم عرفة لغير الحاج أفضل منه للحاج.

وزكاة العين والحرث والماشية فريضة، وزكاة الفطر سنة فرضها رسول الله صلى الله عليه وسلم.

وحج البيت فريضة، والعمرة سنة واجبة، والتلبية سنة واجبة، والنية بالحج فريضة، والطواف للإفاضة فريضة، والسعي بين الصفا والمروة فريضة، والطواف المتصل به واجب، وطواف الإفاضة آكد منه، والطواف للوداع سنة، والمبيت بمنى ليلة عرفة سنة، والجمع بعرفة واجب، والوقوف بعرفة فريضة، ومبيت المزدلفة سنة واجبة، ووقوف المشعر الحرام مأمور به، ورمي الجمار سنة واجبة، وكذلك الحلاق، وتقبيل الركن سنة واجبة، والغسل للإحرام سنة، والركوع عند الإحرام سنة، وغسل عرفة سنة، والغسل لدخول مكة مستحب.

والصلاة في الجماعة أفضل من صلاة الفذ بسبع وعشرين درجة، والصلاة في المسجد الحرام ومسجد الرسول صلى الله عليه وسلم فذا أفضل من الصلاة في سائر المساجد، واختلف في مقدار التضعيف بذلك بين المسجد الحرام ومسجد الرسول عليه الصلاة والسلام، ولم يختلف أن الصلاة في مسجد الرسول صلى الله عليه وسلم أفضل من ألف صلاة فيما سواه وسوى المسجد الحرام من المساجد، وأهل المدينة يقولون: إن الصلاة فيه أفضل من الصلاة في المسجد الحرام

prefer the people of Makkah to do supererogatory prayers rather than *ṭawāf*, but *ṭawāf* is better than the prayer for visitors because of the little opportunity they have to do it.

It is an obligation to lower the eye and not look at forbidden women, but there is no harm in the first glance when it is not deliberate, nor in looking at a woman who does not provoke desire, nor in looking at a young woman for a legitimate reason, such as identifying her and the like. There is a similar allowance for someone proposing marriage.

It is an obligation to guard one's tongue from lying, perjury, obscene language, backbiting, gossiping, and all falsehood. The Messenger ﷺ, said, "Anyone who believes in Allah and the Last Day should speak well or be silent." The Prophet ﷺ said, "Part of the excellence of a person's Islam is his leaving alone what does not concern him."

Allah Almighty has made the blood of Muslims, their property and their honour inviolable except when there is a right involved. The life of a Muslim is not lawful unless he reneges after belief, commits illicit sex after he is *muḥṣan*, kills someone when it is not a case of retaliation, or engages in corruption in the earth or renounces the *dīn*.

You should keep your hands away from what is not lawful to you in respect of property, body or blood. Do not let your feet move after what is not lawful for you. Do not let your private parts, or any part of your body, touch what is not lawful for you. Allah Almighty says, "*those who guard their private parts – except from their wives or those they own as slaves, in which case they are not blameworthy; but those who desire anything more than that are people who have gone beyond the limits.*" (23:5-7) Allah has forbidden obscenity, whether open or secret, and approaching women sexually when they are bleeding from

بدون الألف، وهذا كله في الفرائض، وأما النوافل ففي البيوت أفضل، والتنفل بالركوع لأهل مكة أحب إلينا من الطواف، والطواف للغرباء أحب إلينا من الركوع لقلة وجود ذلك لهم.

ومن الفرائض غض البصر عن المحارم، وليس في النظرة الأولى بغير تعمد حرج، ولا في النظر إلى المتجالة، ولا في النظر إلى الشابة لعذر من شهادة عليها وشبهه، وقد أرخص في ذلك للخاطب.

ومن الفرائض صون اللسان عن الكذب والزور والفحشاء والغيبة والنميمة والباطل كله. قال الرسول عليه الصلاة والسلام: من كان يؤمن بالله واليم الآخر فليقل خيرا أو ليصمت. وقال عليه الصلاة والسلام: من حسن إسلام المرء تركه ما لا يعنيه.

وحرم الله سبحانه دماء المسلمين وأموالهم وأعراضهم إلا بحقها. ولا يحل دم امرئ مسلم إلا أن يكفر بعد إيمانه، أو يزني بعد إحصانه، أو يقتل نفسا بغير نفس، أو فساد في الأرض، أو يمرق من الدين.

ولتكف يدك عما لا يحل لك من مال أو جسد أو دم، ولا تسع بقدميك فيما لا يحل لك، ولا تباشر بفرجك أو بشيء من جسدك ما لا يحل لك. قال الله سبحانه: ﴿ والذين هم لفروجهم حافظون﴾. إلى قوله ﴿ فأولئك هم العادون﴾. وحرم الله سبحانه الفواحش ما ظهر منها وما بطن، وأن يقرب النساء في دم حيضهن أو نفاسهن. وحرم من النساء ما تقدم ذكرنا إياه.

menstruation or lochia. He has forbidden marriage to the women who were already mentioned.

Allah commanded eating what is good, which is the lawful. It is only lawful for you to eat what is lawful or to wear what is lawful or to ride what is lawful or live in what is lawful. Everything else which you use must also be lawful. Besides good things there are doubtful things. If someone leaves them, he is safe, and if someone takes them, he is like someone who grazes around a private preserve: he is likely to stray into it.

Allah has forbidden taking property under false pretences. False acquisition includes misappropriation, transgression, treachery, usury, bribery, gambling, risk, adulteration, deceit and duping.

Allah has forbidden carrion, blood, pork and what is hallowed to other than Allah and what is sacrificed to other than Allah, and that whose death has been caused by falling from a mountain or being hit with a stick or something else, or strangled with a rope or something else. That is unless there is dire need of such meat, such as carrion. When an animal reaches a state after which it cannot live due to those reasons, then there is no slaughter of it. There is no harm in someone compelled by necessity eating carrion and having his fill and taking provision from it. When he has no further need of it, then he must throw it away.

There is no harm in using the skin of carrion when it has been tanned, but one should not pray on it nor sell it. There is no harm in praying on the skins of beasts of prey when they have been slaughtered, and they can be sold. The wool and hair of carrion are used as well as what is removed from them while alive. We prefer that it be washed. Its feathers, horns, claws or teeth may not be used. It is disliked to use the tusks of elephants. Every part of a pig is forbidden, but there is an allowance to use its hair (bristles).

وأمر بأكل الطيب وهو الحلال، فلا يحل لك أن تأكل إلا طيبا، ولا تلبس إلا طيبا، ولا تركب إلا طيبا، ولا تسكن إلا طيبا، وتستعمل سائر ما تنتفع به طيبا. ومن وراء ذلك مشتبهات، من تركها سلم، ومن أخذها كان كالراتع حول الحمى يوشك أن يقع فيه.

وحرم الله سبحانه أكل المال بالباطل. ومن الباطل: الغصب والتعدي والخيانة والربا والسحت والقمار والغرر والغش والخديعة والخلابة. وحرم الله سبحانه أكل الميتة والدم ولحم الخنزير وما أهل لغير الله به، وما ذبح لغير الله، وما أعان على موته ترد من جبل، أو وقذة بعصا أو غيرها، والمنخنقة بحبل أو غيره إلا أن يضطر إلى ذلك كالميتة، وذلك إذا صارت بذلك إلى حال لا حياة بعدها فلا ذكاة فيها. ولا بأس للمضطر أن يأكل الميتة ويشبع ويتزود، فإن استغنى عنها طرحها.

ولا بأس بالانتفاع بجلدها إذا دبغ، ولا يصلى عليه ولا يباع، ولا بأس بالصلاة على جلود السباع إذا ذكيت وبيعها. وينتفع بصوف الميتة وشعرها وما ينزع منها في الحياة، وأحب إلينا أن يغسل، ولا ينتفع بريشها ولا بقرنها وأظلافها وأنيابها. وكره الانتفاع بأنياب الفيل، وكل شيء من الخنزير حرام. وقد أرخص في الانتفاع بشعره.

Allah has forbidden the drinking of wine, either a little or a lot of it. The drink of the Arabs at that time was date wine. The Messenger ﷺ made it clear that if a lot of something intoxicates, then a little of it is unlawful. Any drink which drugs the mind and intoxicates it, whatever it is, is considered to be 'wine'. Furthermore, the Messenger ﷺ, said, "The One who made it unlawful to drink it also made it unlawful to sell it." The Messenger ﷺ also forbade mixing drinks, whether they are mixed when they are set aside for fermentation or are mixed when they are drunk. He forbade storing/fermenting juices in gourds or in pitch-lined containers.

The Messenger ﷺ forbade eating every animal with fangs and the meat of domestic donkeys. Included with donkeys is horse meat and the meat of mules since Allah Almighty says, "*both to ride and for adornment.*" (16:8) None of these are slaughtered except wild asses. There is nothing wrong in eating birds of prey and those with talons.

It is an obligation to be dutiful to one's parents, even if they are evildoers or idolaters. One should speak kindly to them and keep their company with correct politeness, but, as Allah Almighty states, not obey them in disobedience to Allah. A believer must ask for forgiveness for his parents if they are believers.

A believer must always protect believers and give them good advice. No one reaches the reality of faith until "he loves for his brother believer what he loves for himself." That is related from the Messenger of Allah ﷺ. He must maintain ties with his relatives. A believer must greet another believer when he meets him, visit him when he is ill, wish him well when he sneezes, attend his funeral when he dies and defend him when he is absent, publicly and in secret. One must not shun one's brother for more than three days. Greeting ends the shunning, but he should not leave off speaking to him after the

وحرم الله سبحانه شرب الخمر قليلها وكثيرها، وشراب العرب يومئذ فضيخ التمر، وبين الرسول عليه السلام أن كل ما أسكر كثيره من الأشربة فقليله حرام. وكل ما خامر العقل فأسكره من كل شراب فهو خمر. وقال الرسول عليه الصلاة والسلام: إن الذي حرم شربها حرم بيعها. ونهى عن الخليطين من الأشربة، وذلك أن يخلطا عند الانتباذ وعند الشرب، ونهى عن الانتباذ في الدباء والمزفت.

ونهى عليه السلام عن أكل كل ذي ناب من السباع، وعن أكل لحوم الحمر الأهلية، ودخل مدخلها لحوم الخيل والبغال، لقول الله تبارك وتعالى: ﴿لتركبوها وزينة﴾. ولا ذكاة في شيء منها إلا في الحمر الوحشية. ولا بأس بأكل سباع الطير وكل ذي مخلب منها.

ومن الفرائض بر الوالدين، وإن كانا فاسقين، وإن كانا مشركين فليقل لهما قولا لينا وليعاشرهما بالمعروف، ولا يطعهما في معصية، كما قال الله سبحانه وتعالى. وعلى المؤمن أن يستغفر لأبويه المؤمنين.

وعليه موالاة المؤمنين، والصيحة لهم. ولا يبلغ أحد حقيقة الإيمان حتى يحب لأخيه المؤمن ما يحب لنفسه، كذلك روي عن رسول الله صلى الله عليه وسلم. وعليه أن يصل رحمه. ومن حق المؤمن على المؤمن أن يسلم عليه إذا لقيه، ويعوده إذا مرض، ويشمته إذا عطس، ويشهد جنازته إذا مات، ويحفظه إذا غاب في السر والعلانية، ولا يهجر أخاه فوق ثلاثة ليال، والسلام يخرجه من

greeting. Permissible shunning is to shun someone with an innovation or someone who openly commits major wrong actions, provided you cannot punish him and are unable to admonish him or the individual will not accept admonishment.

In these two cases, mentioning the situation of someone is not backbiting nor is it backbiting when someone is consulted about someone's character for the sake of marriage or joint enterprise or the like, nor for the purpose of assessing the character of a witness and the like. It is noble character to pardon someone who wrongs you and to give to someone who refused you and to join the one who cut you off.

The sum of good manners and its peak can be derived from four hadiths:

1. The Prophet ﷺ said, "Anyone who believes in Allah and the Last Day should speak well or be silent."

2. He said ﷺ, "Part of the excellence of a person's Islam is his leaving alone what does not concern him."

3. He ﷺ told the one who asked him for succinct advice, "Do not get angry."

4. He said ﷺ, "A believer wants for his brother believer what he wants for himself."

It is not lawful for you to deliberately listen to all of a falsehood nor to take pleasure in listening to the words of a woman who is not lawful for you nor to listen to musicians and singers. It is not permitted to recite the Qur'an with quavering melodies as in the quavering used in singing. The Mighty Book of Allah must be respected and recited with calm and gravity, with attention and understanding of it, in a way which is certain to please Allah and bring one near to Him.

الهجران. ولا ينبغي له أن يترك كلامه بعد السلام، والهجران الجائز هجران ذي البدعة أو متجاهر بالكبائر لا يصل إلى عقوبته، ولا يقدر على موعظته أو لا يقبلها.

ولا غيبة في هذين في ذكر حالهما، ولا فيما يشاور فيه لنكاح أم مخالطة ونحوه، ولا في تجريح شاهد ونحوه. ومن مكارم الأخلاق أن تعفو عمن ظلمك، وتعطي من حرمك، وتصل من قطعك.

وجماع آداب الخير، وأزمته تتفرع عن أربعة أحاديث.

١ - قول النبي عليه السلام: من كان يؤمن بالله واليوم الآخر، فليقل خيرا أو ليصمت.

٢ - وقوله عليه السلام: من حسن إسلام المرء تركه ما لا يعنيه.

٣ - وقوله عليه السلام للذي اختصر له في الوصية: لا تغضب.

٤ - وقوله عليه السلام: المؤمن يحب لأخيه المؤمن ما يحب لنفسه.

ولا يحل لك أن تتعمد سماع الباطل كله، ولا أن تتلذذ بسماع كلام امرأة لا تحل لك، ولا سماع شيء من الملاهي والغناء، ولا قراءة القرآن باللحون المرجعة كترجيع الغناء. وليجل كتاب الله العزيز أن يتلى إلا بسكينة ووقار، وما يوقن أن الله يرضى به ويقرب منه مع إحضار الفهم لذالك.

It is an obligation for everyone who has authority in the land and whoever can achieve that to command the correct and forbid the wrong. If someone cannot do that physically, then he should do so with his tongue. If he cannot do that, then he should do so in his heart. It is an obligation for every believer to intend the Noble Face of Allah with every word and deed. If someone desires other than Allah in that, his action is not accepted. Showing off is lesser *shirk*.

Repentance from every wrong action and not persisting in it is an obligation. Persisting in it is to continue in the wrong action and intend to return to it. Part of repentance is to right wrongs and avoid forbidden things and to intend not to revert to the wrong action. The one who repents should ask forgiveness of his Lord and hope for His mercy and fear His punishment while remembering His blessings to him. He should thank Him for His favour to him through actions, meaning those things He has made obligatory, and by not doing what is disliked to do. He should draw near to Allah by doing those voluntary acts of good which are feasible for him. He should make up any obligations which he has missed immediately, asking Allah to accept them and turning to Him in repentance for missing them.

He should seek refuge in Allah when he finds it difficult to direct himself or is confused about what to do. He should be certain that Allah can reform his state, grant him success, and direct him. He should not abandon that because of any good or ugliness in him and he must never despair of the mercy of Allah.

Reflection on the affair (creations) of Allah is the key of worship. So seek help by remembering death and reflecting on what comes after it, the blessings of your Lord to You, and His deferring you while punishing others for their wrong actions. Reflect on your past wrong actions and the outcome of your affair and how suddenly and soon your death will come.

ومن الفرائض الأمر بالمعروف والنهي عن المنكر على كل من بسطت يده في الأرض، وعلى كل من تصل يده إلى ذلك، فإن لم يقدر فبلسانه، فإن لم يقدر فبقلبه. وفرض على كل مؤمن أن يريد بكل قول وعمل من البر وجه الله الكريم، ومن أراد بذلك غير الله لم يقبل عمله. والرياء: الشرك الأصغر.

والتوبة فريضة من كل ذنب من غير إصرار، والإصرار المقام على الذنب، واعتقاد العود إليه. ومن التوبة رد المظالم واجتناب المحارم، والنية أن لا يعود، وليستغفر ربه ويرجو رحمته ويخاف عذابه، ويتذكر نعمته لديه، ويشكر فضله عليه بالأعمال بفرائضه وترك ما يكره فعله، ويتقرب إليه بما تيسر له من نوافل الخير، وكل ما ضيع من فرائضه فليفعله الآن، وليرغب إلى الله في تقلبه، ويتوب إليه من تضييعه.

وليلجأ إلى الله فيما عسر عليه من قياد نفسه ومحاولة أمره، موقنا أنه المالك لصلاح شأنه وتوفيقه وتسديده، لا يفارق ذلك على ما فيه من حسن أو قبيح، ولا ييأس من رحمة الله.

والفكرة في أمر الله مفتاح العبادة، فاستعن بذكر الموت والفكرة فيما بعده، وفي نعمة ربك عليك وإمهاله لك، وأخذه لغيرك بذنبه، وفي سالف ذنبك وعاقبة أمرك ومبادرة ما عسى أن يكون قد اقترب من أجلك.

41. The Natural Form (*Fiṭrah*) – Circumcision, Shaving the Hair, Dress, Covering the Private Parts and the Like

Five things are part of the *fiṭrah*: 1. trimming the moustache, which entails removing any hair which curls around the lips, not shaving off the moustache completely, and Allah knows best; 2. trimming the nails; 3. plucking out the hair of the armpits; 4. shaving pubic hair – and there is nothing wrong in shaving the hair off the rest of the body; 5. and circumcision, which is a *sunnah* for men and honourable for women.

The Prophet ﷺ instructed that the beard should be allowed to grow and become thick without being cut off. Mālik said that there is nothing wrong in shortening it if it becomes too long. Many Companions and *Tābi'ūn* said that. It is disliked to dye the hair black, but not forbidden. There is nothing wrong in using henna and *katam*.

The Prophet ﷺ forbade men to wear silk and gold or iron rings. There is nothing wrong in using silver to decorate a seal ring, a sword or a copy of the Qur'an, but it should not be used in bridles, saddles, knives or in other such things. Women may wear gold rings, but he ﷺ forbade men to wear iron rings. What is preferred, according to what is reported about rings, is that they are worn on the left hand, since the right hand is used for taking things. A person takes something with the right hand and puts it into the left. There is disagreement about wearing *khazz* material (woven of silk and wool). Some permit it and others dislike it. The same is true about silk badges on garments except for a thin strip.

٤١ - باب في الفطرة والختان وحلق الشعر واللباس وستر العورة وما يتصل بذلك

ومن الفطرة خمس: قص الشارب وهو الإطار وهو طرف الشعر المستدير على الشفة، لا إحفاؤه والله أعلم، وقص الأظفار، ونتف الجناحين، وحلق العانة، ولا بأس بحلاق غيرها من شعر الجسد. والختان للرجال سنة، والخفاض للنساء مكرمة.

وأمر النبي أن تعفى اللحية وتوفر ولا تقص. قال مالك: ولا بأس بالأخذ من طولها إذا طالت كثيرا، وقاله غير واحد من الصحابة والتابعين، ويكره صباغ الشعر بالسواد من غير تحريم، ولا بأس به بالحناء والكتم.

ونهى الرسول عليه السلام الذكور عن لباس الحرير وتختم الذهب، وعن التختم بالحديد، ولا بأس بالفضة في حلية الخاتم والسيف والمصحف، ولا يجعل ذلك في لجام ولا سرج ولا سكين ولا في غير ذلك. وتختم النساء بالذهب، ونهي عن التختم بالحديد. والاختيار مما روي في التختم في اليسار،لأن تناول الشيء باليمين، فهو يأخذه بيمينه ويجعله في يساره، واختلف في لباس الخز، فأجيز وكره، وكذلك العلم في الثوب من الحرير إلا الخط الرقيق.

When women go out, they should not wear thin clothing which allows their shape to be seen. A man should not drag his waist-wrapper out of pride nor his garment out of arrogance. His garment should reach the ankles, as that is cleaner for the garment and shows greater *taqwā*. It is forbidden to wear a *ṣammā'* garment over nothing else, which is one lifted up by the arm on one side and hanging down on the other. That is when there is nothing under it. There is disagreement about when there is another garment under it.

It is mandatory to cover the private parts. The waist-wrapper of a believer should reach mid-calf. The thigh is one of the private parts, but not intrinsic to them. A man should not enter the bathhouse without wearing a waist wrapper. A woman should only enter it with a genuine reason for doing so. Two men or two women should not be together under a single cover. A woman should not go out unless she is covered and then only for such necessary matters as being present at the death of her parents or relatives or other such things which are permitted. Furthermore she should not attend a funeral where there are women wailers or gatherings with playing of flutes or lutes or similar instruments, except for the tambourine at weddings. There is disagreement about *kabar* drums.

A man should not be alone with a woman for whom he is not a *maḥram*. There is no harm in him seeing a woman for some reason such as identifying her or similar things, or when he proposes marriage to her. As for a woman who does not provoke desire because of her age, there is nothing wrong in him seeing her face in any case. Women are forbidden to add someone else's hair to their own or to tattoo themselves.

When putting on a sock or sandal, begin with the right and when removing it, begin with the left. There is nothing wrong in putting on sandals while standing. It is disliked to walk in only one sandal. It is

ولا يلبس النساء من الرقيق ما يصفهن إذا خرجن، ولا يجر الرجل إزاره بطرا، ولا ثوبه من الخيلاء، وليكن إلى الكعبين فهو أنظف لثوبه وأتقى لربه. وينهى عن اشتمال الصماء وهي على غير ثوب يرفع ذلك من جهة واحدة ويسدل الأخرى، وذلك إذا لم يكن تحت اشتمالك ثوب، واختلف فيه على ثوب.

ويؤمر بستر العورة ، وأزرة المؤمن إلى أنصاف ساقيه، والفخذ عورة، وليس كالعورة نفسه. ولا يدخل الرجل الحمام إلا بمئزر، ولا تدخله المرأة إلا من علة، ولا يتلاصق رجلان ولا امرأتان في لحاف واحد، ولا تخرج امرأة إلا مستترة فيما لابد لها منه من شهود موت أبويها، أو ذي قرابتها أو نحو ذلك مما يباح لها ، ولا تحضر من ذلك ما فيه نوح نائحة أو لهو من مزمار أو عود أو شبهه من الملاهي الملهية إلا الدف في النكاح. وقد اختلف في الكبر.

ولا يخلو رجل بامرأة ليست منه بمحرم، ولا بأس أن يراها لعذر من شهادة عليها أو نحو ذلك أو إذا خطبها. وأما المتجالة فله أن يرى وجهها على كل حال. وينهى النساء عن وصل الشعر، وعن الوشم.

ومن لبس خفا أو نعلا بدأ بيمينه، وإذا نزع بدأ بشماله. ولا بأس بالانتعال قائما، ويكره المشي في نعل واحدة. وتكره التماثيل في الأسرة

disliked to make images on beds, tents, walls and rings. Designs on clothing are not included in that but it is better not to do it.

When you eat or drink, it is mandatory for you to say, "In the name of Allah – *Bismillāh*" and to take the food using your right hand. When you finish, you should say, "Praise be to Allah – *al-ḥamdu lillāh*." It is good to lick your hand before wiping it. The manners of eating include leaving a third of your stomach for food, a third for drink and a third for breath. If you are eating with others, you should eat from what is in front of you. Do not take another bite until you have finished the previous one. Do not breathe into the vessel while you are drinking. Take the cup away from your mouth and then return it if you wish. Do not drink in gulps but rather sip your drink.

Chew your food properly before swallowing it. Clean your mouth after eating. It is good to wash any grease and milk off your hands. It is good to pick out any food from between your teeth. The Messenger ﷺ forbade eating or drinking with the left hand. When you drink from a vessel, you should pass it to the one on your right. It is forbidden to blow on food or drink or on a book, or to drink from a gold or silver vessel. There is nothing wrong in drinking standing up. It is not permitted for someone who has eaten raw leeks, garlic or onions to enter a mosque. It is disliked to eat reclining. It is disliked to start eating from the top of *tharīd* (bread soaked in broth).

It is forbidden to eat two dates at the same time, but it is said that this prohibition only applies to co-owners of the dates they are eating. There is nothing wrong in doing that with your own family or people you are feeding. When eating dates and other fruits, there is nothing

والقباب والجدران والخاتم، وليس الرقم في الثوب من ذلك، وتركه أحسن.

وإذا أكلت أو شربت فواجب عليك أن تقول: بسم الله، وتتناول بيمينك، فإذا فرغت فلتقل الحمد لله، وحسن أن تلعق يدك قبل مسحها. ومن آداب الأكل أن تجعل بطنك ثلثا للطعام وثلثا للشراب وثلثا للنفس. وإذا أكلت مع غيرك أكلت مما يليك، ولا تأخذ لقمة حتى تفرغ الأخرى، ولا تتنفس في الإناء عند شربك ولتبن القدح عن فيك ثم تعاوده إن شئت، ولا تعب الماء عبا، ولتمصه مصا.

وتلوك طعامك وتنعمه مضغا قبل بلعه، وتنظف فاك بعد طعامك، وإن غسلت يدك من الغمر واللبن فحسن، وتخلل ما تعلق بأسنانك من الطعام. ونهى الرسول عليه السلام عن الأكل والشرب بالشمال، وتناول إذا شربت من على يمينك، وينهى عن النفخ في الطعام والشراب والكتاب، وعن الشرب في آنية الذهب والفضة، ولا بأس بالشرب قائما، ولا ينبغي لمن أكل الكراث أو الثوم أو البصل نيئا أن يدخل المسجد، ويكره أن يأكل متكئا، ويكره الأكل من رأس الثريد.

ونهي عن القران في التمر: وقيل: إن ذلك مع الأصحاب الشركاء فيه، ولا بأس بذلك مع أهلك أو مع قوم تكون أنت أطعمتهم. ولا بأس في التمر وشبهه أن تجول يدك في الإناء لتأكل ما تريد منه، وليس

wrong in reaching your hand around the dish to choose those of them you want to eat. Washing one's hands before eating is not *sunnah* unless they are dirty.

After eating, a person should wash his hands and mouth free of grease and rinse any milk from his mouth. It is not liked for the hands to be cleaned with food or any bean flour or even the chaff of grain, but there is disagreement about the latter. If you are invited to a wedding feast, you should go unless there is well-known or objectionable entertainment there. It is up to you whether you eat. Mālik stated that it is allowed not to go if it is too crowded.

غسل اليد قبل الطعام من السنة إلا أن يكون بها أذى.

وليغسل يده وفاه بعد الطعام من الغمر، وليمضمض فاه من اللبن، وكره غسل اليد بالطعام أو بشيء من القطاني، وكذلك بالنخالة. وقد اختلف في ذلك. ولتجب إذا دعيت إلى وليمة العرس إن لم يكن هناك لهو مشهور ولا منكر بين، وأنت في الأكل بالخيار. وقد أرخص مالك في التخلف لكثرة زحام الناس فيها.

42. Rulings concerning speech
greetings, asking permission to enter, conversation, recitation, supplication, *dhikru-llāh*, and travel

Returning a greeting is mandatory. Initiating it is *sunnah* and desirable. The form of the greeting is that a man says, "Peace be upon you – *as-salāmu 'alaykum*" and the reply is, "And upon you peace – *wa 'alaykumu-s-salām*" or "Peace be upon you – *salāmun 'alaykum*" as was said to him. A fuller greeting which ends with blessing is that you say in reply, "Upon you peace and the mercy of Allah and its blessings – *wa 'alaykumu-s-salāmu wa raḥmatu-llāhi wa barakātuh*." Do not say in your reply, "The peace of Allah be upon you – *salamu-llāhi 'alayk*."

If one of a group makes the greeting, that suffices for all of them. The same applies when one of them returns the greeting. Someone riding should greet someone walking, and someone walking someone sitting. Shaking hands is good. Mālik disliked embracing but Ibn 'Uyaynah allowed it. Mālik disliked kissing another's hand and did not accept what is related about it.

You should not initiate the greeting to a Jew or Christian. But if a Muslim inadvertently greets a *dhimmī*, he should not take it back. If a Jew or Christian greets a Muslim, he should answer, "On you – *'alayk*." It is also said that one may answer with "And on you *silām*." "*Silām*" means a stone. That used to be said.

Asking permission to enter people's houses is mandatory. Do not enter a house where someone is present without asking his permission three times. If you are given permission, enter. Otherwise, go away. It is recommended to visit the sick.

٤٢ - باب في السلام والاستئذان والتناجي والقراءة والدعاء وذكر الله والقول في السفر

ورد السلام واجب، والابتداء به سنة مرغب فيها. والسلام أن يقول الرجل: السلام عليكم، ويقول الراد وعليكم السلام، أو يقول: سلام عليكم كما قيل له، وأكثر ما ينتهي السلام إلى البركة. أن تقول في ردك: وعليكم السلام ورحمة الله وبركاته، ولا تقل في ردك: سلام الله عليك.

وإذا سلم واحد من الجماعة أجزأ عنهم، وكذلك إن رد واحد منهم. وليسلم الراكب على الماشي، والماشي على الجالس. والمصافحة حسنة، وكره مالك المعانقة، وأجازها ابن عيينة، وكره مالك تقبيل اليد، وأنكر ما روي فيه.

ولا تبتدأ اليهود والنصارى بالسلام، فمن سلم على ذمي فلا يستقيله، وإن سلم عليه اليهودي أو النصراني فليقل: عليك. ومن قال: عليك السلام بكسر السين، وهي الحجارة فقد قيل ذلك.

والاستئذان واجب، فلا تدخل بيتا فيه أحد حتى تستأذن ثلاثا، فإن أذن لك وإلا رجعت. ويرغب في عيادة المرضى.

Two people should not converse together to the exclusion of a third. Nor may a larger group do that while excluding one of them. It is also said that they should only do that with his permission. Shunning people was already mentioned in an earlier chapter (40).

Mu'ādh ibn Jabal said, "No action of a human being is more likely to save him from the punishment of Allah than *dhikru-llāh*." 'Umar (ibn al-Khaṭṭāb) said, "Better than the remembrance of Allah on the tongue is the remembrance of Allah by obeying His commands and prohibitions." One of the supplications of the Messenger of Allah ﷺ morning and night was:

Allāhumma bika nuṣbiḥu wa bika numsī, wa bika naḥyā wa bika namūt

"O Allah, by You we start the day and by You we end it, and by You we live and by You we die."

He also used to add in the morning:

Wa ilayka-n-nushūr

"To You is the gathering," and in the evening;

Wa ilayka-l-maṣīr

"To You is the return."

Also related in that context is:

Allāhumma-j'alnī min a'ẓami 'ibādika 'indaka ḥaẓẓan wa naṣīban fī kulli khayrin tuqsimuhu fī hādha-l-yawmi wa fīmā ba'dahu min nūrin tahdī bihi aw raḥmatin tanshiruhā, aw rizqin tabsuṭuhu, aw ḍurrin takshifuhu, aw dhanbin taghfiruhu, aw shiddatin tadfa'uhā, aw fitnatin taṣrifuhā, aw mu'āfātin tamunnu bihā bi raḥmatika, inna-ka 'alā kulli shay'in qadīr

"O Allah, grant me a portion in every blessing with Your slaves who have the greatest portion with You which You distribute on this day and afterwards, of light by which You guide, mercy which You spread, provision which You expand, harm which You

ولا يتناجى اثنان دون واحد، وكذاك جماعة إذا أبقوا واحدا منهم، وقد قيل: لا ينبغي ذلك إلا بإذنه. وذكر الهجرة قد تقدم في باب قبل هذا.

قال معاذ بن جبل: ما عمل آدمي عملا أنجى له من عذاب الله من ذكر الله. وقال عمر: أفضل من ذكر الله باللسان، ذكر الله عند أمره ونهيه.

ومن دعاء رسول الله صلى الله عليه وسلم كلما أصبح وأمسى:

اَللَّهُمَّ بِكَ نُصْبِحُ وَبِكَ نُمْسِي، وَبِكَ نَحْيَا، وَبِكَ نَمُوتُ

ويقول في الصباح:

وَإِلَيْكَ النُّشُورُ وفي المساء:

وَإِلَيْكَ الْمَصِيرُ

وروي مع ذلك:

اَللَّهُمَّ اجعَلْنِي مِنْ أَعْظَمِ عِبَادِكَ عِنْدَكَ حَظًّا وَنَصِيباً فِي كُلِّ خَيْرٍ تَقْسِمُهُ فِي هَذَا الْيَوْمِ وَفِيمَا بَعْدَهُ مِنْ نُورٍ تَهْدِي بِهِ أَوْ رَحْمَةٍ تَنْشُرُهَا، أَوْ رِزْقٍ تَبْسُطُهُ، أَوْ ضُرٍّ تَكْشِفُهُ، أَوْ ذَنْبٍ تَغْفِرُهُ، أَوْ شِدَّةٍ تَدْفَعُهَا، أَوْ فِتْنَةٍ تَصْرِفُهَا، أَوْ مُعَافَاةٍ تَمُنُّ بِهَا بِرَحْمَتِكَ، إِنَّكَ عَلَى كُلِّ شَيْءٍ قَدِيرٌ

remove, wrong actions which You forgive, hardship which You drive away, trials which You avert and pardon which You bestow by Your mercy. You have power over all things."

One of his supplications ﷺ when he went to sleep was that, putting his right hand under his right cheek and his left hand on his left thigh, he then said:

Allāhumma bismika waḍaʿtu janbī wa bismika arfaʿuh. Allāhumma in amsakta nafsī fa-ghfir lahā wa in arsaltahā fa-ḥfaẓhā bimā taḥfaẓu bihi-ṣ-ṣaliḥina min ʿibādik. Allāhumma innī aslamtu nafsī ilayk, wa aljaʾtu ẓahrī ilayk, wa fawwaḍtu amrī ilayk, wa wajjahtu wajhī ilayk, rahbatan minka wa raghbatan ilayk, lā manjā walā maljaʾa minka illā ilayk, astaghfiruka wa atūbu ilayk, āmantu bikitābika-lladhī anzalt, wa bi nabīyika-lladhī arsalt, fa-ghfir lī mā qaddamtu wa mā akhkhart, wa mā asrartu wa mā aʿlant, anta ilahī lā ilāha illā ant, rabbi qinī ʿadhābaka yawma tabʿathu ʿibādak.

"O Allah, in Your Name I have lain down and in Your Name I will rise. O Allah, if You keep my self, then forgive it. If You release it, then guard it as You guard the righteous among Your slaves. O Allah, I have surrendered myself to You and I commend myself to You. I entrust my affair to You and have turned my face towards You, fearing You and desiring You. There is nowhere to flee or refuge from You except to You. I ask for your forgiveness and I turn to You. I have believed in Your Book which You sent down, and in your Prophet whom You sent, so forgive me what I have sent ahead and what I have left behind, what I conceal and what I make public. You are my Lord. There is no god but You. My Lord, protect me from Your punishment on the Day You resurrect Your slaves."

It is related that when he ﷺ left the house, he said:

ومن دعائه عليه السلام عند النوم، أنه كان يضع يده اليمنى تحت خده الأيمن، واليسرى على نخده الأيسر، ثم يقول:

اَللَّهُمَّ بِاسْمِكَ وَضَعْتُ جَنْبِي وَبِاسْمِكَ أَرْفَعُهُ. اَللَّهُمَّ إِنْ أَمْسَكْتَ نَفْسِي فَاغْفِرْ لَهَا وَإِنْ أَرْسَلْتَهَا فَاحْفَظْهَا بِمَا تَحْفَظُ بِهِ الصَّالِحِينَ مِنْ عِبَادِكَ. اَللَّهُمَّ إِنِّي أَسْلَمْتُ نَفْسِي إِلَيْكَ، وَأَلْجَأْتُ ظَهْرِي إِلَيْكَ، وَفَوَّضْتُ أَمْرِي إِلَيْكَ، وَوَجَّهْتُ وَجْهِي إِلَيْكَ، رَهْبَةً مِنْكَ وَرَغْبَةً إِلَيْكَ، لاَ مَنْجَا وَلاَ مَلْجَأَ مِنْكَ إِلاَّ إِلَيْكَ، أَسْتَغْفِرُكَ وَأَتُوبُ إِلَيْكَ، ءَامَنْتُ بِكِتَابِكَ الَّذِي أَنْزَلْتَ، وَبِنَبِيِّكَ الَّذِي أَرْسَلْتَ، فَاغْفِرْ لِي مَا قَدَّمْتُ وَمَا أَخَّرْتُ، وَمَا أَسْرَرْتُ وَمَا أَعْلَنْتُ، أَنْتَ إِلَهِي لاَ إِلَهَ إِلاَّ أَنْتَ، رَبِّ قِنِي عَذَابَكَ يَوْمَ تَبْعَثُ عِبَادَكَ.

ومما روي في الدعاء عند الخروج من المنزل:

Allāhumma innī a'ūdhu bika an aḍilla aw uḍalla aw azilla aw uzalla aw aẓlima aw uẓlama aw ajhala aw yujhala 'alayya

"O Allah I seek refuge with You from straying or being misled, or slipping or being caused to slip, or wronging [anyone] or being wronged, or behaving ignorantly or that anyone should behave ignorantly towards me.""'

It is related that he ﷺ said that after every prayer you should say, "*Subḥāna-llāh*" 33 times, "*Allāhu akbar*" 33 times and "*al-ḥamdu lillāh*" 33 times and end the hundred with:

Lā ilaha illa-llāhu waḥdahu lā sharīka lah, lahu-l-mulku wa lahu-l-ḥamd, wa huwa 'alā kulli shay'in qadīr

"There is no god but Allah alone with no partner. His is the kingdom and praise is His and He has power over all things."

After going to the lavatory, you should say:

Al-ḥamdu lillāhi-lladhī razaqanī ladhdhatahu wa akhraja 'annī mashaqqatahu wa abqā fī jismī quwwatah

"Praise be to Allah who provided me with its pleasure and removed from me its discomfort and let its nutrition remain in my body." You should seek protection from everything you fear.

And when you camp in a place or sit in a place or sleep somewhere you should say:

A'ūdhu bikalimāti-llāhi-t-tāmmāti min sharri mā khalaq

"I seek refuge with the complete words of Allah from the evil of what He created."

Or you may say:

A'ūdhu biwajhi-llāhi-l-karīmi wa bikalimāti-llāhi-t-tāmmāti-llatī lā yujāwizuhunna barrun walā fājirun, wa bi asmā'i-llāhi-l-ḥusnā kullihā mā 'alimtu minhā wa mā lam a'lam min sharri mā khalaqa wa dhara'a wa bara'a, wa min sharri mā yanzilu mina-s-samā'i wa min sharri mā ya'ruju

اَللَّهُمَّ إِنِّي أَعُوذُ بِكَ أَنْ أَضِلَّ أَوْ أُضَلَّ أَوْ أَزِلَّ أَوْ أُزَلَّ أَوْ أَظْلِمَ أَوْ أُظْلَمَ أَوْ أَجْهَلَ أَوْ يُجْهَلَ عَلَيَّ

وروي في دبر كل صلاة أن يسبح الله ثلاثا وثلاثين، ويكبر الله ثلاثا وثلاثين، ويختم المائة بـ:

لاَ إِلَهَ إِلاَّ اللهُ وَحْدَهُ لاَ شَرِيكَ لَهُ، لَهُ الْمُلْكُ وَلَهُ الْحَمْدُ، وَهُوَ عَلَى كُلِّ شَيْءٍ قَدِيرٌ

وعند الخلاء تقول:

اَلْحَمْدُ لِلَّهِ الَّذِي رَزَقَنِي لَذَّتَهُ وَأَخْرَجَ عَنِّي مَشَقَّتَهُ وَأَبْقَى فِي جِسْمِي قُوَّتَهُ

وتتعوذ من كل شيء تخافه.

وعندما تحل بموضع أو تجلس بمكان أو تنام فيه. تقول:

أَعُوذُ بِكَلِمَاتِ اللهِ التَّامَّاتِ مِنْ شَرِّ مَا خَلَقَ

ومن التعوذ أن تقول:

أَعُوذُ بِوَجْهِ اللهِ الْكَرِيمِ وَبِكَلِمَاتِ اللهِ التَّامَّاتِ الَّتِي لاَ يُجَاوِزُهُنَّ بَرٌّ وَلاَ فَاجِرٌ، وَبِأَسْمَاءِ اللهِ الْحُسْنَى كُلِّهَا مَا عَلِمْتُ مِنْهَا وَمَا لَمْ أَعْلَمْ مِنْ شَرِّ مَا خَلَقَ وَذَرَأَ

fīhā, wa min sharri mā dhara'a fi-l-arḍi wa min sharri mā yakhruju minhā, wa min fitnati-l-layli wa-n-nahāri, wa min ṭawāriqi-l-layli wa-n-nahāri illā ṭāriqan yaṭruqu bi khayrin yā Raḥmān

"I seek refuge with the noble face of Allah and with the complete words of Allah which neither a pious or impious person can overlook, and with all the Most Beautiful Names of Allah, what I know of them and what I do not know, from the evil of what He created, originated, and produced, and from the evil of what descends from the sky and from the evil of what ascends into it, and from the evil of what He created on the earth and from the evil of what emerges from it, and from the evil of the trials of the night and day, and from the evil of every visitant at night except that which knocks with good, O All-Merciful."

One may add:

wa min sharri kulli dābbatin rabbī ākhidun bi nāṣīatihā, inna rabbī 'alā ṣirāṭi-m-mustaqīm

"And from every beast whose forelock my Lord has taken, My Lord is on a Straight Path."

When someone enters his house, it is recommended that he say:

Mā shā'a-llāhu lā quwwata illā billāh

"As Allah wills. There is no strength except by Allah."

In mosques it is disliked to do work such as sewing and similar things. People should not wash their hands in a mosque nor eat in it unless it is something light, like a gruel of parched barley or similar grains (*sawīq*). They should not trim their moustaches or nails there. If they do so, they should collect the clippings in their garment. They should not kill lice or fleas there. There is an allowance for strangers to spend the night in mosques in the countryside.

In bathhouses you should recite no more than a few verses. One

وَبَرَأَ، وَمِنْ شَرِّ مَا يَنْزِلُ مِنَ السَّمَاءِ وَمِنْ شَرِّ مَا يَعْرُجُ فِيهَا، وَمِنْ شَرِّ مَا ذَرَأَ فِي الْأَرْضِ وَمِنْ شَرِّ مَا يَخْرُجُ مِنْهَا، وَمِنْ فِتْنَةِ اللَّيْلِ وَالنَّهَارِ، وَمِنْ طَوَارِقِ اللَّيْلِ وَالنَّهَارِ إِلاَّ طَارِقًا يَطْرُقُ بِخَيْرٍ يَا رَحْمَٰنُ

ويقال في ذلك أيضا:

وَمِنْ شَرِّ كُلِّ دَابَّةٍ رَبِّي ءَاخِذٌ بِنَاصِيَتِهَا، إِنَّ رَبِّي عَلَى صِرَاطٍ مُسْتَقِيمٍ

ويستحب لمن دخل منزله أن يقول:

مَا شَاءَ اللهُ ، لاَ قُوَّةَ إِلاَّ بِاللهِ

ويكره العمل في المساجد من خياطة ونحوها، ولا يغسل يديه فيه، ولا يأكل فيه إلا مثل الشيء الخفيف كالسويق ونحوه، ولا يقص فيه شاربه، ولا يقلم فيه أظفاره، وإن قص أو قلم أخذه في ثوبه، ولا يقتل فيه قملة ولا برغوثا. وأرخص في مبيت الغرباء في مساجد البادية.

ولا ينبغي أن يقرأ في الحمام إلا الآيات اليسيرة، ولا يكثر، ويقرأ

can recite Qur'an riding, lying down, or walking from one town to another, but it is disliked to recite it while walking to the market, although it is said that a learner can do that. It is good for someone to recite the entire Qur'an in seven nights but to recite less with understanding is better. It is related that the Prophet ﷺ never recited it in less than three nights.

It is recommended for a traveller to say when he mounts:
Bismi-llāhi, Allāhumma anta-s-ṣāḥibu fī-s-safari wa-l-khalīfatu fī-l-ahl. Allāhumma innī a'ūdhu bika min wa'thā'i-s-safari, wa ka'ābati-l-manqalabi, wa sū'i-l-manẓari fī-l-ahli wa-l-māl
"In the Name of Allah. O Allah, You are the Companion in the journey and my substitute in the family. O Allah, I seek refuge with you from the hardship of the journey and from the trouble of reversal and finding family and possessions in a poor state."
When a traveller is upright on his mount, he should say:

Subḥāna-lladhī sakhkhara lanā hādhā wa mā kunnā lahū muqrinīna wa innā ilā rabbinā lamunqalibūn
"Glory be to Him who subjected this to us. We could never have done it by ourselves. Indeed we are returning to our Lord!" (43:12-13)

It is disliked to trade in the land of the enemy or the land of the blacks. The Prophet ﷺ said, "Travel is a portion of punishment." A woman should not make a journey of a day and a night or more without a relative except in the case of the obligatory *ḥajj* according to the position of Mālik. Then she may travel in a safe group, even if she has no relative with them.

الراكب والمضطجع والماشي من قرية إلى قرية، ويكره ذلك للماشي إلى السوق. وقد قيل: إن ذلك للمتعلم واسع. ومن قرأ في سبع فذلك حسن، والتفهم مع قلة القراءة أفضل. وروي أن النبي عليه السلام لم يقرأه في أقل من ثلاث.

ويستحب للمسافر أن يقول عند ركوبه:

بِسْمِ اللهِ، اَللَّهُمَّ أَنْتَ الصَّاحِبُ فِي السَّفَرِ وَالْخَلِيفَةُ فِي الْأَهْلِ، اَللَّهُمَّ إِنِّي أَعُوذُ بِكَ مِنْ وَعْثَاءِ السَّفَرِ، وَكَآبَةِ الْمُنْقَلَبِ، وَسُوءِ الْمَنْظَرِ فِي الْأَهْلِ وَالْمَالِ

ويقول الراكب إذا استوى على الدابة:

سُبْحَـٰنَ ٱلَّذِى سَخَّرَ لَنَا هَـٰذَا وَمَا كُنَّا لَهُۥ مُقْرِنِينَ وَإِنَّآ إِلَىٰ رَبِّنَا لَمُنقَلِبُونَ

وتكره التجارة إلى أرض العدو وبلد السودان. وقال النبي عليه السلام: السفر قطعة من العذاب. ولا ينبغي أن تسافر المرأة مع غير ذي محرم منها سفر يوم وليلة فأكثر إلا في حج الفريضة خاصة، في قول مالك في رفقة مأمونة، وإن لم يكن معها ذو محرم فذلك لها.

43. Medical treatment

CHARMS, OMENS, STARS, CASTRATION, BRANDING, DOGS, AND COMPASSION TO SLAVES

There is nothing wrong in using charms (*ruqā*) against the evil eye and other things, nor in using prayers for refuge. There is nothing wrong in undergoing medical treatment, drinking medicine, being bled and cauterisation. Cupping is good. It is permitted for men to use kohl for treatment and it is a cosmetic for women. Wine, impurities, that which comes from carrion, or anything which Allah Almighty has forbidden, are not to be used for medical treatment. There is nothing wrong in cauterisation and using charms containing the Book of Allah or using good words. There is no harm in amulets which contain something of the Qur'an.

If the plague breaks out in a land no one should enter it and those there should not flee from it. The Messenger ﷺ said about evil omens, "If they exist, they are in houses, women, and horses." The Prophet ﷺ disliked bad names and liked good omens.

The manner of washing on account of the evil eye is that the person responsible for inflicting the evil eye should wash his face, hands, elbows, knees, the ends of his feet and under his waist-wrapper over a basin. Then that water should be poured over the one afflicted. You should only look at the stars to find the direction of *qiblah* and the time of the night and not other things.

Dogs should not be kept in houses in either town or country except

٤٣ - باب في التعالج وذكر الرقى والطيرة والنجوم والخصاء والوسم والكلاب والرفق بالمملوك

ولا بأس بالاسترقاء من العين وغيرها والتعوذ والتعالج، وشرب الدواء والفصد والكي. والحجامة حسنة، والكحل للتداوي للرجال جائز، وهو من زينة النساء. ولا يتعالج بالخمر، ولا بالنجاسة، ولا بما فيه ميتة، ولا بشيء مما حرم الله سبحانه وتعالى. ولا بأس بالاكتواء والرقى بكتاب الله وبالكلام الطيب. ولا بأس بالمعاذة تعلق، وفيها القرآن.

وإذا وقع الوباء بأرض قوم فلا يقدم عليه، ومن كان فلا يخرج فرارا منه. وقال الرسول عليه السلام في الشؤم: إن كان ففي المسكن والمرأة والفرس. وكان عليه السلام يكره سيء الأسماء، ويحب الفأل الحسن.

والغسل للعين أن يغسل العائن وجهه ويديه ومرفقيه وركبتيه وأطراف رجليه وداخلة إزاره في قدح، ثم يصب على المعين. ولا ينظر في النجوم إلا ما يستدل به على القبلة وأجزاء الليل، ويترك ما سوى ذلك.

ولا يتخذ كلب في الدور في الحضر، ولا في دور البادية إلا لزرع

those used for guarding crops or livestock, when the dog accompanies the flock into the desert and then comes home with them, or dogs used for hunting for livelihood, but not for sport.

There is nothing wrong in castrating sheep and goats if it improves their meat. It is forbidden to geld horses. It is disliked to brand animals on the face. There is nothing wrong in branding them elsewhere.

One should be kind to slaves and not oblige them to do work they are incapable of doing.

أو ماشية يصحبها في الصحراء، ثم يروح معها، أو لصيد يصطاده لعيشه، لا للهو.

ولا بأس بخصاء الغنم لما فيه من صلاح لحومها، ونهي عن خصاء الخيل. ويكره الوسم في الوجه، ولا بأس به في غير ذلك. ويترفق بالمملوك، ولا يكلف من العمل ما لا يطيق.

44. Dreams, yawning, sneezing, playing backgammon and other games, racing horses, shooting and the like

The Messenger of Allah ﷺ said, "A good dream of a righteous man is a forty-sixth portion of Prophethood. If any of you has a dream he dislikes, when he wakes up, he should spit three times to his left and say:

Allāhumma innī a'ūdhu bika min sharri mā ra'aytu fī manāmī an yaḍurranī fī dīnī wa dunyāya

'O Allah, I seek refuge in You from the evil of what I have seen in my dream lest it harm me in my *dīn* or worldly affairs.'"

If someone yawns, he should place his hand over his mouth. If someone sneezes, he should say:

Al-ḥamdu lillāh

"Praise be to Allah,"

and the one who hears him praise Allah should say:

Yarḥamuka-llāh

"May Allah have mercy on you."

The sneezer then replies:

Yaghfiru-llāhu lanā wa lakum

"May Allah forgive us and you" or

Yahdīkumu-llāhu wa yuṣliḥu bālakum

"May Allah guide you and make you thrive"

Playing backgammon and chess is not permitted but there is nothing wrong in greeting someone who is playing them. It is, however,

٤٤ - باب في الرؤيا والتثاؤب والعطاس واللعب بالنرد وغيرها، والسبق بالخيل والرمي وغير ذلك

قال رسول الله صلى الله عليه وسلم: الرؤيا الحسنة من الرجل الصالح جزء من ستة وأربعين جزءا من النبوة، ومن رأى منكم ما يكره في منامه فإذا استيقظ فليتفل عن يساره ثلاثا، وليقل:

اَللَّهُمَّ إِنِّي أَعُوذُ بِكَ مِنْ شَرِّ مَا رَأَيْتُ فِي مَنَامِي أَنْ يَضُرَّنِي فِي دِينِي وَدُنْيَايَ

ومن تثاءب فليضع يده على فيه. ومن عطس فليقل:

اَلْحَمْدُ لِلّٰهِ

وعلى من سمعه يحمد الله أن يقول له:

يَرْحَمُكَ اللّٰهُ

ويرد العاطس عليه:

يَغْفِرُ اللّٰهُ لَنَا وَلَكُمْ، أو يقول:

يَهْدِيكُمُ اللّٰهُ وَيُصْلِحُ بَالَكُمْ

ولا يجوز اللعب بالنرد ولا بالشطرنج، ولا بأس أن يسلم على من يلعب بها، ويكره الجلوس إلى من يلعب بها، ويكره الجلوس إلى من

disliked to sit with someone playing them and to watch them. There is nothing wrong in racing horses and camels and in holding archery competitions. If two contestants stake a prize, they should put another contestant between them. If the third party wins, he takes the stake. If one of the other two wins, the third party owes nothing. This is the opinion of Ibn al-Musayyab.

Mālik said that it is allowed for a man to set a stake. If someone beats him, then that winner takes the prize. If the one who set the stake wins, it goes to the one who came after him. If there is only the one who put the stake and one other and the one who put the stake wins, then the stake goes to the spectators.

It is reported that when the snakes of Madīnah appear they are asked to leave for three days. Doing that in other places is good but this is not done in the desert and they are killed when they appear. Killing lice and fleas by fire is disliked. There is nothing wrong, Allah willing, in killing ants when they cause harm and cannot be removed but it is better not to kill them. Geckos should be killed. It is disliked to kill frogs.

The Prophet ﷺ said, "Allah has removed from you the stupidity of the *Jāhiliyyah* and their boasting of their ancestors. Whether you are godfearing believers or wretched deviants, you are the sons of Adam, and Adam came from dust." The Prophet ﷺ said about a man who learned the genealogies of people, "A useless knowledge and ignorance of it will not harm you." 'Umar said, "Learn about your lineages enough to be able to maintain ties of kinship." Mālik said, "I dislike tracing genealogies back to ancestors before Islam."

A good dream is a forty-sixth part of prophethood. If someone has a bad dream he should spit to his left and seek the protection of Allah

يلعب بها، والنظر إليهم. ولا بأس بالسبق بالخيل والإبل وبالسهام بالرمي، وإن أخرجا شيئا جعلا بينهما محللا يأخذ ذلك المحلل إن سبق هو، وإن سبق غيره لم يكن عليه شيء، هذا قول ابن المسيب.

وقال مالك: إنما يجوز أن يخرج الرجل سبقا، فإن سبق غيره أخذه، وإن سبق هو كان للذي يليه من المتسابقين، وإن لم يكن غير جاعل السبق وآخر فسبق جاعل السبق أكله من حضر ذلك.

وجاء فيما ظهر من الحيات بالمدينة أن تؤذن ثلاثا، وإن فعل ذلك في غيرها فهو حسن، ولا تؤذن في الصحراء، ويقتل ما ظهر منها. ويكره قتل القمل والبراغيث بالنار، ولا بأس إن شاء الله بقتل النمل إذا آذت ولم يقدر على تركها، ولم تقتل كان أحب إلينا. ويقتل الوزغ، ويكره قتل الضفادع.

وقال النبي عليه الصلاة والسلام: إن الله أذهب عنكم غبية الجاهلية ونخرها بالآباء، مؤمن تقي أو فاجر شقي، أنتم بنو آدم، وآدم من تراب. وقال النبي عليه وآله الصلاة والسلام في رجل تعلم أنساب الناس: علم لا ينفع، وجهالة لا تضر. وقال عمر: تعلموا من أنسابكم ما تصلون به أرحامكم. وقال مالك: وأكره أن يرفع في النسبة فيما قبل الإسلام من الآباء.

والرؤيا الصالحة جزء من ستة وأربعين جزءا من النبوة، ومن رأى

from the evil which he has seen. Someone who has no knowledge of the science of dreams should not interpret them, nor should he interpret it as indicative of something good when he knows that it indicates something disliked.

There is nothing wrong in reciting poetry but a small amount is better. One should not spend too much time reciting or composing it. The best and most fitting type of knowledge, and the closest to Allah, is knowledge of His *dīn* and His laws regarding what He commanded, forbade, summoned to and encouraged in His Book and on the tongue of His Prophet ﷺ. One must have understanding and a grasp of that and be concerned with observing it and acting according to it.

Acquiring knowledge is the best of actions. The scholar closest to Allah and most entitled to Him is the one with the greatest fear of Him and desire for what is with Him. Knowledge directs to good things and guides to them. Salvation lies in seeking protection in the Book of Allah Almighty and the Sunnah of His Prophet ﷺ and following the path of the believers and that of the best of generations of the best community produced for mankind. Reliance on that is protection. Salvation lies in following the righteous Salaf. They are the model with regard to the interpretations which they made and the results of their deductions. Even though they differed in respect of secondary rulings, no one should leave their group.

Praise belongs to Allah who guided us to this and were it not that Allah had guided us, we would not have been guided.

Abū Muḥammad 'Abdullāh ibn Abī Zayd says:

We have now done what we stipulated for ourselves to do in this book of ours. Allah willing, it will be of use to those children who

في منامه ما يكره فليتفل عن يساره ثلاثا، وليتعوذ من شر ما رأى، ولا ينبغي أن يفسر الرؤيا من لا علم له بها ولا يعبرها على الخير وهي عنده على المكروه.

ولا بأس بإنشاد الشعر وما خف من الشعر أحسن، ولا ينبغي أن يكثر منه ومن الشغل به. وأولى العلوم وأفضلها وأقربها إلى الله علم دينه وشرائعه مما أمر به ونهى عنه، ودعا إليه وحض عليه في كتابه وعلى لسان نبيه، والفقه في ذلك والفهم فيه والتهمم برعايته، والعمل به.

والعلم أفضل الأعمال، وأقرب العلماء إلى الله تعالى وأولاهم به أكثرهم له خشية، وفيما عنده رغبة، والعلم دليل إلى الخيرات وقائد إليها. واللجأ إلى كتاب الله عز وجل وسنة نبيه، وإتباع سبيل المؤمنين وخير القرون من خير أمة أخرجت للناس نجاة، ففي المفزع إلى ذلك العصمة، وفي إتباع السلف الصالح النجاة، وهم القدوة في تأويل ما تأولوه، واستخراج ما استنبطوه، وإذا اختلفوا في الفروع والحوادث لم يخرج عن جماعتهم.

والحمد لله الذي هدانا لهذا وما كنا لنهتدي لولا أن هدانا الله.

قال أبو محمد عبد الله ابن أبي زيد:

قد أتينا على ما شرطنا أن نأتي به في كتابنا هذا مما ينتفع به إن شاء

desire to learn what it contains and adults who are in need of it. What it contains will lead the ignorant to knowledge of what to believe in his *dīn* and what obligations they must perform. It will give them much understanding of the basic principles and secondary rulings of *fiqh* as well as the *sunnah*s, desirable practices and manners.

I ask Allah Almighty to enable us and you to benefit by what He has taught us and to help us and you perform what we owe Him with respect to what He has made obligatory for us. There is no power nor strength except by Allah, the All-Knowing, the Immense. May Allah bless our master Muḥammad, His Prophet, and his family and Companions and grant them much peace.

الله من رغب في تعليم ذلك من الصغار، ومن احتاج إليه من الكبار، وفيه ما يؤدي الجاهل إلى علم ما يعتقده من دينه، ويعمل به من فرائضه، ويفهم كثيرا من أصول الفقه وفنونه، ومن السنن والرغائب والآداب.

وأنا أسأل الله عز وجل أن ينفعنا وإياك بما علمنا، ويعيننا وإياك على القيام بحقه فيما كلفنا، ولا حول ولا قوة إلا بالله العلي العظيم، وصلى الله على سيدنا محمد نبيه وعلى آله وصحبه وسلم تسليما كثيرا.

People and places mentioned in the text

'Abd al-Malik 'Abd al-Malik ibn Marwān, the *khalīfah* of Banī Umayyah, many of whose judgements and decisions were highly influential

'Aṭā' 'Aṭā' ibn Yasār, one of the most eminent Followers. He was from Makkah.

'Umar ibn 'Abd al-'Azīz the *khalīfah* from Banī Umayyah universally acknowledged as one of the Rightly Guided Khalīfahs

Ashhab Ashhab ibn 'Abd al-'Azīz, one of the leading pupils of Imam Mālik. He lived in Cairo and was one of those whose judgements are found in the *Mudawwanah.*

Bakkah Makkah

Banū Umayyah the descendants of Umayyah ibn 'Abd Shams of Quraysh, and thus often a shorthand for the *khalīfah*s who succeeded the first Rightly Guided Khalīfahs

Ibn 'Uyaynah Ṣufyān ibn 'Uyaynah, a contemporary of Imam Mālik, and one of the eminent Followers of the Followers (*Tābi'ūn*). From Makkah, he lived in Kufa.

Ibn al-Musayyab Sa'īd ibn al-Musayyab was one of the foremost Followers (*Tābi'ūn*) of the Companions in Madīnah. He was one of the 'seven *fuqahā*' of Madīnah.

Ibn al-Qāsim 'Abd ar-Raḥmān ibn al-Qāsim, the *faqīh* from Egypt who spent nineteen years with Imam Mālik until the latter's death, and whose verdicts recorded by Ṣaḥnūn in the *Mudawwanah* are a foundation of later Mālikī fiqh

Ibrāhīm ﷺ The Prophet and Messenger of Allah who is the ancestor of the Messenger of Allah ﷺ and the Prophets of Banī Isrā'īl

Jamrat al-'Aqabah the Jamrah that the people on Ḥajj stone after returning to Minā from Muzdalifah and before entering Makkah for the *Ṭawāf al-Ifāḍah*

Magian Zoroastrian, a fire-worshipper. They are dualists who posit a force of good and an opposite force of evil.

Mālik ibn Anas the well known Imam of the Abode of the Hijrah. He was of the generation of the Followers of the Followers.

Mash'ar al-Ḥarām the open-roofed mosque at Muzdalifah

People of the Book those who have a revealed scripture, most particularly the Jews and Christians. The Zoroastrians were included among them except that it is not permissible to marry their women or eat their meat.

Ṣaḥnūn the *faqīh* who travelled from Qayrawān to Cairo to compile the *Mudawwanah* – the main source for Imam Mālik's judgements after the *Muwaṭṭa'* – from the main companions of Imam Mālik such as Ashhab, Aṣbagh, 'Abdullāh ibn Wahb, but principally 'Abd ar-Raḥmān ibn al-Qāsim

Salaf the Companions and the right-acting among their Followers and the Followers of the Followers.

Valley of Muḥassir a valley between Muzdalifah and Minā where the people on Ḥajj must go quickly

Zayd ibn Thābit the Companion entrusted both by Abū Bakr and 'Uthmān in the compilation of the *muṣḥāf*, who was regarded widely as the Imam of Madīnah during his lifetime

Glossary of Arabic Terms

A

adab	courtesy
adhān	the call to prayer
'alas	a small grain similar to wheat
'aqīqah	marking the birth of a new-born child
āmīn	Amen. Said after the Fātiḥah.
'āqilah	the tribe of a person, who sometimes bear the burden of reparations for his corporal and capital crimes
'āriyah	a gift, for example, of the fruit of palm trees from a garden; a loan for temporary use
'Āshūrā'	the tenth day of the month of Muḥarram whose fasting is desirable
'awl	proportionate adjustment of the shares of inheritance when the total of the fixed shares exceeds the sum of the estate
awliyā'	see *walī*
'awrah	the private parts; that of the body which must not be seen by others

B

bint makhāḍ	a female camel in its second year
bint labūn	a female camel in its third year

C

consanguine siblings	those from the same father but from different mothers

D

danī f. *daniyyah* a lowly person

Dār al-Ḥarb the land of war – beyond the frontiers of Dār al-Islam (the Abode of Islam)

Day of Tarwiyah "The day of providing oneself with water", 8th Dhu-l-Ḥijjah which people on Ḥajj spend at Minā before proceeding to 'Arafah on the 9th

dhikru-llāh the mention/remembrance of Allah

dhimmah the contract made with people of the Book living under Muslim governance

dhimmī one of the people of the *dhimmah*

dīn life transaction comprising Islam, *Īmān,* and *Iḥsān,* Islam itself comprising both *'ibādah* – acts of worship and *mu'āmalah* – ordinary transactions

dirham a standard weight of 2.97 g, as well as a silver coin of that weight

dinar a standard weight of 4.24 g, also known as a *mithqāl,* as well as a gold coin of that weight

F

farḍ obligatory

Fātiḥah The Opener, the first sūrah of the Qur'ān

fiqh detailed understanding, specifically of what behaviour is obligatory, recommended, permissible, disliked and forbidden

faqīh pl. *fuqahā'* people of fiqh

G

gharar uncertainty or lack of clarity in a transaction

ghusl the complete washing of the body

H

ḥadd pl. *ḥudūd*	both limit-parameters and the punishments for contravening them
hady	animal to be sacrificed as part of the *ḥajj*
ḥalāl	permissible
ḥarām	prohibited or forbidden
ḥawḍ	basin or pond of the Prophet ﷺ from which his followers will drink on the Last Day
ḥiqqah	a female camel in its fourth year capable of carrying loads and bearing children
ḥirābah	aggravated robbery
ḥubus	endowed property dedicated to a charitable end, a *waqf*

I

ibn labūn	a male camel in its third year
'Īd	a recurring periodic festival
'Īd al-Fiṭr	the festival marking the end of Ramadan
'Īd al-Aḍḥā	the festival marking the end of Ḥajj
'iddah	the term marked by a divorced or widowed woman before remarriage
ifrād	doing *Ḥajj* by itself
iḥrām	entering into the state to perform the *ṣalāt,* by saying the *takbīrat al-iḥām*; or into the Ḥajj or 'Umrah, which for men entails wearing two simple cloths
iḥsān	excellence, kindness, and "that you worship Allah as if you see Him, for if you do not see Him, He sees you"
ijārah	hiring services
ijtihād	discretion; the exercise of intellect in reaching judgements when confronted with new situations or

on deciding on matters that are the province of the person in authority

iqāmah the call to gather people for prayer. In a mosque it is performed after the *adhān*

īlā' when a man swears not to have intercourse with his wife for more than four months; he is considered to have pronounced a divorce if he fails to retract it

imām someone who leads others in prayer; when capitalised as *Imām* it can refer to the leader of the Muslim community, the *Khalīfah*

istibrā' the waiting period in the case of a slave-girl whose ownership changes. It is one menstruation

istiḥāḍah vaginal bleeding which extends beyond the ordinary term of menstrual bleeding

istijmār cleansing of the private parts after urination or defecation with dry materials such as stones

istinjā' cleansing of the private parts after urination or defecation with water

J

jadha'ah a female camel in its fifth year

Jāhiliyyah the time before Islam

jā'ifah an abdominal wound

jamrah lit. a small walled place, but in this usage a stone-built pillar

Jamrat al-'Aqabah the largest of the three *jamrah*s at Minā

janābah in a state requiring a ghusl because of sexual intercourse or nocturnal ejaculation

jihād fighting or struggling in the Way of Allah

jizyah annual tax on adult male non-Muslims living under Muslim governance

K

kaffārah atonement or expiation for a major wrong action or violation of an obligation or an oath

katam a dye-plant which has a red colour and which is mixed with *wasmah* – either indigo or woad – to dye hands and hair

khalifah a pregnant camel

khazz a material woven of silk and wool

khifāḍ female circumcision, not to be confused with pagan African, female genital mutilation

khul' is a type of divorce which takes place when the husband accepts remuneration from his wife in return for her release from marriage; it precludes any possibility of remarriage

khuṭbah a formal address, most often that delivered by the *imām* on Jumu'ah

kitābah a contract made by a slave to purchase his freedom

kitābī one of the People of the Book

L

laḥd a grave in which, after having dug the basic trench, a place is dug out for the body at the bottom of the side which faces *qiblah* so that the body is protected by an overhang

li'ān when a husband accuses his wife of adultery, four times, laying a curse upon himself if he is lying. She may repudiate it four times, calling down the anger of Allah on herself if she is lying. They are divorced by that and can never remarry under any circumstances.

M

madhhab — a way taken in fiqh and thus a 'school'

madh-y — a thin, white liquid which comes out of the penis at times of sexual arousal

maḥārim — any marriage bars

ma'mūmah — a wound that reaches the brain

maniy — is the white liquid ejaculated at orgasm

mawlā — both the emancipator and the slave emancipated, as well as people in the first generations who became *mawlā*s when they entered Islam

mile (*mīl* pl. *amyāl*) — the Arabic mile was based on the Roman, derived from *mille passus,* a thousand paces. It is 1.855 km according to Malikis and Hanafis. The British mile is 1.609 km.

mīqāt pl. *mawāqīt* — the locations where people embarking on Ḥajj or 'Umrah enter *iḥrām*

mu'akkadah — a Sunnah, such as the *witr rak'ah* after 'Ishā', that is stressed because the Messenger of Allah ﷺ was not known to leave it out in any circumstances

mudabbar — a slave whose master has decided to set him or her free upon his own death

mudd — a measure equivalent to that which two cupped hands contain, as defined by the hands of the Prophet ﷺ

mūḍiḥah — a head wound that exposes the skull

Mufaṣṣal — the *sūrah*s at the back of the Qur'ān, often considered to begin at Sūrat al-Ḥujurāt

muḥṣan/muḥṣanah — a man or woman who is or has been in a marriage that was consummated

mukātab — a partially freed slave who has made a *kitābah* agreement to purchase his freedom

munaqqilah a wound that affects the skull

musāqāh a cropsharing contract in which a worker takes his share in exchange for irrigating the crops

mushrik someone who associates a partner with Allah

musinnah or *thaniyyah* a cow in its fourth year

muzābanah buying something whose number, weight and measure is not known with something whose number, weight or measure is known, for example buying dates on the tree with dried dates

N

nāfilah supererogatory, optional and voluntary extra acts

nifās the post-natal period of bleeding

nabīdh an infusion, usually of dates or raisins, that is allowed to stand, thus sometimes fermenting

Q

qafīz 48 *ṣāʿ*, approximately 97.32kg

qasāmah in the absence of sufficient witnesses of integrity to a murder, based on a single witness or the testimony of the deceased, fifty male relatives of the deceased may each swear an oath as to the guilt of the accused

qiblah the direction faced for prayer, i.e. the Kaʿbah

qarḍ a loan for business or for other reasons

qirāḍ profit-sharing investment loan in trade

qirān *ḥajj* and *ʿumrah* together

qunūt the silent supplication made in the second *rakʿah* of Ṣubḥ

qurʾ pl. *qurūʾ* the period of purity between two menstruations

R

raghībah desirable acts

rak'at — a unit of prayer comprising standing and reciting, bowing, standing again, prostrating, sitting and prostrating

ribā — usury, increase in the transaction even if it should amount to a handful of grass

ribāṭ — guarding a frontier post

rikāz — treasure

riṭl — a weight corresponding to 128 dirhams, 380.16 g

rukhṣah — allowance or concession

rukū' — bowing

ruqā — charms

S

ṣā' — a volumetric measure of 4 *mudd*s, approximately equal to 2.028 kg

ṣadaqah — charitable giving in the Cause of Allah

Ṣaḥābah — the Companions of the Prophet ﷺ

sahūlī cloth — cloth that has been beaten, washed and whitened

sahw — leaving something out inadvertently

sā'ibah — a slave without a *walī*

sajdah/sujūd — prostration

salaf — payment in advance; when capitalised (Salaf) it refers to the Companions and the right-acting of the Followers and the Followers of the Followers of the Companions in *iḥsān*

salām — peace itself and the greeting of peace

salam — payment in advance

salas — urinal incontinence

ṣammā' — *ishtimāl aṣ-ṣammā'* is, while having no lower garment on, one wraps a cloth around the shoulders and then brings one's left hand out from underneath the garment

sawīq	a gruel of parched barley or similar grains
sa'y	to walk briskly and vigorously, particularly during Ḥajj and 'Umrah between Ṣafā and Marwah
seemga	a grain: *raphanus oleifer*
shaf' (even)	two *rak'ahs* after 'Ishā' or at the end of the night, that are followed by the single *witr rak'ah*
shaqq	a type of grave that has a simple trench at the bottom of the grave
sharī'ah	the legal modality of a people based on the revelation of their Prophet. The final *sharī'ah* is that of Islam.
shighār	a marriage in which there is a direct exchange of daughters without any dowry
shuf'ah	pre-emption
shuhadā'	witnesses; also martyrs, those who die fighting in jihad in the way of Allah
ṣirāṭ	path; and specifically the Bridge in the *Ākhirah* on which the *mu'minūn* pass over the Fire into the Garden
siwāk	toothstick, preferably from a twig of the Arak tree
sujūd	synonymous with *sajdah*, prostration
Sunnah	the customary practice of a person or group of people. It has come to refer almost exclusively to the practice of the Messenger of Allah ﷺ.
sunnah	an act that is less than obligatory but more than recommended
sūrah	a chapter of the Qur'ān containing three or more *āyahs*

T

ta'ālā	*"exalted is He"* – sometimes said after the Divine Name

tabī'	a calf in its third year
tadbīr	the contract when a man says to his slave, "You are *mudabbar*" or "You are free afterwards," (i.e. after my death
Tābi'ūn	the followers or successors of the Companions who followed them in *iḥsān*
takbīrat al-iḥrām	the *takbīr* that begins the prayer
tamattu'	*'umrah,* then coming out of *iḥrām,* then later returning to *iḥrām* and performing *ḥajj* separately all in the same season
tashahhud	the supplication said while seated in the prayer
ṭawāf	seven circuits around the Ka'bah performed in a counter-clockwise direction
Ṭawāf al-Ifāḍah	the *ṭawāf* performed after stoning the Jamrat al-'Aqabah
Ṭawāf of Farewell	the *ṭawāf* performed after completing the rites of Ḥajj before returning to one's land
tayammum	the dry purification performed in lieu of *wuḍū'* when the latter is not possible for various reasons
thaniyyah	of cattle a male in its fourth year, and of camels a six-year-old male
tharīd	bread soaked in broth

U

umm walad	a slave woman who gives birth to her master's child; neither she nor her child may be sold
'umrā	the gift of the use of a house for a specific period of time
'umrah	the lesser pilgrimage that may be performed at any time
ūqiyyah	40 dirhams, a weight of 118.8 g

uterine siblings — those from the same mother but different fathers

W

wadīʿah — something deposited with another person

wady — a thick white liquid which comes out, usually after urinating

waqf pl. *awqāf* — synonymous with *ḥubus*, a property endowed to charitable ends

walī pl. *awliyāʾ* — a guardian

wasq pl. *awsuq* — a volumetric measure of 60 *ṣāʿ* equivalent to 121.65 kg.

witr — odd, i.e. the single *rakʿat*, either after the two *shafʿ* (even) *rakʿat*s after ʿIshāʾ or at the end of the prayers of the night

wuḍūʾ — purification with water preparatory to the prayer

Z

ẓihār — a man's statement that sex with his wife is tantamount to incest is considered a divorce, which may be retracted along with the *kaffārah*

zinā — illicit sexual intercourse, fornication or adultery

zindīq — someone who conceals disbelief while making an outward display of Islam